The Women
Who Shaped Politics

The Women
Who Shaped Politics

*Empowering stories of women who
have shifted the political landscape*

Sophy Ridge

CORONET

First published in Great Britain in 2017 by Coronet
An imprint of Hodder & Stoughton
An Hachette UK company

1

A CIP catalogue record for this title is available from the British Library

Hardback ISBN: 978 1 473 63876 1
Ebook ISBN: 978 1 473 63878 5

Typeset in Sabon by Hewer Text UK Ltd, Edinburgh

Printed and bound by CPI Group (UK) Ltd, Croydon, CR0 4YY

Hodder & Stoughton policy is to use papers that are natural, renewable
and recyclable products and made from wood grown in sustainable
forests. The logging and manufacturing processes are expected to
conform to the environmental regulations of the country of origin.

Hodder & Stoughton Ltd
Carmelite House
50 Victoria Embankment
London EC4Y 0DZ

www.hodder.co.uk

Contents

Introduction

We are at a tipping point. As I type these words, the UK has its second female prime minister, Germany has its first ever female chancellor, Scotland and Northern Ireland both have female first ministers, women currently lead the Green Party, Plaid Cymru, Scottish Labour and the Scottish Conservatives and Hillary Clinton came closer than any woman before to the White House. At what point do feminists declare victory? Women achieving political equality no longer feels like a distant mirage but a firm and achievable target. Female leaders are not only strutting the world stage but shaping it.

It was on 20 July 2016 that, for me, the new political reality sank in. Theresa May's first trip as prime minister had been to see Nicola Sturgeon in Holyrood; now she was in Germany on her first overseas visit, meeting another female leader. Angela Merkel was playing host at the Chancellery, the post-modern Berlin building that has looked sternly down on a dull stream of suited politicians. As the gathered journalists weighed up what questions to ask at the press conference, the men asked their female colleagues: can we mention that they are two women? Or is that sexist? Over the next two days, three out of the four questions put to the prime minister would come from female members of the travelling press pack. Sitting in the press conference, I remember feeling a strong sense that the tectonic plates of history were shifting. Margaret Thatcher is no longer a blip. There is no better time to write a book celebrating women in politics.

The female politicians winning elections and changing countries are standing on the shoulders of generations of women who have gone before. Writers, campaigners, suffragists, suffragettes, pioneers, change-makers and ceiling smashers have made the new reality possible, from the glamorous society darling Caroline Norton, who campaigned for the rights of married women in the nineteenth century, to the elderly servant who cast the first female vote in 1867. From the aristocratic suffragette Lady Constance Lytton to the bomb-making dancer from Leicester – both women's health was wrecked in the force-feeding chambers at Holloway Prison. From the American whirlwind Lady Astor, the first MP to take her seat in the House of Commons, to the class warriors Margaret Bondfield, Barbara Castle and Ellen Wilkinson; from the no-nonsense fighters Edwina Currie and Ann Widdecombe, to the parliamentary change-makers Harriet Harman and Yvette Cooper. From the first female prime minister to the first female speaker of the House of Commons. This book is an attempt to tell their story.

History, as marginalised women know only too well, is shaped by what is left out. For the glaring gaps – and there are many – I can only apologise. What follows is a personal narrative that centres unashamedly on Westminster, my own area of knowledge and expertise. That inevitably means there will be unforgivable omissions from Welsh, Irish and Scottish politics and – in our increasingly global world – across different countries and continents as well. It has proved tricky, in addition, to know where to draw the arbitrary start line. I begin my story with Queen Mary II and the Bill of Rights, a point at which Parliament begins to emerge from the clouds of history in a recognisable form. Again, that means inevitable omissions. The second female prime minister, Theresa May, and the first female speaker of the House of Commons, Betty Boothroyd, have both said their personal heroine is the towering colossus Queen Elizabeth I, commander of ships, men and empire. But the political world she inhabited is too distant and foreign for this book.

We are at a critical moment in women's history and now is the time to lean forward rather than rest back. To be a woman in Westminster is to be among a minority. Whether MPs, senior civil servants, backroom spin-doctors or political journalists, men outnumber women. In the claustrophobic atmosphere of the Chamber or the breezy riverside terrace bar, you may still feel as though you are an intruder in a world where women remain the exception. I first got my lobby pass back in 2008, the coveted card that allows you to wander – almost – freely through the Palace of Westminster. Strolling through the airy atrium of Portcullis House with a fellow newspaper hack, I allowed my surroundings to soak in: the restaurants, coffee bars and trees beneath the sky-lit roof. My (male) colleague bumped into a (male) MP he knew and thought he would do his cub reporter a favour by introducing us. The Honourable Member reacted by jumping up, offering his hand, and saying: 'So you must work for the fashion pages?'

Six years later, at the 2014 Labour Party conference in Brighton, I was standing at the bar of the Midland Hotel with a group of broadcast journalists, winding down after a relentless day's work and hoping to bump into a few contacts. Rightly or wrongly, bars are still the most fruitful place for political hacks to pick up stories. A Labour MP bounded up to say hello to a correspondent he knew. When he turned to me, he said: 'You do the weather, don't you?' In both cases I was in places where no weather girl or fashion journalist would be. You need a political pass to get into Portcullis House or the party conferences. And yet, somewhere in the deepest regions of their subconscious, the two MPs thought it was more likely that a fashion journalist should be in Parliament's atrium or a weather presenter at the Labour Party conference than that a political reporter should be a woman.

That, too, is changing, thanks to the trail-blazing work of women like Julia Langdon, who joined the lobby in the 1970s and became the first ever female political editor in Westminster in 1984, and Elinor Goodman, political editor of Channel 4 News in the eighties and nineties. Women were only accepted as lobby journalists in 1945 – well after the first female MPs – with the appointment of Eirene Jones as political correspondent at the *Manchester Evening News*, but Langdon and Goodman remained the only two women well into the eighties. Now, among other leading female journalists, we have a female political editor at the BBC, Laura Kuenssberg, and two women job-sharing the role of political editor of the *Guardian*, Anushka Asthana and Heather Stewart. Elinor Goodman, Catherine McLeod, formerly of the *Glasgow Herald*, and Beth Rigby, formerly of the *Financial Times* and now at Sky News, have all been chairman (or woman?) of that most dusty of Westminster establishments, the Lobby.

Even in my relatively short time working in Parliament, there has been a shift in the corridors of power. Women may still be a minority but are no longer outsiders, and Westminster is mostly a brilliant, exhilarating place to work. Walking around the rabbit warren of stairs and corridors, paintings and statues of women are beginning to punctuate the images of men who document the history of British democracy. Statues of Winston Churchill and David Lloyd George flank the archway in the Members' Lobby that leads to the House of Commons chamber, but opposite is a larger-than-life statue of Margaret Thatcher. Statesmen usually have to wait until they are dead before being immortalised in Westminster, but an exception was made for this stateswoman. Thatcher is depicted mid-debate, her finger pointing towards the House of Commons chamber. The bronze Maggie is now such an ingrained part of Westminster's fabric that it is tradition for Conservative MPs to rub her foot for luck before debates (technically banned to avoid wearing down her shoe but an edict roundly ignored).

Baroness Thatcher's statue represents female achievements in the pulsing heart of Westminster, the debating Chamber and Number 10 itself. Away from Parliament's hallowed lobbies, in a public park that skirts the Palace of Westminster and the River Thames, there is a very different statue. Emmeline Pankhurst attempted to force female voices into Westminster when the establishment was determined to keep them out. The leader of the Women's Social and Political Union (WSPU) looks more like an elderly and benevolent school teacher than a militant suffragette. But appearances can be deceiving. The two statues symbolise the disparate battles fought over hundreds of years for women to have a voice in Parliament. The fight has not yet been won. But I hope the following pages will be a celebration of women in Parliament, rather than a complaint about the distance still to travel.

I have been asked about the thesis of this book, but it is not intended to be a dense text of academic theory. Instead I hope it will be seen as a simple celebration of women in politics and the compelling, tragic, uplifting stories of the shoulders on which our current leaders stand. In the research of this book I have been privileged to speak to some of the most inspiring women in British political life, individuals who have not only borne witness to history being made but helped to shape it. Uncovering their stories, and the remarkable tales of the women who have gone before them, has been an honour and a joy. I can only hope a fraction of the pleasure of the writing will be felt in the reading.

The Queens

'She was the prince's wife, and never meant to be other than in subjection to him.'

– Queen Mary II

'Were women to unsex themselves by claiming equality with men, they would become the most hateful, heathen and disgusting of beings.'

– Queen Victoria

In the beginning were the queens, their myths passed down through generations like a game of Chinese whispers. The medieval monarch's consort Eleanor of Aquitaine, wealthy and wilful with a prodigious sex life. Queen Elizabeth I, the rusty-haired virgin, conqueror of countries and commander of ships. The Catholic Mary I, who executed her God-given purpose in the bloodiest of ways. These women held considerable political power, but this is not their history. The story of women and politics can only begin when Parliament emerges in recognisable form. In the country known as the Mother of Parliaments, the birth of modern politics came on 13 February 1689, when a woman decided that duty to her husband outweighed loyalty to her father.

The streets were packed with people. Rippling towards Westminster's resplendent Banqueting House, a sea of heads filled the road from Whitehall to Charing Cross. Inside, preparations had been made for a great ceremony. A cluster of chubby cherubs, lovingly painted by the great artist Rubens, looked down on it from above. The heavenly scene, *The Apotheosis of James I*, was a luscious glorification of the monarchy. Ironically, however, the painted angels celebrating the divine right of kings would observe two events that heralded the triumph of Parliament over the monarchy.

The first happened on a chilly day in January 1649. King Charles I downed a glass of claret and slipped on a second shirt, then stepped out of a window at the Banqueting House and onto the executioner's wooden scaffolding. Proud even when moving towards certain death, the King didn't want the gathered crowds to see him shiver in case they assumed he was shaking from fear. The brutal beheading in the end changed very little. The civil war raged on until 1651 and the merry King Charles II acted as if his father had never been executed. 'You had better have one King than five hundred,' he cheerily declared in 1681, breezily dismissing the authority of Parliament. But in 1689, forty years later, the men from the House of Commons and the House of Lords who gathered at the Banqueting House bore witness to an event that would elevate their role for ever.

In that room stuffed with men, there was a solitary woman. Her role was instrumental that day, so it seems fitting that the story of women in politics starts in the same chapter as the birth of the modern British Parliament.

Centre stage, the twenty-six-year-old woman was sitting beside her husband, a short man with black hair so thick he did not need to wear a wig. Members of the House of Lords had assembled on one side of the couple, with men from the House of Commons on the other. The speaker was standing by, holding his mace – a five-foot silver club symbolising royal authority, without which Parliament still cannot meet or pass laws. Traditionally the speaker was an agent of the sovereign, tasked with imposing his will on the House of Commons. But that had changed when, in 1642, Charles I stormed into Parliament to arrest five members for treason. The speaker point-blank refused, and uttered the words that would reverberate through centuries: 'I have neither eyes to see, nor tongue to speak in this place, but as the House is pleased to direct me, whose servant I am here.'[1] Forty-seven years later, as the speaker looked from the gathered MPs to the seated woman – a direct descendant of

Charles I – there was no question of whom he was there to serve.

The royal couple, surrounded by parliamentarians, must have felt as if they were in enemy territory. The elected representatives had spent decades wrestling for power with the monarchy, and today they were determined to secure the supremacy of Parliament for ever.

The Declaration of Rights, read aloud by the clerk to the House of Lords, was a remarkable document setting out the rights of every citizen. William and Mary, sitting shoulder to shoulder in the Banqueting House, had to sign up to its demands before they could become king and queen. From that point on, the monarch had to obey the law rather than be above it. She or he could no longer meddle with the legal system, levy taxes or maintain an army in peacetime without the consent of Parliament. Freedom of speech in parliamentary debate was guaranteed – one of the founding principles of democracy. The monarch's ability to act as an independent authority, ignoring the will of others, was stifled and she or he would be forced to call Parliament regularly.

After the Rights had been read out, William of Orange declared: 'We thankfully accept what you have offered us!' The assembled politicians answered with a shout of joy, loud enough to be heard in the streets below, where the huge crowd cheered back. To the sound of trumpets, William and Mary were offered the Crown and nothing would ever be quite the same again.

The moment marked the birth of modern British politics. Finally the power struggle between Parliament and Crown had been settled. But the curious thing about that historic day in the Banqueting House was that there was not one monarch sitting in the room but two. It was not just the new king, William III, who had to sign up to one of the most important terms and conditions in history, but the queen also. Mary was not there merely as William's wife, for moral support and window-dressing. She was of equal status, and what became known as the Glorious Revolution could not have happened without her.

So who was Mary? And why did a very personal choice, between her father and her husband, change the course of British history?

In the seventeenth century, the only route to political power for women was one over which they had no control: an accident of birth that made them queen. Even then the establishment did everything possible to stop them, with male heirs superseding female, and male monarchs desperate for sons. Born in 1662, Mary was the eldest daughter of James II and her father's favourite child. There was, however, a split between them that would grow into a destructive chasm: religion.

Mary was brought up as a devout Protestant at the insistence of Charles II, despite the Catholicism of both her parents. It was an upbringing that stubbornly stuck. Her father's attempts to convert her fell on deaf ears, and she resisted the Catholic writings that he doggedly sent to her. Aged just fifteen, she was married to her Protestant cousin William and moved to Holland to be with him. Of course, this was no love match: it was one of Charles II's attempts to build alliances with other Protestant powers. The teenage Mary was deeply unhappy at the prospect of spending her life with an unfamiliar man twelve years older and four inches shorter than her. She wept throughout the ceremony.

William was an awkward man, outwardly aloof and unpopular. To make matters worse, he was having an affair with one of Mary's ladies in waiting. Elizabeth Villiers – known as 'Squinting Betty' – was no beauty, but she was witty, intelligent and had a grip on William that his new wife had no hope of prising off. Within a year of marriage, Mary had her first miscarriage. She was to remain childless. Despite the unpromising beginnings, however, Mary and William's marriage lasted until death. William could appear callous and dismissive in public, but contemporaries claim he was devoted to Mary, whose own sense of duty meant she was determined to be the perfect loyal wife. That mattered.

Back in England, religious tensions were rising. Protestants were increasingly restless about the Catholic James II, and when his son was born (bumping Protestant Mary down the pecking order as the new heir to the throne), they decided to act. At the invitation of James's opponents, William of Orange landed in Devon with 25,000 soldiers. It was the largest force ever to invade England, and James had no chance of resisting. Deserted by his generals, he soon realised the game was up and fled to France.

That was where Mary came in. William had wealth, power and brute military strength, but his wife gave him the missing ingredient that would make him acceptable to the public. As the daughter of the man her husband had humiliated, she had blood legitimacy. Mary was also wildly popular in England, while William was a physically unimpressive and socially awkward asthmatic. Parliament ruled that if William wanted the Crown he must act as a joint sovereign with his wife. Otherwise the deal was off.

The ever-devoted Mary decided she would do her bit to make the Dutchman palatable to the public. When it was suggested to her that she could take the Crown herself, she replied 'that she was the prince's wife, and never meant to be other than in subjection to him, and she did not thank anyone for setting up for her an interest divided from that of her husband'.[2]

Those may sound like the words of a woman who wielded little political power and hid in the shadow of her husband, but the reality was very different. Mary was the first woman to hold serious influence in the modern Parliament. Her husband was a part-time King of England, who spent much of his time travelling around Europe, fighting long and expensive battles against the Catholics while the Queen reigned in his absence. Although she remained meek and deferential at all times, she was seen as a quietly skilled politician. Her chaplain once commented 'that if her husband ever retained his throne, it would be by her skill and talents for governing'.[3]

Mary's power meant defeat and humiliation for the father she had loved deeply as a child. History remains frustratingly silent on her inner thoughts when her husband won the Crown and sent her father scuttling into hiding. We know she prayed four times a day while the invasion took place, and took the advice of a fortune-teller. When she travelled to England to take the throne and effectively usurp her father, onlookers were shocked that she seemed outwardly gleeful. When she moved into Whitehall Palace after the Glorious Revolution that had overthrown James, it was said that she looked as jolly as if she was going to a wedding. The Duchess of Marlborough sniffed at Mary for rummaging through closets and turning up quilts 'as people do when they come to an inn', adding: 'For whatever necessity there was in deposing King James, he was still her father who had so lately been driven from that chamber and that bed; and, if she felt no tenderness, I thought that she should still have looked grave, or even pensively sad, at so melancholy a reverse of his fortunes.'[4]

Mary claimed that she was trying to put a brave face on an overwhelming situation. In a letter to her cousin, she explained she had to 'force myself to more mirth than became me at that time, and was by many interpreted as ill nature, pride, and the great delight I had to be a Queen. But alas they did little know me, who thought me guilty of that . . . My heart is not made for a kingdom and my inclination leads me to a quiet life.'[5] Mary's piercing sense of duty to her husband trumped all other considerations, but James never forgave what he saw as a heartless betrayal. As she was dressing to go to her coronation, a missive arrived from her father. Mary makes no reference to it in her diary, so it may have been intercepted before she could read it: 'I have been willing to overlook what has been done, and thought your obedience to your husband and compliance to the nation might have prevailed. But your being crowned is in your own power; if you do it while I and the Prince of Wales are living, the curses of an angry father will fall on you, as well as those of a God who commands obedience to parents.'[6]

In 1694, just five years after signing the Declaration of Rights,

Mary died of smallpox. She was thirty-two, and still estranged from her father. Her husband was devastated. William had often seemed indifferent to his wife, but he had made up a bed so he could sleep in her sick room and even suppressed his cough for fear it would irritate her. When she finally died, he fainted at her bedside.

Mary's choice transformed the political landscape and redefined the power of the monarch. After the Declaration was passed and became the Bill of Rights in December 1689, Parliament has met at least once every year. By modern standards an annual session hardly feels like democracy, particularly in a country where no women and just one in four men were eligible to vote. At the time, it was more representation than any other country in the world offered.

When Mary signed the Bill of Rights, the struggle for supremacy between Parliament and the Crown did not end automatically. Her sister Anne was an autocratic queen who would become the first sovereign of Great Britain and the last monarch to veto a bill passed by Parliament.

A sickly child who grew into a perennially ill adult, nobody expected Mary's sister Anne to reach the throne. She was pregnant for most of her adult life, yet not a single child from her seventeen pregnancies survived into adulthood. However, she presided over a piece of legislation that led to the creation of the United Kingdom of Great Britain: the Act of Union.

When Anne, an Anglican Tory, took the throne in 1702 she recommended uniting the two kingdoms of England and Scotland in her very first speech. To the horror of many nobles and conservatives, the historic motion was placed in front of a deeply divided Parliament and the law was passed by just a handful of votes. Scotland's future was decided by a few MPs and a very determined queen. It is the perfect example of how the first real political power that women managed to grab was in the hands of a female monarch.

In April 1706, Scottish commissioners travelled to Westminster to clash with their English counterparts in crucial negotiations, both sides driven to secure the most advantageous deal. Generous concessions were transacted, and the Scots came back with an agreement for full freedom and trade with England, which they had desired for many years. The bargain was done, and from then on Scotland would send thirty-eight MPs and sixteen peers to Westminster. Queen Anne, the Union's chief cheerleader, was presented with the full text of the agreement on 3 July. In the spring of 1707 the Act of Union was passed by the Scottish and English Parliaments.

As the summer leaves turned golden and autumnal winds swept the newly unified country, Scottish MPs started the long ride from Holyrood to Westminster. They travelled in grand pomp and ceremony for Parliament's October session, the first in which English and Scottish MPs were to cram together, knees brushing, on the green benches.

Queen Anne's dream of a United Kingdom was in place but not secure. Fierce public opposition spilled out into the streets, and petitions containing tens of thousands of signatures were angrily marched to the gates of Westminster. 'The mob of this town are mad and against us,' declared the Whig MP John Erskine, as politicians balked at the vehement opposition.[7]

The most violent reaction exploded in Scotland. On 23 October protesters stormed the Edinburgh house of the Scottish commissioner, Sir Patrick Johnstone, who had played a key role in the negotiations, throwing stones at the windows and breaking open doors. They were searching, of course, for Sir Patrick but he had narrowly made his escape before they reached him. On 20 November, 200 angry men publicly burned a copy of the treaty, watched by a crowd of thousands.

Queen Anne quickly realised her Union was hanging by a thread. As a sop to the protesters, she promised to take robust action against Catholics in Scotland and vowed to support Protestantism and Presbyterianism. Her secret weapon, though, was financial. Scotland was weak and struggling economically, and Anne took her chance to bulldoze through reform. A proud nation had, in the end, little choice.

If William and Mary's reign transferred power from king and queen to Parliament, Anne marked the end of the era of autocratic monarchs imposing their will. She had championed legislation and dictated the make-up of her government, picking Tories for the plum jobs whether it was the Whigs who had won more seats in elections or not. In the eighteenth century, though, times were changing. Anne was the last monarch to use the right to veto a bill, when she rejected the Scottish Militia Bill in 1708. Passed by both Houses of Parliament, it would have given weapons to the Scottish army. After Anne's death the royal assent, by which the monarch agrees to make Parliament's bills into laws, or acts, became a mere formality.

Since 1714, women have managed to grasp political power without being monarchs. Ever since the Glorious Revolution, and the shift in the balance of power between Crown and Parliament, new avenues of influence had opened and, as a result, the political weight of the monarchy waned. Queen Victoria and Queen Elizabeth II boast far longer reigns than the women who went before them, but much less parliamentary influence.

Victoria reigned over nearly a quarter of the earth's land mass and was a celebrity monarch: doting wife, mother and figurehead. Her subjects named waterfalls, lakes and cities after her and she was the first monarch to be immortalised at Madame Tussaud's and the first to be officially photographed. Despite the glitz and adulation, she stepped away from the direct political influence of her predecessors, and her contribution to women's rights, in particular, is complex. Millions of men were given the right to vote during her reign, as the franchise was extended to the middle and skilled-working classes, but no women.

Queen Victoria was no champion of female suffrage. In a letter, published in 1908 by the Men's League for Opposing Woman Suffrage, she wrote:

The Queen is most anxious to enlist everyone who can speak or write to join in checking this mad wicked folly of 'Woman's Rights', with all its attendant horrors on which her poor sex is bent, forgetting every sense of womanly feeling and propriety. Were women to unsex themselves by claiming equality with men, they would become the most hateful, heathen and disgusting of beings and would surely perish without male protection . . . God created men and women different – then let them remain each in their own position.[8]

Despite her opposition to women's equality, Victoria may unwittingly have broken down barriers for others. Benjamin Disraeli, who would later become prime minister, told the House of Commons in 1848: 'In a country governed by a woman . . . I do not see, where she has as much to do with State and Church, on what reasons, if you come to right, she has not a right to vote.'[9]

In September 2015 Elizabeth II overtook Queen Victoria as Britain's longest-serving monarch and reigns over a nation transformed since her predecessor Mary II sat under the chubby cherubs at the Banqueting House. On paper, she wields immense political power as the world's longest-serving leader and representative of a thousand-year-old monarchy. She is queen of the United Kingdom of Great Britain and Northern Ireland, plus fifteen other countries, including Canada, New Zealand and Australia. A little red box of government papers lands on her desk daily and she signs off on every law passed by Parliament. The royal veto may not have been used since the days of Queen Anne, but the potential power remains. The Queen is the Defender of the Faith and Supreme Governor of the Church of England, able to appoint bishops and archbishops. She is head of the armed forces, so soldiers, sailors and air personnel pledge allegiance to her and sometimes die in her service. The Queen's political power, however, slumbers. She does not meddle in the affairs of her lawmakers, and when she reads her legislative programme annually at the state opening of Parliament she acts as the mouthpiece of the current government. Her opinions are expertly masked.

Despite relinquishing the political power deployed by her ancestors, Elizabeth II retains her emotional power. The modern monarch is the ultimate diplomat, creating positive relationships, smoothing tensions and forging powerful links. Her life is a whirl-wind of dinners, lunches, military ceremonies, charity events and gloved handshakes. She welcomes popes, prime ministers and presidents to the United Kingdom, and still engages in weekly private meetings with prime ministers. On all of these occasions, therapist-like, she listens more than she speaks. Tradition is the lifeblood of the royal family, and the root of its mystery. The insti-tution is bigger than any individual. Politicians are temporary lodgers in Parliament. The monarch remains.

The Writers

'*Why does* Mrs James trouble her Head about these matters,
She is but a Woman. *Why that is true:* I am but a Woman: *you
cannot but think I must be something more than ordinary.*'

– Elinor James

'*If all Men are born free, how is it that all Women are born
Slaves?*'

– Mary Astell

'*I am not born to tread in the beaten track.*'

– Mary Wollstonecraft

In the seventeenth century, Newgate Prison was a five-storey hell-
hole. Hundreds of inmates died of disease, shackled together in
overcrowded wards where the floor crunched with lice and
bedbugs. Inside one of the dark and dirty cells in London's most
notorious prison a middle-aged woman had had the audacity to
try to project her political voice. Elinor James, a printer and
devout Catholic, was being punished for a pamphlet that had
upset the establishment. Elinor James had neither wealth nor
influence, but her pamphlets had frightened the authorities so
much that they had locked her up. Appalled that the Catholic
James II had been deposed in the Glorious Revolution, she
suggested William III was an interim monarch who should hand
the throne back to his father-in-law. Elinor didn't make it difficult
for the authorities to trace her: she signed her explosive missive
'Mrs James'. The insubordinate writer was sent straight to
Newgate.

For women who were excluded from the dusty corridors of
Westminster, writing allowed them to wedge a foot through the
door until that point firmly closed by the male establishment. If

the pen was the first feminised political weapon, the rapidly spreading printing presses of the seventeenth century were a veritable arsenal, allowing women to voice their opposition to a society whose rules were set by male politicians, judges and juries, and in which a wife had no separate legal identity from her husband. The radical Levellers, who campaigned for a more democratic Parliament and equality under the law, used secret presses to create petitions with thousands of signatures. On a spring morning in 1649, an emerald snake of women from the Leveller movement marched on Parliament wearing striking green dresses and carrying one such petition:

> Since we are assured of our creation in the image of God, of an interest in Christ equal unto men, we cannot but wonder and grieve that we should appear so despicable in your eyes as to be thought unworthy to petition this honourable House. Have we not an equal interest to the men of this nation, in those liberties and securities and other good laws of the land?[1]

They were curtly dismissed by the serjeant-at-arms, who said parliamentary business was too difficult for women to understand. When twenty women gained access to the lobby and were told by one MP to go home and wash their dishes, one petitioner replied that they had scarcely any dishes left to wash.

Individual women, as well as politicised organisations, were also grabbing the opportunity afforded by the printing presses, and Elinor James was one of the most prolific users, distributing more than ninety pamphlets. The large, single-printed pages were known as broadsides and she directed them at public figures, from kings to parliamentarians. She was given the means to express her opinions when, in 1662, aged seventeen, she married the London printer Thomas James. As the family business expanded, Elinor James was so efficient in formulating her opinions on everything from business tax to public fireworks displays that she was able to respond to parliamentary debates within twenty-four hours in typically fiery style. One 1695 broadside reads: 'I can assure Your Honours, I could not have thought that anyone could have dared to give such a Bill against Printing. Sure it must have been a Firebrand of Hell that presumed it? For it wholly aims at the ruin of *Printers, Booksellers and Stationers*; and it is as if they designed to destroy the whole nation.'[2]

Elinor James's incessant lobbying of MPs made her a familiar face around Westminster, where she was met with derision. One of her petitions bears a scrawled note in the margins: 'A Mad Woman who used to attend at the Doors of the House of Lds and Commons.'[3]

The influential author and bookseller John Dunton was also alarmed by her politicising, praising Thomas James in 1705 as 'a competent printer and a well-read man', then lamenting that he was 'something the better known as being the husband of that *She State Politician*, Miss Elianor James'.[4]

The mad woman with a printing press in her home was clearly well known in seventeenth-century London, her writings irritating politicians and sending her to prison. In 1706 she speculated that some would think: 'Why does *Mrs James* trouble her Head about these matters, *She is but a Woman*. Why that is true: *I am but a Woman:* you cannot but think I must be something more than ordinary.'[5]

The political voices of early female writers have been persistently marginalised and sometimes erased altogether. In her lifetime Mary Astell was a well-known political thinker with considerable influence, but she has been almost written out of the history books. Just four of her letters survive, preserved simply because they were addressed to wealthy male aristocrats, who passed them down among their effects. Until Florence M. Smith published a 1916 biography of her, she had faded into insignificance, and it is only recently that revisionists have revived her reputation, with some considering her to have been one of the first British feminists.

Astell was born in 1666 into a proudly middle-class family that was sliding down in the world. Their descent quickened when she was twelve because her father died, leaving her without a dowry and with little prospect of marriage. Incredibly for a woman of letters, Astell had no formal education. Her family's savings were invested in her brother's schooling, leaving her to be taught by her alcoholic uncle, an ex-clergyman. When her mother also died, she moved to London to try to make her fortune. At twenty-one she found herself destitute and, in despair, penned a letter to the Archbishop of Canterbury:

> I have pawned all my cloathes & now am brought to my Last Shift. I am a gentlewoman & not able to get a liflyhood . . . to beg I am ashamed, but meer necessaty forces me to give grace the trouble hoping charity will consider me, for I have heard a very great and good character of charity you have done and do dayly.'[6]

The letter had been the act of a young woman with nowhere else to turn, but it worked. When the archbishop had given Astell the money she so desperately needed, she sent him a hand-sewn book containing her poetry. He was so impressed that he helped her find a publisher. The unmarried orphan now had a livelihood and set up home in fashionable Chelsea. It was an astonishing turn-around.

In that relatively rural corner of south-west London, Astell found herself surrounded by an intellectual circle of wealthy families tired of city grime. Many literary ladies shared her concerns about the lack of education and opportunity for women. With her new friends prepared to give her financial backing, Astell starting writing letters and pamphlets that would form the crucial foundations of feminist political thought in the UK.

Letter-writing was a marginalised form of political discourse at the end of the seventeenth century, but at that time women could operate only on the margins. Sending communications to influential men was, for many early female writers, the most effective way of influencing political debate when public speaking was frowned upon. In addition, women did not need a public position or reputation to get a hearing. Astell's use of rhetoric and logic to win her political battles was soon raising eyebrows. At a dinner party with Dr Francis Atterbury, later the Bishop of Rochester, she said she would be pleased to read one of his sermons. After printing and sending her a copy, he was little prepared for the sheet of remarks she sent back:

> I take them to be of an extraordinary nature, considering they came from the pen of a woman [he wrote in a letter to a friend]. Indeed one would not imagine a woman had written them. There is not an expression that carries the least air of her sex from the beginning to the end of it . . . She has not the most decent manner of insinuating what she means, but is now and then a little offensive and shocking in her expressions; which I wonder at, because a civil turn of words is what her sex is always mistress of. She, I think, is wanting in it. But her sensible and rational way of writing makes amends for that defect, if indeed anything can make amends for it. I dread to engage her, so I only wrote a general civil answer to her, and leave the rest to an oral conference.[7]

In 1694 Astell wrote the work that would become her most famous and influential. *A Serious Proposal to the Ladies for the Advancement of their True and Greatest Interest* argued passionately for more educational opportunities for women. 'Ladies,' begins the author who describes herself only as 'a Lover of Her SEX' before outlining her proposal: 'Its aim is to fix that Beauty, to make it lasting and permanent, which Nature with all the helps of Art cannot secure: and to place it out of the reach of Sickness and Old Age, by transferring it from a corruptible Body to an immortal mind.'[8] She asks her readers, 'How can you be content to be in the World like Tulips in a Garden, to make a fine *shew* and be good for nothing' while their souls 'lye fallow and neglected?'[9]

Later Astell started a charity school for girls in Chelsea that flourished until the nineteenth century. Its founder, however, would live to see only its first two years. Mary Astell died of breast cancer in 1731, a few months after a failed operation to remove the tumour.

Her close friend and patron Lady Elizabeth Wilson described her last days in a letter:

> The great and good Mrs. Astell died at Chelsea the 9th of this
> month; she was five days actually a dying. Lady Catherine Jones
> was with her two days before her death; she then begged to see
> no more of her old acquaintances and friends, having done
> with the world, and made her peace with God; and what she
> had then to do was to bear her pains with patience, cheerful-
> ness, and entire resignation to the Divine Will.[10]

Nearly a century after Mary Astell's death, another Mary was born. She would become the towering female political writer of the pre-Victorian era and write the text that would become a blueprint for future feminism. It is not known whether Mary Wollstonecraft was influenced by Mary Astell's works. They both passionately believed that women's education was the route out of oppression, although their vision had some crucial differences, with Astell's rooted in religion and Wollstonecraft's in secular solutions.

When Mary Wollstonecraft was born in 1759, little progress had been made towards educational equality, and the reality of life for women was bleak. Marriage laws were essentially prop-erty rights and everything a woman owned belonged to her husband – even her children. Killing your husband was consid-ered treason, not murder.

From childhood, Wollstonecraft was angry at the injustice she saw everywhere.

Her father, Edward, was a handkerchief weaver, who had married a pretty young Irish wife, Elizabeth. In 1757 she gave birth to a son, named after his father but called Ned, and Mary followed two years later. The family split their time between the bustling industry of Bishopsgate in east London and the comparatively idyllic setting of a farmhouse in Epping. Looking back on her childhood, though, Wollstonecraft felt hard done by. Her father was bad-tempered and unaffectionate with a weakness for alcohol and gambling. Worse still, he could be violent. Wollstonecraft would sleep on the landing outside her parents' room in the hope it would stop him assaulting her mother. At the age of twelve she decided that she would never marry.

Elizabeth was a submissive wife who doted on Ned, leaving her daughter jealous and resentful. While Mary was sent to the local village day school, Ned went to a grammar school with a big library. When her wealthy grandfather died, Ned received a third of his estate while Mary wasn't left a penny. As soon as she turned eighteen, Wollstonecraft left home and never returned.

Directionless and with limited options, she took up work as a ladies' companion in Bath, then travelled to Ireland to work as a governess for the wealthy Kingsborough family. Always convinced of her own intellectual superiority, she was ill-suited to the deferential demands of her new role. In 1787, she was dismissed.

Returning to London, Wollstonecraft fell on her feet when she was employed as a translator for the bookseller Joseph Johnson. He printed, published and sold radical literature and dissenting religious texts from his shop in St Paul's Churchyard, the largest in a row of bookshops. Just a few miles from the respectable MPs of Westminster, a network of underground politicians was nourished by the radical discussions around Johnson's dining table. Leading writers, philosophers and artists would gather in his apartment above the shop to discuss progressive ideas, inspired by the French Revolution, fearless of the iron fist of the establishment. Mary Wollstonecraft was disillusioned by her family, exasperated by the employment opportunities afforded to her and shut out of conventional politics on account of her sex. In Joseph Johnson's radical bookshop, she finally felt she belonged.

Johnson gave Wollstonecraft work writing for his *Analytical Review*, lent her money and even found her a place to stay. In 1787 he advanced funds to allow her to publish the first of her revolutionary feminist works. *Thoughts on the Education of Daughters* argues that women would make a more effective contribution to society – and become better wives and mothers – if they received a proper education. At the time the majority of teaching women received focused on conduct and social grace.

Without the grounding of a solid education, Wollstonecraft argues, young women make bad choices: 'Many women, I am persuaded, marry a man before they are twenty, whom they would have rejected some years after. Very frequently, when the education has been neglected, the mind improves itself, if it has leisure for reflection, and experience to reflect on; but how can this happen when they are forced to act before they have time to think, or find that they are unhappily married?'[11]

While her radical friends were demanding rights for men, Wollstonecraft decided it was time to write a rallying call to her own sex. She wrote three hundred pages in just three months, working at an unprecedented speed and making little attempt to do any background reading or research. The text poured from her fingers. When *A Vindication of the Rights of Women* was published in 1792, it was an immediate success and the thirty-two-year-old Wollstonecraft became famous – or infamous – overnight. Polite society was scandalised by the eruption of a female voice but readers consumed it voraciously. A second edition swiftly followed, with copies published in France, Ireland, Germany and America. Booksellers struggled to keep up with demand, and there was such a turnover in library copies that some complained they couldn't keep their hands on the book long enough to digest it properly.

Readers were scandalised and delighted in equal measure. Wollstonecraft was hailed as part of a brave generation of radicals and mocked as something less than a woman. Either way, her name was now inseparable from the political struggle for women's rights.

The poet and critic Anna Seward wrote to a friend: 'Have you read that wonderful book, *The Rights of Women*? It has by turns, pleased and displeased, startled and half convinced me that its author is oftener right than wrong.'[12] On the other hand, contemporary male writers, such as Horace Walpole, scoffed at Wollstonecraft's feminism, and the dramatist Hannah Cowley was appalled: 'Will Miss Wolstonecraft [*sic*] forgive me . . . if I say that politics are *unfeminine*? I never in my life could attend to their discussion.'[13]

The book was the most comprehensive argument to date that women should receive the same educational opportunities as men. 'It is time to effect a revolution in female manners – time to restore them to their lost dignity – and make them as a part of the human species,' Wollstonecraft declares.

Women are not innately weaker or less rational than men, *A Vindication* argues, but society suppresses them in a childlike state by limiting their education and expectations. The proffered solution is co-educational day schools at which boys and girls would receive an identical education until the age of nine. Inspired by the French Revolution, which promised a new kind of politics and a more equal future in which the old constructs of class and society have been torn down, *A Vindication* was a radical vision rooted in women's rights.

For Wollstonecraft, the revolution in female manners must start early. 'Respecting the first dawn of character,' she writes, 'I will venture to affirm that a girl whose spirits have not yet been damped by inactivity, or innocence tainted by false shame, will always be a romp, and the doll will never excite attention unless confinement shows her no alternative.'[14]

Imprisoned by the expectations of their elders, young women are further shackled by the lack of educational opportunities afforded to them as they grow up. As a result their intellect is stunted, their interest centres on appearances, and they live limited, self-gratifying lives. Reason, according to *A Vindication*, is the escape route from this empty existence.

'There are some loopholes out of which a man may creep, and

dare to think and act for himself, but for a woman it is a Herculean task, because she has difficulties peculiar to her sex to overcome which require almost superhuman powers,' Wollstonecraft writes.[15]

In 1792 Mary Wollstonecraft stood at the peak of her powers. Even though she was barred from voting in an election, she had successfully shaped the political debate of her time through her radical writing. It was to be another hundred years, however, before women were admitted to university, despite her call for equality in education. Female literacy rates remained stubbornly low.

Wollstonecraft herself, however, threw herself into a lifestyle uninhibited by society's expectations. Living in Paris, swept up in the exhilarating freedoms promised by the city, Wollstonecraft met the dashing American speculator Captain Gilbert Imlay. Scorning the old conventions of marriage, the couple soon conceived a child. The handsome captain's eye, though, had already begun to wander, and when she followed him back to London, he refused to set up home with her. The confident and rebellious Wollstonecraft was now a discarded mistress. When the captain asked her to travel to Scandinavia, alone with their tiny daughter Fanny, to further his business interests, she obediently agreed. The letters she wrote during her visits to Sweden, Norway and Denmark chronicle the splintering relationship: 'But you will say that I am growing bitter, perhaps, personal. Ah! Shall I whisper to you – that you – yourself, are strangely altered . . .'[16]

By the time she had returned, Gilbert Imlay had set up house with an actress from the local travelling circus. The hope of a new, modern type of relationship was shattered, and Wollstonecraft found herself in the familiar despair that women had known for centuries. She was an abandoned single woman, with a young child. Desperate, she offered to live with the couple in a *ménage* à *trois*. Even that offer was spurned.

Sexual politics at the time were stacked against women. An

unmarried mother faced prostitution or the workhouse, her reputation in tatters. It was clear that laws were made by men: the age
of consent was just twelve years old (and wasn't raised to thirteen
until the 1870s) and child prostitution was rife. Fanny was the
creation of two human beings, but the dashing captain was able
to skip lightly away to another woman, his reputation not only
intact but potentially enhanced.

Mary Wollstonecraft had always lived a revolutionary life and
defied society's expectations, but now she felt weak and depressed.
Surrendering the fight for a better future, she made her way to
Putney Bridge.

On an October night in 1795, it was pouring with rain. The low
marshes of the Thames near Battersea were even muddier than
usual, the riverbanks and bridges deserted. A solitary woman
could be seen walking slowly down one side of Putney Bridge,
before turning and coming back. Mary Wollstonecraft had left
her daughter Fanny with the maid Marguerite before making
her lonely journey. She paced up and down the bridge for half an
hour until her long skirts were saturated with rainwater. Then
she clambered up the railings and threw herself into the river.
She had hoped that if she was drenched in the downpour, her
clothes would be heavy enough to drag her down to the silty
floor of the Thames. Instead, as dirty water filled her lungs and
she choked, the long dress billowed. The swirling skirts saved
her: a boatman saw the commotion and hauled her unconscious
out of the water.

If anyone was born in the wrong century, it was Mary
Wollstonecraft. Defiant and indignant at the way others saw fit to
tell women how to behave, she refused to be constrained by society's expectations. But that October afternoon, she crumbled.
Wollstonecraft was the most radical British feminist of her time –
perhaps of any time before her, too. She was also human.

Pulled back from the murky depths of the Thames, she had a
second chance at happiness. She refused, though, to stop picking

at society's most uncomfortable places. Her last book, *Maria, or the Wrongs of Women*, was a novel arguing that women's sexual desires can be as strong as men's.

In 1796 she fell in love with William Godwin, the critic and reformer, a political radical, who was also a friend of Joseph Johnson. Godwin was a renowned bachelor who, like Wollstonecraft, had criticised the institution of marriage. Within months, they were husband and wife. Their intense romance is all the more moving for its brevity. It lasted just seventeen months.

On 30 August 1797, a heavily pregnant Wollstonecraft felt the contractions begin. Climbing the stairs of their house, she told her husband she would join him to eat later, expecting a straightforward birth. The placenta did not fully expel itself and a doctor was called to rip out the rest in a botched four-hour operation without anaesthetic. She said afterwards that she had not known pain before. Eleven days later she was dead, killed by a resulting infection. She was thirty-eight.

The little girl would grow up as Mary Wollstonecraft Shelley, author of *Frankenstein*.

Godwin's diary entry on the day his wife died records the precise time of her death, followed by three trailing wordless lines. The next day he sat with a copy of *Thoughts on the Education of Daughters*, which he could not bring himself to read. Blinded by grief, he placed a portrait of his late wife above his desk and began work on a candid biography of the woman he had adored. He faithfully told of Wollstonecraft's affair with Captain Imlay, the birth of Fanny and her suicide attempt. When Joseph Johnson published the memoir in 1798, readers were outraged. William Godwin had hoped to immortalise his revolutionary wife. Instead he killed her reputation for a hundred years. The feminist vision she had put forward in *A Vindication* was now seen only through the lens of her own misery and what was considered to have been a failed, scandalous life. Only relatively recently has her work been reinstated to its rightful place in political history.

A hundred and thirty years after her death another great writer, Virginia Woolf, said of Mary Wollstonecraft: 'One form of immortality is her undoubtedly: she is alive and active, she argues and experiments, we hear her voice and trace her influence even now among the living.'[17]

The Campaigners

'It is a strange and crying shame that the only despotic right an Englishman possesses is to wrong the mother of his children.'

— Caroline Norton

'I understand, I too have suffered.'

— Josephine Butler

'I will speak for the dumb. I will speak of the small to the great, and of the feeble to the strong. I will speak for all the despairing silent ones.'

— Annie Besant

In the early nineteenth century, gentlemen politicians debating with each other in the House of Commons Chamber were not aware they were being secretly watched. If they had glanced upwards, even if they knew where to look, it would have been hard to make out the eight pairs of eyes peering down through the small gaps in the roof of St Stephen's Chapel. Women were banned from watching parliamentary debates and witnessing men making the laws over which they had no say. However, a determined group of ladies had discovered a secret vantage point where they could peer down on the tops of the heads below.

Reaching the viewing spot was not easy. The infiltrators had to climb up into the attic above St Stephen's Chapel, which housed the green benches of the House of Commons. In the dimness, lit by a single lantern with one candle, they would gather around a ventilation shaft fixed in the gap between Sir Christopher Wren's false ceiling and the original Gothic roof. The eight small openings were just large enough to admit a head.

The Irish novelist Maria Edgeworth visited the attic gallery in 1822, and described the limited view:

We saw half the Table, the Mace lying on it, and papers, and, by peering hard, two figures of clubs at the father [sic] end; but no eye could see the Speaker or his chair – only his feet; his voice and terrible 'ORDER' was soon heard. We could see part of the Treasury Bench and the Opposition in their places – the tops of their heads, profiles and gestures perfectly.[1]

The attic was dusty and draughty and, squinting down on the debates, the women could see only a fraction of what was happening below. Despite that, the intruders were grateful for the snatches they could glean. Alicia Payne was a regular visitor:

Ladies who were privileged to go there could catch a glimpse of speakers within a certain radius. When tired of peering through these pigeon-holes we roamed about our prison, and it was very refreshing to look out on a summer's evening upon the Thames. We were locked up, and every now and then our custodian came to tell us who was 'on his feet'.[2]

It was not until a fire swept through Parliament in 1834 and the entire Chamber had to be rebuilt that a Ladies' Gallery was established for the first time. Women were kept separate so the men wouldn't be distracted by them as they listened to debates. There was a two-week waiting list when the Ladies' Gallery first opened, and it could no longer be claimed that women weren't interested in politics.

The parliamentary debates that women were so desperate to see might have been an all-male affair, but outside the Palace of Westminster, in the nineteenth century, women were effecting significant political change. The names of some of the campaigners in this chapter may not be as familiar as those ingrained in the feminist conscience, such as Mary Wollstonecraft, Emmeline Pankhurst or Florence Nightingale. Yet women like Caroline Norton and Josephine Butler achieved political reform that impacted on the lives of hundreds of thousands, if not millions, of people. Despite being banned from voting or sitting in Parliament, they managed to change the law.

Women like Mary Carpenter were part of a new generation of female campaigners. Carpenter, who immersed herself in the most notorious slums in Bristol, did more than any woman before her to further the cause of education. In early-nineteenth-century Britain an army of urchins was working up to sixteen hours a day in factories, up chimneys or down mines without any formal education. In 1844 the Ragged Schools Union was set up, dedicated to providing free education, clothing and lodging for the destitute, with classrooms in stables, lofts or railway arches, to teach reading, writing, arithmetic and Bible studies. Two years later, Carpenter set up her own ragged school in the Bristol slum of Lewin's Mead and, in 1854, she opened a school for girls involved in crime, at Red Lodge House. Things did not always go smoothly: in 1857 three female absconders were jailed only for one to be released pregnant after a liaison with the prison governor. Carpenter was drawn to tackle those most in need, whom she called 'the perishing and dangerous classes'.[3]

Hundreds passed through Carpenter's ragged schools, but her real influence was on Parliament. In 1851 she published *Reformatory Schools: For the Children of the Perishing and Dangerous Classes, and for Juvenile Offenders*. In it she writes, 'Love must be the ruling sentiment of all who attempt to influence and guide these children. The enormity and amount of juvenile depravity . . . must make every Christian heart tremble . . . Education – the early nurture and the sound religious, moral, and industrial training of the child is the only curative that can strike at the root of the evil.'[4]

Carpenter identified three classes of school urgently needed: free day schools for the general population, industrial schools with free meals for children in need, and reformatory schools for young offenders – in other words, universal free education.

The book's influence was immediate. Carpenter found herself being contacted by leading reformist thinkers, and she was

consulted by politicians drafting education bills. She was invited
to conferences and gave evidence before the House of Commons
Select Committee on Criminal and Destitute Juveniles. Her 1852
work, *Juvenile Delinquents, their Condition and Treatment*,
contributed to the passing of the Juvenile Offenders Act in 1854.
Later her lobbying helped lead to the passing of the Industrial
Schools Acts of 1857, 1861 and 1866.

However, some female campaigners were pressing for far more
controversial changes – to the laws that focused on women.

On 22 June 1836, Westminster Hall was pounding with people.
Inside there was standing room only; outside, crowds of voyeurs
stood in the drizzle, hoping to push their way inside. Charles
Dickens was perched on the reporters' bench, about to witness a
very public scandal that would inspire his first novel, *The Pickwick
Papers*.

Norton v Melbourne was an extraordinary trial: a Tory MP
accusing the prime minister of having sex with his wife. He was
seeking a divorce and damages of £10,000 (close to £1 million in
today's money).

The details were splashed across all of the next day's papers,
including the *Morning Chronicle*:

> At an early hour yesterday morning, both the public and private
> entrances to the Court were thronged with people eager to
> procure a place from which they could hear the smallest portion
> of a trial which has excited so much interest. Their patience and
> perseverance, however, were but ill-rewarded, for the galleries of
> the body of the court were filled before the public doors were
> thrown open, so high a sum as five and even in some cases we
> believe ten guineas given for a seat.[5]

The one person who wasn't there was the alleged adulteress at the
centre of it. In nineteenth-century trials, women were not permitted to defend themselves. Caroline Norton was accused of
'criminal conversation' with Lord Melbourne, then in his fifties

and old enough to be her father. In other words, the glamorous society darling was accused of seducing someone else's spouse.

The details were lurid enough to delight the spectators. The court heard how Lord Melbourne was a frequent visitor to Caroline Norton's house when her husband, George, was away, and there was explosive laughter when a lawyer said he invariably went in by the 'passage behind'. Every one of Caroline's actions was scrutinised – apparently she would rouge her face and pencil in her eyebrows before his visits. One servant even claimed to have seen 'the thick part of her thigh' when the pair were in a room together.[6]

After eight and a half hours of testimony, the court threw out the case despite the prosecution's best efforts. The evidence was circumstantial and some suspected it was a political set-up.

Caroline Norton had been found innocent, but her reputation was shattered. She was left incensed by a legal system stacked against women, and wives in particular. The nineteenth-century legal system relegated women to the status of an object, not a person. The trial was essentially about damage to a man's property, with Caroline the ruined possession. A 'criminal conversation' charge was also the only reliable way to get a divorce, but it could be initiated only by the husband. Wives could be controlled by law, but had no control over it. Caroline was bruised by a trial that had made her feel like 'a painted Prostitute in a Public Court'.[7] Now, she was spoiling for a fight.

Caroline Norton was an unlikely radical. She was an outrageous flirt and would certainly not have identified herself as a feminist. But this dark-eyed and dark-haired beauty did more than anyone before her in support of the rights of a most discriminated-against group: wives.

The Sheridans were an aristocratic family with a proud lineage of playwrights and politicians, but by the time Caroline was born in 1808, their star was fading. After her father died, the family had fallen on hard times (although not so hard that they had to give up the grace-and-favour home in Hampton Court). As a result, Mrs Sheridan fretted about her daughters marrying well and vetoed any love affairs driven by the heart rather than the head.

George Norton was immediately infatuated when he first met the nineteen-year-old woman who would become his wife. Caroline was underwhelmed by her suitor, but her mother thought it was a good match, and when he wrote to ask for her daughter's hand, she accepted on Caroline's behalf. The pair was profoundly mismatched from the start. Caroline Norton was beautiful, intelligent, vivacious, and loved being the centre of attention. She was also successful: her popular poems, songs and novels earned her the nickname 'the female Byron'. The limp-wristed George didn't know how to cope with her. Caroline might have looked good on his arm, but she was far from the demure damsel he had expected. As the feminist scholar Mary Lyndon Shanley puts it: 'He was not very bright and had few social graces; she was quick-witted, a dazzling beauty, and loved to be in society. He had a fearsome temper, which was exacerbated by Caroline's lack of subservience and her biting wit. He was not wealthy, and resented his need for the money that Caroline's growing career as a poet and novelist brought them. George's temper led on occasion to outbreaks of brutal violence, especially when he was drunk.'[8]

As their relationship disintegrated, the violence got worse. One night George kicked her in the stomach after a drunken fight and Caroline spent the night awake and alone in the spare room. Later he beat her so badly she miscarried her fourth child. She buried herself in her work as a distraction, even though, under contemporary marriage law, everything she earned was her husband's.

The fragile stack of cards was soon to tumble. In the 1830s, exasperated and humiliated by his flirtatious wife, George publicly accused the prime minister, Lord Melbourne, of adultery with her.

Everything was calculated in advance. When Caroline was away from home visiting her sister, George took their children, aged seven, five and eighteen months, to a secret location and locked his wife out of the house. As the husband, he had complete control over the property they lived in, everything they owned and – most painfully – their children. From now on, he told her, the children would live with him and she would be forced to move in with her brother. Caroline was to receive no allowance, and he would keep all her possessions, down to the last pearl necklace.

There was nothing Caroline could do about it. Women were taught that marriage was their ticket to a better life. In fact, it was the end of an autonomous existence. A married couple was considered to be one legal person and the husband had all the rights.

Ironically, it might have been easier for Caroline if the celebrity trial on 22 June 1836 had found her guilty of criminal conversation with Lord Melbourne. Until 1857, a criminal-conversation conviction was the only way for a couple to divorce without an Act of Parliament. Many unhappy couples were stuck with each other, and Caroline was trapped with the powerless status of wife. George still refused to let her see her children and under common law had complete custody rights. He also failed to pay her a regular allowance and grabbed any money she made from writing.

George was immovable and Caroline was desperate. She could not change her husband's mind, so she turned her intellect to changing the law. First, she used her literary talent to write a pamphlet explaining the unfairness of the law, called *The Natural Claim of a Mother to the Custody of her Children as affected by the Common Law Rights of the Father*. Once again, political pamphlets were to prove a key weapon to women desperate for change. She argued that under the present law, mothers had no rights whereas fathers had all the powers of an autocratic dictator. Legally, a man could abandon his wife and hand over any children to his mistress. It was the first open challenge to the marriage laws.

The one thing that George couldn't touch was Caroline's connections. She persuaded Thomas Talfourd, MP for Reading, to introduce a bill allowing mothers to appeal for custody of their children under seven years old and sent pamphlets to every MP aiming to persuade them to support it.

The lobbying paid off. In 1839, just three years after the trial, Parliament passed the Infant Custody Act. It was a huge blow to the web of legislation suppressing the rights of women. Children were no longer automatically the property of fathers: mothers could be awarded custody as long as the children were under seven. Women didn't get equal custody rights until 1925.

Despite the victory, women remained the property of their husbands. Under common law, when a couple got married the woman transferred all her possessions to her husband, including anything that she should later earn or inherit. She couldn't hold a property in her own name, and at any time George could claim her earnings and her body.

In 1848, George and Caroline signed a separation deed that finally entitled her to a small allowance (a small price to pay, you might think, for someone who routinely pocketed the money Caroline earned through her successful writing career). When Lord Melbourne died and left her some money, though, George flipped and said that the separation deed was now invalid. To her horror, Caroline discovered that the contract wasn't worth the paper it was written on. In another example of the law being stacked against one sex, a wife's signature had no legal weight unless it was co-signed by her husband. Although they were living apart, the couple were still legally married. You can almost hear her disbelief in the 1853 pamphlet she circulated, *English Laws for Women in the Nineteenth Century*: 'I propose to take a lease; and am told, that being "non-existent" in law, *my* signature is worthless!'[9]

After transforming women's rights over their children, she set her sights on female property rights. In her highly influential 1855 pamphlet, *A Letter to the Queen on Lord Chancellor Cranworth's Marriage and Divorce Bill*, she was careful not to frame it as a feminist argument.

The natural position of women is inferiority to men. Amen!
That is a thing of God's appointing, not of man's devising . . . I
am Mr Norton's inferior, I am the clouded moon of that sun. Put
me then (my ambition extends no further) in the same position
as all his other inferiors! . . . Put me under some law of protection; and do not leave me to the mercy of one who has never
shown me mercy . . .[10]

Using her own bitter experience to argue for a change in the law,
she continued:

Why is England the only country obliged to confess she cannot
contrive to administer justice to women? . . . Simply because our
legists and legislators [will never] succeed in acting on the legal
fiction that married women are 'non-existent', and man and wife
are still 'one' in cases of alienation, separation, and enmity, when
they are about as much 'one' as those ingenious twisted groups
of animal death we sometimes see in sculpture; one creature wild
to resist, and the other fierce to destroy.[11]

Caroline spent her adult life twisted in her own battle-to-the-
death with her husband, George. By furiously fighting back, her
efforts led to the 1870 Married Woman's Property Act, which
allowed wives to keep their own earnings and inherit small sums
of money. She transformed the status of married women in a legal
system that saw them as a mere chattels, but she was not to benefit
from her own reforming zeal. A life that had shown such promise
was never to recover from one bad mistake: marrying the wrong
man.

The change in child-custody law that Caroline had fought for
applied only in England and Wales, and George promptly took
their children to his brother's estate in Scotland. Their devastated
mother was still unable to see them. In 1842, Caroline's youngest
son, William, fell from a pony when he was out riding with his
brother. The eight-year-old received a minor cut to his arm but it
went untreated and he contracted blood poisoning. When

Caroline eventually found out that her son was gravely ill, she sped to his bedside, but it was too late. He was dead by the time she arrived.

Caroline had transformed the law surrounding marriage, but it took William's death for George to allow the two remaining children, Fletcher and Brinsley, to live with her.

In a fine Regency house in central Cheltenham, a six-year-old girl was rushing to say goodnight to her parents. She slipped from the second floor banister in the family home and cracked her head on the stone floor below. Josephine Butler would never forget the image of her husband with their daughter, Eva, in his arms, the little head resting on his shoulder, the golden hair stained with blood. Three hours later she died of her injuries.

Until that moment Butler had led a seemingly charmed life. Born into an idyllic family home in Northumberland, her progressive parents believed in educating their daughters as well as their sons. She had married George, a Church of England clergyman, in 1852 and the well-matched couple had four children.

Josephine Butler was inconsolable after the death of her daughter, but losing her little girl left her with a deeper religious faith and the conviction that she needed a new purpose. She explained that she 'became possessed with an irresistible desire to go forth and find some pain keener than my own . . . to plunge into the heart of human misery and to say . . . to afflicted people, "I understand, I too have suffered."'[12]

Soon after the tragedy the Butlers moved to Liverpool, their family home reminding them too much of the daughter they had lost. It was there, in the industrial northern city, that Josephine started to visit the infamous Brownlow Hill workhouse. A grim, imposing building, it held thousands of women, mainly prostitutes, but also unmarried mothers. The upper-middle-class lady would sit alongside them, picking oakum – a punishment for misbehaviour that involved collecting the fibres from old pieces of ropes.

She became one of her era's most zealous campaigners and chose to shine a light into the murkiest back-streets and alleyways of nineteenth-century London. She did not devote herself to improving the aspirations of women from the upper and middle classes, turning instead to the weakest and most discriminated against – the poor. It may be the reason why she is far less known than some of her contemporaries, who chose more wholesome campaigns to focus on. 'I have a certain feeling that the love & sacred souls of these poor girls are given to us in return for the loss of little Eva,' Butler said. '*Nothing* can repair *that* loss. Still, it seems as if God wd give us souls while he gives us sorrows.'[13]

Butler grew obsessed with the lives of the women. She went with them to the back streets of Liverpool to see their reality: gin shops, sex in dark alleys. At the time prostitutes were seen as wicked temptresses who seduced innocent men, but Butler found a very different situation. They were overwhelmingly either domestic servants, seduced by their male employers, then cast out when they became pregnant, or girls forced into prostitution because of economics. They couldn't get by as dressmakers or shop assistants and needed to find a way of eking out their meagre salaries.

One prostitute, Mary Lomax, stood out. Butler first met her in the workhouse hospital, where she was seriously ill. Lomax soaked up the hope promised in the Bible extracts that Butler read at her bedside. Feeling a connection, Butler invited her into her home to be treated by the family doctor. Lomax's death had a transformative effect on Butler. She opened her two spare rooms to other destitute and dying women or girls, not even closing the door on a mother who had killed her illegitimate baby. Later she opened the thirteen-bed House of Rest. The family doctor, who had been moved to tears by the death of Mary Lomax, gave his services free of charge.

Inspired and appalled by the experiences of the women and girls she met, Butler brought the darkness of Victorian Britain into the spotlight where politicians could no longer ignore it. She told of child virgins being sold for as little as five pounds and girls being chloroformed and raped. Days later they would be 'patched up' and resold as virgins. Butler argued that the age of consent should be raised because children were being targeted by sex-trafficking gangs. In 1885 Parliament voted to make it illegal to have sex with a child of less than sixteen – a huge success.

Immersed in the world of buying and selling bodies, Butler realised that a particular piece of legislation made almost unbearable the lives of the women she worked with. The 1866 Contagious Diseases Act was intended to tackle the spread of sexually transmitted infections. In reality it discriminated solely against women, while allowing – and even encouraging – male promiscuity. Under the law, an autonomous group of police and magistrates were set up effectively to license prostitution in garrison towns, where soldiers frequently paid women for sex. This newly created police group, consisting of officers from the Metropolitan Police, could order any woman – frequently a prostitute but also the wife or girlfriend of a soldier – in front of a magistrate, who would then force her to undergo a genital examination to see if she had an infection. If the woman refused, she would be imprisoned. If she was found to have a disease, she would be locked up in a special hospital for up to nine months. After that, her reputation was in tatters. If she was not a prostitute before the ordeal, the likelihood was that she would be afterwards.

As Butler's biographers explain:

She learned that long-term girlfriends or common-law wives of soldiers were forcibly registered by the police; that police spies showed no respect for registered women, using any tricks to incriminate a woman, even intruding into their bedrooms to force sick women to attend the examination; and that menstruating or pregnant women were examined despite the exemption clauses in the 1869 Act. Such horrors they told Butler through their tears, their faces covered with their hands.[14]

The double standards incensed Butler, who believed the law should look at the men buying sex, not the women forced to sell it. In the words of one prostitute: 'It did seem hard, ma'am, that the Magistrate on the bench who gave the casting vote for my imprisonment had paid me several shillings, a day or two before, in the street, to go with him.'[15] The Act denied women trial by jury and allowed them to be convicted by hearsay alone, which often amounted to little more than gossip. Unlike any other criminal, they were guilty until proven innocent. The legislation itself was open about the double standards: 'With the one sex [women] the offence is committed as a matter of gain; with the other it is an irregular indulgence of a natural impulse.'[16]

In Victorian society where intimate matters were rarely discussed in public – particularly by upper- and middle-class women – Butler regularly made unflinchingly direct speeches about sex. She had seen too clearly the consequences of leaving the discussion and law-making to men. An upper-class middle-aged mother, she visited brothels, theatres and prisons, and did a tour of the garrison towns of Kent, Chatham, Canterbury and Dover. It was dangerous work. Butler was physically attacked and had to attend meetings in disguise because her opponents had posted descriptions of her dress around the towns. At one meeting pimps pelted her with cow dung; on another occasion men smashed the windows of the hotel where she was staying, trying to get to her.

Despite the violence, Butler's speeches attracted huge crowds and many women risked a great deal to support her publicly. On 8 March 1870, in Nottingham, a thousand people were listening as she told them: 'The present crisis would show what the women of England were made of.'[17]

After seventeen years of activism, the Contagious Diseases Act was finally repealed in 1886. Josephine Butler was watching from the Ladies' Gallery when the hated legislation was finally overturned in Parliament at 1.30 a.m., by 182 votes to 110. Victorious, she went out onto the terrace that overlooked the River Thames:

'The fog had cleared away and it was very calm under the starlit sky. All the bustle of the city was stilled and the only sound was that of dark water lapping against the buttresses of the broad stone terrace . . . it almost seemed a dream.'[18]

Towards the end of the nineteenth century the campaigning spirit had infiltrated the foggy air around Westminster. Thanks to the determination of people like Mary Fildes and Josephine Butler, politicians could no longer ignore the working classes filling the cotton mills of Manchester or London's sugar refineries. In 1888 the pressure cooker atmosphere came to a head in perhaps the most famous campaign of the nineteenth century. It was led by a woman.

At the Bryant & May match factory in London's Bow, female employees worked from 6.30 a.m. in summer until 6 p.m. at night, with half a day's pay docked from their wages if they were late. They earned just a few shillings a week, with fines deducted for talking too much, dropping matches or going to the toilet without permission. The women paid a heavy price to earn a pathetic wage. The ends of the matchsticks were dipped in a paste made of white phosphorus – a substance that would later be deployed as a devastating chemical weapon in Afghanistan and Vietnam. It acts like something out of a horror movie, causing skin to melt and bones to decay while the victim is still alive. An increasing number of young women working in Victorian factories were struck by what they called 'phossy jaw'. First, the victim complained of toothache. Next came painful smelly abscesses as the bones around the mouth began to rot. Eventually, the remains of the phosphorus-infected jaw glowed a greenish-white in the dark. Without surgery, internal organs would fail and the sufferer would die. The factory girls were poor; many were Irish and looked down on as migrant labour. There was little public outcry at their fate.

Without Annie Besant, this would have remained just one of the many untold stories of working-class London. A forty-year-old journalist, she published a halfpenny weekly journal called the *Link*, with a motto: 'I will speak for the dumb. I will speak of the small to the great, and of the feeble to the strong. I will speak for all the despairing silent ones.'[19]

After hearing of the disparity between the enormous dividends paid to Bryant & May shareholders and the pitiful wages doled out to employees, Besant waited outside the factory to speak to some workers. She listened to the stories of the despairing, silent ones and gave them a voice. In June 1888, she published an article entitled 'White Slavery in London':

> But who cares for the fate of these white wage slaves? Born in the slums, driven to work while still children, undersized because underfed, oppressed because helpless, flung aside as soon as worked out, who cares if they die or go on the streets, provided only that the Bryant and May shareholders get their 23 per cent, and Mr Theodore Bryant can erect statues and buy parks?[20]

A few days after the article appeared, around two hundred match girls turned up to the *Link*'s office in Fleet Street and started shouting Annie Besant's name. Three girls had been sacked for speaking out in the article and the others, mainly teenagers, had marched out in protest. The shareholders intended to sue for libel, and when the girls had refused to sign letters saying they were happy at work, one of the ringleaders was sacked. All 1,400 workers went on strike. It was a brave move for women who were so poor they lived on bread and tea. The young workers had no trade union to turn to, so they went to Annie Besant for help.

The small but indefatigable journalist used protest techniques that remain a guide on how to lobby politicians successfully. She took a delegation of teenagers to the House of Commons, making sure they wore their filthiest rags so that the press could not help but note the contrast between the poverty-stricken workers and the opulent dress of the male politicians and society ladies who stalked Westminster's streets. As they spoke to the MPs, a thirteen-year-old girl took off her bonnet to show her raw, bald scalp from carrying heavy pallets on her head. 'A pretty hubbub we created,' Besant later wrote.[21]

Facing a public outcry and a barrage of articles in the press, Bryant & May were forced to climb down. They agreed to abolish the fines and provide a breakfast room for workers. The next day, the girls returned to the factories. The dangerous white phosphorus was banned and replaced by red. It worked just as well and had the advantage of not killing people.

The 1888 match girls' strike was a landmark in history, and inspired a ripple of trade unions representing the unskilled workforce. The working poor – and working women in particular – gained fresh sympathy and attention from the middle classes, and subsequently from politicians. Five years later, the Independent Labour Party was set up – it became the modern Labour Party – representing working people. Annie Besant had – quite literally – changed political history.

The story of the campaigners is not one of privileged ladies locked away in luxurious houses, but gutsy women who opened their eyes and doors to the society around them. Besant was denied the education her brothers enjoyed and was brought up in a family that struggled to get by after her father died when she was just five. She had little choice but to accept a marriage proposal from the Lincolnshire vicar Frank Besant. Two children followed in as many years, leaving their mother increasingly isolated and unhappy. As their union disintegrated, Frank asked her to leave. Annie Besant was now that most unacceptable of women: a single mother. To make matters worse she was an atheist – despite, or because of, her husband's devout faith. 'If the Bible and Religion stand in the way of women's rights then the Bible and Religion must go,' she said.[22]

More than ten years before she successfully lobbied for the match girls, Besant was campaigning for women's rights over their own bodies. In 1877 she was convicted of publishing an 'obscene' pamphlet on birth control. In the Victorian era 40 per cent of families had seven or more children, leaving women in a perpetual cycle of childbirth, breastfeeding and pregnancy. *The Fruits of Philosophy* explained the reproductive system and gave advice on contraception, complete with diagrams that outraged the Victorian sense of decorum. The solicitor general described it as a 'dirty, filthy book . . . the object of it is to enable persons to have sexual intercourse, and not to have that which in the order of Providence is the natural result of that sexual intercourse'.[23]

In court Besant pointed out that she was only trying to give working-class women access to information for sixpence that richer ladies were already buying at W. H. Smith's for a few shillings. She added: 'It is more moral to prevent the birth of children than it is after they are born to murder them . . . by want of food, and air, and clothing, and sustenance.'[24] The court disagreed. She was found guilty, fined two hundred pounds and sentenced to six months in prison.

Besant was eventually let off on a technical point on appeal, but she had to pay an even heavier price. As a result of the scandal, Frank gained custody of their daughter Mabel, along with their son who was already living with him. A decade later the woman considered unfit to bring up her own daughter saved the lives of many match girls, who looked upon her as a mother.

Meanwhile, sales of Besant's supposedly scandalous pamphlet on birth control spiralled from a few thousand copies before the court case to 185,000 afterwards. Shut out of Parliament and suppressed by the legal system, the women campaigners carved out their own channels of influence to make lasting political change.

The Suffragists

'The cowardly dastards who let loose their bloodhounds to plunge their sabres into our bosoms, and trample us under their horses' hoofs, shall find, when the day of retribution arrives, that the wrongs which they have heaped upon our heads shall recoil on their own.'

– Mary Fildes

'However benevolent men may be in their intentions, they cannot know what women want and what suits the necessities of women's lives as well as women know these things themselves.'

– Millicent Garrett Fawcett

On 16 August 1819, a public meeting was called at St Peter's Field in Manchester. The city had ballooned, thanks to industrialisation, but it still had no parliamentary representation beyond two MPs for the whole of Lancashire. The purpose of the gathering was to try to work out how to get a city representative onto a green bench in St Stephen's Chapel. The meeting was legal, pre-arranged and well organised. That would make no difference. One of the most shameful and bloody suppressions of a peaceful gathering was about to take place.

As the sun rose on a pleasant morning, 60,000 people from across the North-West made their way to St Peter's Field. Female spinners and weavers marched alongside the working men. The radical politician Henry Hunt was to speak from a specially erected stage. But – unlike the closed male ranks of Westminster – a female voice was to address the tens of thousands of disenfranchised workers.

Mary Fildes was a radical activist and leader of the Manchester Female Reform Group, which campaigned for universal suffrage.

Beyond that, we know frustratingly little about a woman considered so extraordinary by her contemporaries that she was invited
to speak in front of the 60,000. A radical revolutionary woman
has been effectively written out of history.

Fildes was a Chartist, passionately in favour of universal
suffrage. She also believed in birth control – which liberated
women by giving them control over their lives – and the books she
sold on contraception were angrily branded pornography. But,
more than anything, Fildes was ordinary. Her husband William
was a journeyman manufacturer, a contemporary description of
a worker who had completed an apprenticeship but was not yet a
master. They had two sons, John and Henry, and ran a pub. We
know little else about her.

Mary Fildes was politically engaged, passionate, and ultimately voiceless – just like the 60,000 working-class people who
gathered in Manchester. At the beginning of the nineteenth
century the vast majority of people were still locked out of democracy, powerless to have a say over the 658 MPs who crammed onto
the green morocco-leather benches in the thirteenth-century
chapel of St Stephen to decide on the country's laws. Voting was
a postcode lottery, corruption was rife and 'rotten boroughs'
made a mockery of Parliament. In the seaside constituency of
New Shoreham, for instance, eighty-one men decided to sell their
votes as a block to the highest bidder. Old Sarum continued to
return two MPs to Parliament even though it was a ghost town
with no constituents. Meanwhile, rapid industrialisation was
causing mass movement across Britain, as the working class
moved to the new cotton-mill towns springing up across the
north. Those new heavily populated towns had no parliamentary
representation at all.

A rotten voting system produced rotten politics. A deep
economic recession was causing real hardship: wages slumped
while food became ever more expensive. By the beginning of the
nineteenth century, the excluded were not prepared to put up
with it any longer. Trade unions were illegal but working-class

women and men started organising protests demanding political reform. In 1811 workers were smashing textile machines in Nottinghamshire and Derbyshire, and a year later there were riots in Sheffield. Women were excluded from Parliament but were embraced by the protesters. In 1818 the first female political-reform societies sprang up in Lancashire and women spinners went on strike shoulder to shoulder with men. This was seen not just as a threat to the class system but to male authority as a whole.

Wealthy parliamentarians – insulated from the recession and a poor harvest – were unmoved. Working-class men and women had no vote, so MPs had no obligation to represent them. Instead they passed a new law, which meant that a worker who broke a machine faced death. It was not long before the true horrors of the legislation were felt. In January 1813, seventeen men were executed in Yorkshire.

Chartism was born of the realisation that the only way to be heard in nineteenth-century Britain was to have the vote – which working-class men and all women were denied. The corrupt and complacent parliamentarians might have not realised it, but the mob was about to get organised. As a result, the backdrop to the protest at Peterloo was one of rising tension between a politicised working class and an increasingly nervous establishment.

As the sun edged towards the middle of the sky, rows of women, men and children, led by brass bands, wove their way into Manchester from the surrounding towns and villages. Some had walked nearly thirty miles to attend, holding banners and wearing their Sunday best. Many of the women had dressed in white, to signal their virtue. In several towns they had practised the march, to make sure they were in perfect time.

For the skittish local magistrates, the organised marching, banners and music seemed militaristic. Whether this was a genuine mistake or a feeble excuse to break up the meeting with violence is a matter for historical interpretation. However, it is hard to see how a group that even banned walking sticks for being too dangerous could be seen as a genuine threat. The authorities planned to arrest Henry Hunt and other speakers at the meeting, and decided to send in the armed forces.

As the men and women continued to march in perfect order, soldiers on horseback rode through the crowds, pulled out their swords and slashed. There was no chance to get away. Eleven people were killed and several hundred pierced by the soldiers' swords or trampled beneath hoofs and thousands of feet as the protesters tried desperately to escape.

Disturbing evidence suggests that women were deliberately targeted. According to contemporary reports, some soldiers tried to disfigure female marchers by slashing their breasts and faces. A third of casualties were female, even though they made up a relatively small percentage of the marchers. Four women are listed as losing their lives: Margaret Downes, sabred; Mary Heys, trampled by cavalry; Sarah Jones, truncheoned on the head by special constables; and Martha Partington, crushed to death in a cellar. A total of 168 women were listed as injured. The female Chartists were a double threat, transgressing not only the class order but the gender order.

Eye-witnesses claim the constables were specifically hunting for the audacious female speaker Mary Fildes. She was travelling in a coach and holding a banner for the Manchester Female Reform Group when they found her. When she refused to let go of the flag, she was bludgeoned with a truncheon. According to one eye-witness, her white dress was caught on a nail as she was dragged out of the carriage, leaving her suspended and helpless. The cavalry didn't miss the opportunity – cutting her exposed flesh with a sword.

Fildes was no coward and the experience merely fuelled her determination. In a letter to the radical politician Henry Hunt a year later, she wrote:

> *We are but Women, it is true, but if our unnatural enemies chose to despite us on that account – we have only to instance the case of our brave and matchless Queen.*

The cowardly dastards who let loose their bloodhounds to plunge their sabres into our bosoms, and trample us under their horses' hoofs, shall find, when the day of retribution arrives, that the wrongs which they have heaped upon our heads shall recoil on their own. They shall find, too, that their cowardly attempts to intimidate us are in vain and futile; – in spite of all their efforts –

Still will we keep our course – still speak, and even fight –
Till death shall plunge us in the shades of night.[1]

The immediate legacy of the Peterloo Massacre was a depressing reassertion of the old order. It wasn't the killers who were prosecuted but the working-class organisers, imprisoned for sedition. When Parliament reassembled in November, the men elected supposedly to represent the public responded to the deaths by passing six Acts banning gatherings of more than fifty people.

But democracy's flame had been lit. Out of the ashes of the Peterloo Massacre, Chartism was born, Britain's best-known working-class movement, mobilising the excluded. After sustained pressure the June 1832 Great Reform Act allocated constituencies more fairly and increased the number of men who could vote, but the women who had marched in white to St Peter's Field were still disenfranchised. As the vote began slowly to trickle through to their brothers, husbands and sons, the injustice was felt more keenly. The long and difficult campaign for female enfranchisement had begun.

On 3 August 1832, two months after the passing of the Great Reform Act, the House of Commons echoed with laughter and smutty jokes. Parliament has always been raucous and rowdy but on this occasion the innuendos were so *risqué* they were written up in most of the next morning's papers. The clustered MPs, knocking knees on the green benches, could hardly contain themselves as a petition was read out by Henry Hunt, the radical politician who had been the star speaker at what had become known as the Peterloo Massacre. Hunt acknowledged that the document 'might be a subject of mirth to some hon. Gentlemen' but despite that, it 'was one deserving for consideration'.[2]

The petition was authored by Mary Smith, who owned a house in Stanmore, Yorkshire, and argued that unmarried women who paid their taxes, obeyed the law and met the property requirements should be allowed to vote. Her impassioned petition called on Members of Parliament to 'raise the female sex from the degradation to which it was depressed by the ancient heathens', adding that since women are 'taxed by the Legislature equally' and are 'liable to every punishment (that of death not excepted) appointed by the law', preventing them from voting is 'a most flagrant tyranny and cruel oppression'.[3]

The petition was met with laughter, and the proceedings quickly descended into sexual slurs and vulgar jokes (contemporary observers of Parliament might notice that, when it comes to innuendo, not much has changed). The following day, the newspapers reported the proceedings with relish.

According to the broadsheet *Bell's Life*, Sir Francis Trench MP joked that if juries were to consist of an equal number of men and women there might be a problem 'in locking them up all night without fire or candle'. As the politicians fell about laughing, another MP quipped that, if that were the case, they might take months before reaching any decisions. As cheers echoed around the Chamber, Hunt replied that he 'saw no objection to the mixture of men and women on Juries' and joked that Sir Francis Trench 'had often been all night in the company of women, without doing them least harm'.

'But we were not locked up!' came Trench's reply.[4]

The newspapers were universal in their condemnation of 'Mrs SMITH'S foolish petition'. The *Age* speculated whether it was an elaborate ruse to find a husband, while *The Times* concluded: 'In all affairs of civil rights, women are the gainers in their being administered solely by men.'[5]

Mary Smith's petition might have been laughed out of

Parliament but it was an early ripple in what would be an unstoppable stream of pressure. Female reform societies, like that of Mary Fildes, were central to the Chartist movement and had demonstrated on an equal footing with men. Now the genie could not be put back into the bottle. 'We have been told that the province of woman is her home, and that the field of politics should be left to men,' the Female Political Union from Newcastle upon Tyne argued in 1839. 'This we deny; the nature of things renders it impossible . . . Is it not true that the interests of our fathers, husbands, and brothers, ought to be ours? If they are oppressed and impoverished, do we not share those evils with them?'[6]

On the coat-tails of the 1832 Act came the 1867 Reform Act, doubling the electorate and giving the vote to what was seen as the respectable male working class, those who owned property or paid more than ten pounds in annual rent. But it did nothing for women.

The champions of equality were still patiently trying to change minds in the House of Commons. On 20 May 1867, the Liberal MP John Stuart Mill tabled an amendment forcing the first House of Commons debate on women's suffrage. He demanded a change so simple it could be done with the stroke of a pen: replacing the word 'man' with 'person' in the new legislation so men and women would be given the vote on an equal footing. Mill tried to reassure his fellow MPs that women wouldn't suddenly desert their families and stop being homemakers once they were given the vote. 'The ordinary occupations of most women are, and are likely to remain, principally domestic,' he said, but 'the notion that these occupations are incompatible with the keenest interest in national affairs, and in all the great interests of humanity, is as utterly futile as the apprehension, once sincerely entertained, that artisans would desert their workshops and factories if they were taught to read.'[7]

The MPs roundly rejected the argument. Just seventy-two voted in favour of the amendment and 196 against.

As the general election rolled around on 26 November 1867, it seemed inevitable that the new Parliament would be decided exclusively by male voters. But, incredibly, one woman managed to exercise the democratic right she had been denied. The story of the first British woman to vote in a general election has dropped out of the history books, but it is an incredible chapter in the history of women's suffrage.

In the one surviving photograph of Lily Maxwell, a doughty-looking elderly woman stares into the distance just to the left of the camera. She wears a capacious black gown, her grey hair neatly pinned back from her face under a bonnet. Written on the back of the picture is: 'Lily – an old servant of the family'.

Lily Maxwell was neither well-connected, well-off nor well-educated. She was an ordinary woman who found herself in an extraordinary situation. Born in Scotland in 1801, she moved to Manchester for work and found employment as a servant for the prominent businessman Sir Bosdin Thomas Leech. After decades of the tough, physical demands of servitude, she had saved enough money to open a small business.

At the time of her vote, she is recorded as owning a chandler's shop – selling candles and wax – on Ludlow Street, Chorlton-upon-Medlock. It was a terraced road in a relatively middle-class suburb of Manchester, known for its cotton mills. Her neighbours included a watchmaker, a butcher and a boot-maker. The former servant was going up in the world. A prompt rate-payer who never missed an instalment, Lily Maxwell was respectable, aspirational but ultimately unremarkable. She found herself in the history books by pure chance: her name ended up on the electoral register.

The mistake was discovered just a couple of days before the vote and seized upon by the formidable Lydia Becker, the secretary of the Manchester Suffrage Society, one of many organisations springing up across the country dedicated to getting women the vote. Lydia Becker was a severe-looking woman, with spectacles, who wore her hair in a tight bun at the back of her head. She was mocked in the press for her appearance, but was a brilliant speaker – the fourteen-year-old Emmeline Pankhurst joined the suffragist cause after hearing her oratory. On the day of the vote, Becker and Maxwell made their way to Chorlton Town Hall, the local polling station. The two women were escorted by a group of men, but no protection was needed. Nobody tried to stop Lily Maxwell casting her vote. In fact, the reaction was quite the opposite.

After noting her name on the electoral roll, the returning officer duly recorded her vote and the room erupted with three cheers for Britain's first ever female voter. Next to Maxwell's name in the electoral register is written a single word: 'Woman!!' Maxwell knew exactly whom she would support: Jacob Bright, the local Liberal MP. A bushy-bearded radical, he worked in his family's cotton-spinning business, providing many jobs in the local area, and supported Chartism and women's suffrage.

In his victory speech, Jacob Bright was effusive: 'This woman is a hard-working, honest person who pays her rates as you do . . . if any woman should possess a vote, it is precisely such a one as she.'[8]

Lily Maxwell's story ends in sadness. A year after her historic vote, she was forced to give up her little shop, falling into ill-health and poverty. Once such a prompt and reliable rate-payer, her dream of running a small business was over. But she is more than an intriguing aside in the history of female suffrage, more than a mistake on the electoral roll.

In January 1868, the *Englishwoman's Review* wrote about the extraordinary case of Lily Maxwell, who it described as 'an intelligent person of respectable appearance'. The article continued: 'It is sometimes said that women, especially those of the working class, have no political opinion at all. Yet this woman, who by chance was furnished with a vote, professed strong opinions and was delighted to have a chance of expressing them.'[9]

It was strong political conviction – rather than a feminist passion for female suffrage – that compelled Lily to head to the polling station. Lydia Becker admitted: 'She was rather timid at first – and I believe I should never have got her to come, only that she was so strongly in favour of Mr Bright.'[10]

Lily had no history of campaigning or politics – but she knew passionately whom she wanted to vote for. If she had had twenty votes, she said, she would have given them all to him.

The Suffragists attempted to use Lily Maxwell's vote to kick-start wider reform. The indefatigable Lydia Becker arranged house-to-house visits to try to get women's names on the register. On 7 November 1868, the 5,346 female householders of Manchester had their case heard in the court – represented by one Dr Pankhurst, whose wife would later be the most famous women's suffrage campaigner in British history. Inevitably, perhaps, it was thrown out.

The suffragette Ray Strachey remembered: 'Dr Pankhurst made a desperate effort to get these cases heard: "It is so great a subject," he said, "there is so much to urge, it involves so vast a mass of material." But there was laughter in the court, and the judges would not hear him. The decision was given and the matter was at an end.'[11]

The campaigners did not know it at the time, but there had been a turning point in the struggle for universal suffrage. The slowly shifting tectonic plates of society, or rippling political movements, can spark change. Sometimes, however, it is individuals who can be the most transformative of all. When Millicent Garrett came spluttering into the world on 11 June 1847, the daughter of a successful merchant and ship-owner, nobody could have been aware that the baby girl would arguably do more than anyone in the fight for votes for women.

When Millicent was just thirteen, the family was living in a newly built mansion on a hill overlooking the coastal town of Aldeburgh in Suffolk. In a scene of deceiving domesticity, three young women were sitting by the bedroom fire brushing each other's long hair. The two older girls were fast friends. Emily, a twenty-nine-year-old with mousy hair, was visiting Elizabeth, Millicent's elder sister. Both had the breezy confidence of young women determined to make their mark on the world.

As they brushed, the older girls debated. Women could get nowhere, they complained, unless they were as well educated as men. They couldn't become independent and earn their own money because most professions were barred to them. Emily finally pronounced: 'Well, Elizabeth, it's quite clear what has to be done. I must devote myself to securing higher education, while you open the medical profession to women. After these things are done, we must see about getting the vote.' Then she turned to Millicent, who was watching quietly from a stool, and said: 'You are younger than we are, Millie, so you must attend to that.'[12]

Emily Davies indeed devoted herself to securing higher education: she founded Girton College, Cambridge, Britain's first women's university college. Elizabeth Garrett Anderson became the first British woman to qualify as a doctor. The pair also did their bit for female suffrage, organising a Ladies' Petition to Parliament with 1,499 signatures in 1866. But it was Millicent Garrett Fawcett who perhaps did more to secure the vote than any other British woman. She did not chain herself to railings and was not force-fed. Her quiet diplomacy was not as scintillating or romantic as the suffragettes' violence – perhaps that is why she's inspired fewer films and books. But long before the Pankhursts were pouring ink through letterboxes and spitting on policemen, Fawcett was patiently and persistently building a logical, constitutional argument for the vote to be extended to women.

As the young women carved up their futures in Alde House, society's sands were shifting.

The thirteen-year-old girl grew into an amber-haired young lady, whose slight figure masked an intimidating intellect and a keen sense of humour. In 1866, at just nineteen, she became secretary of the London Society for Women's Suffrage, a group of influential women based in affluent Kensington. Meetings were held in drawing rooms and gentlemen's clubs. Feminist pamphlets were printed and distributed. Speeches were made – Millicent Fawcett was so nervous in front of an audience that she often threw up before taking the platform. Despite her fears, she spoke in public up to four times a week. Her first speech – made to a mixed audience in 1869 alongside another suffragist – outraged prudish society because she was the wife of an MP. The spectacle was described by an MP as 'two ladies, wives of Members of this House, who have disgraced themselves by speaking in public'.[13]

In 1867 Millicent Garrett had married Henry Fawcett, the MP for Brighton, who was a keen supporter of women's suffrage. Henry had been blind ever since a misfired shot snuffed out his sight when he was twenty-five, out hunting with his father. It did not stop him becoming a Cambridge professor, a radical Liberal MP and a happily married man. Millicent, who had been warned against chaining herself to a disabled man fourteen years her senior, acted as his eyes from their wedding day until his death.

As an MP's wife, Fawcett believed in parliamentary democracy and felt the only way to secure female suffrage was to get enough men to vote for a change in the law. She devoted her life to pushing and persuading MPs to join her cause. The first chance came in 1870, when the Liberal MP Jacob Bright brought the first Women's Suffrage Bill before the House of Commons. The man for whom Lily Maxwell had cast her vote was a determined supporter of universal suffrage, and he managed – incredibly – to get a majority of thirty-three. The jubilation was short-lived. When the then prime minister, William Gladstone, opposed the legislation the Liberal vote crumbled, and the bill was thrown out at committee stage. For nine of the next ten years, bills were brought forward demanding votes for women. They all failed.

While attempts to change the law floundered in Parliament, the nineteenth-century suffragists started looking at other routes to political power. In 1875, Martha Merrington became the first woman Poor Law guardian in South Kensington. The guardians were elected annually to supervise workhouses and collect taxes to fund them, and in 1894 Emmeline Pankhurst, the founder of the suffragette movement, joined their ranks. It had a profound impact on her. On one occasion she was walking through a workhouse infirmary when she saw a little girl of thirteen lying in bed playing with a doll. 'I was told she was on the eve of becoming a mother, and she was infected with a loathsome disease, and on the point of bringing, no doubt, a diseased child into the world,' she later recalled, in a famous speech in London's Royal Albert Hall. 'Was not that enough to make me a Militant Suffragette?'[14]

While women secured their first foothold on elected office, Westminster remained stubbornly resistant. In 1884, a third Reform Act was passed, which enfranchised a further eight million male voters. The Representation of the People Act targeted working-class men in rural areas but, again, did precisely nothing for women. It was another disappointment for the long-suffering suffragists.

Later that year, as the nights became longer and autumn faded into winter, Henry Fawcett died of pleurisy. The passionate MP and radical thinker had been seriously ill with diphtheria two years previously, and although his health had improved, the illness had marked the end of his distinguished and brave political career. Millicent had stopped acting as his secretary and become his nurse. His thirty-seven-year-old widow was bereft.

For two decades Millicent Garrett Fawcett had poured her relentless energies into her talented, high-flying husband, a keen supporter of women's rights. After his death she found a new outlet for her passions. Fawcett moved to London to live with another elder sister, Agnes Garrett, and became a revolutionary organisational force in the movement she had joined when she was just a teenager.

For the women's suffrage agitators, an unexpected opportunity presented itself in 1889. When the London County Council was created, the legislation setting it up was woolly at best, and failed to stipulate that only men were eligible to stand for office. Jane

Cobden, a prominent suffragist, jumped at the chance to put herself forward to represent Bow and Bromley. With the backing of the local Liberal Party, she stood on a platform promising to fight for fairer wages and better homes for the poor. Incredibly, she won the seat.

As Cobden set to work, trying to improve conditions in local schools and asylums, her enemies on the council refused to accept her victory. As soon as she began actively to participate in the committee work, a legal writ was filed by the Tory council member Sir Walter de Souza. When the Court of Appeal heard the case in 1891, the male judges found in his favour. Bizarrely, Cobden's membership of the council remained valid but she was not allowed to do her job. Relegated to a no man's land, Cobden continued to attend meetings but was unable to vote.

The suffragists campaigning for women to be represented in local government were finally victorious in 1907. There was stiff opposition to the idea of women becoming councillors, including from the Earl of Halsbury, who said women were 'too hysterical' and 'guided by feeling and not cold reason' to be elected councillors.[15] But Halsbury was in the minority. MPs voted in favour of the Qualification of Women (County and Borough Councils) Act. It was a huge boost for the suffragists who felt their efforts to win reform by peaceful and constitutional means were finally starting to pay off. Later that year, women in Oldham couldn't contain their excitement when a Mrs C. E. Lees won the Hollinwood ward with 727 votes for the Liberal Party. According to contemporary accounts: 'Immediately the poll opened yesterday in Hollinwood there was a rush at St John's School by women who each wished to be the first to vote for Mrs Lees.'[16] By 1934, 23 per cent of the London County Council Labour group was female.

Despite the battles of women like Jane Cobden, at the end of the nineteenth century women were no closer to securing the vote. Around nineteen separate groups had been fighting for female suffrage and had achieved little. It was time for women to unite.

In 1897, when the London Society for Women's Suffrage, the Manchester Society for Women's Suffrage and the Central Committee for Women's Suffrage joined forces to become the National Union of Women's Suffrage Societies (NUWSS), Millicent Fawcett played the role of organisational kingpin. Within three years she had become the group's leader.

Fawcett believed change could happen constitutionally only through the Houses of Parliament, and began an indefatigable campaign of lobbying MPs, speaking out in public meetings and organising petitions. The tactics of the NUWSS were the opposite of the violence and disobedience encouraged by the suffragette movement, which Emmeline Pankhurst founded, in 1903, as the Women's Social and Political Union (WSPU). Some of the more radical suffragettes looked down their noses at its peaceful, conciliatory efforts.

Even some feminists who worked closely with Fawcett were sceptical. Ray Strachey, a member of the NUWSS and a close friend of its leader, admits the organisation was 'strong and of old standing but quiet and uninteresting'. The group's tactics, according to Strachey, were 'decorous public meetings, unnoticed in the press, petitions from women (which MPs consigned, without glance, to their wastepaper baskets) and private letters to candidates at election times'.[17]

In reality, the unglamorous NUWSS was making steady if slow progress. It attracted an enormous membership – far higher than Pankhurst's militant group. Just before the First World War, at the height of campaigning, it boasted 100,000 members in comparison to 2,000 at the WSPU. While the militant suffragettes attacked the establishment, Fawcett tried to burrow into the system to effect change. She painstakingly identified MPs who were likely to be sympathetic to the cause, then relentlessly lobbied them to back bills supporting women's right to vote. In 1908, when the Liberal Herbert Asquith was elected prime minister, Fawcett must have felt a surge of hope. She was a committed member of the party, which had a proud record in pushing for equal rights. Surely, she thought, the suffragists were on the verge of a breakthrough.

Herbert Asquith was to become a major roadblock for the women campaigning to get the vote and a bitter disappointment for Millicent Garrett Fawcett. She was constantly meeting with Asquith and the home secretary, David Lloyd George, leading delegations of suffragists to their offices. As she diligently sent the prime minister letters outlining the arguments for female enfranchisement, he prevaricated and made excuses. While the majority of his party backed women having the vote, others were worried that the middle-class women who would be enfranchised were more likely to vote Conservative than Liberal.

In 1910 a petition supporting the Conciliation Bill gathered more than 250,000 signatures. It was named thus because it would have given the vote to just a million women, in an attempt to reassure opponents of female suffrage. Fawcett met Asquith to warn him that the more militant campaigners were close to revolution and it would provoke huge anger if he refused the bill time. After it passed its second reading, Asquith panicked. Using the excuse of a looming general election, he sent the Conciliation Bill to a committee of the whole House – a delaying tactic that ensured it would run out of time and come to nothing.

Fawcett's warning proved prescient. Hundreds of furious women marched to the House of Commons on 18 November 1910, a day that became known as Black Friday. The home secretary, now Winston Churchill, was alarmed, and ordered the police to keep the protesters well away from Parliament. That command was seen as a green light for six hours of police brutality to begin. Arms were twisted, skin was pinched, and officers forced women to the ground, pressing their faces against the black railings surrounding Parliament. In the chaos some men saw the opportunity for sexual assault, with women reporting that their breasts were grabbed and skirts lifted.

The ugly day triggered a campaign of violence sponsored by Emmeline Pankhurst's WSPU. For the suffragette leader, Fawcett's patient diplomacy and compromise had not worked. 'The argument of the broken pane of glass is the most valuable argument in modern politics,' Pankhurst pronounced.[18]

Fawcett regarded the outbreak of violence with horror; she considered it would undo the results of her many years' lobbying and persuading MPs: 'The continued violence of the militants – smashing windows, slashing the canvas of valuable paintings, burning the contents of letterboxes, letting off explosives in empty churches, etc, – caused intense irritation and resentment among the general public, and afforded an excuse to those MPs who had promised their support to our movement to break their word.'[19]

Meanwhile, her efforts to persuade Asquith were falling on deaf ears. In May 1911 MPs debated another Conciliation Bill and voted to give it a week of government time. Again, Asquith changed his mind and announced he was in favour of a bill introducing universal suffrage for men. The legislation was dropped, as he had known it would be. For the third time in three years, a Conciliation Bill was introduced in 1912. This time it was narrowly defeated by MPs.

Fawcett was not only devastated – she was angry. How could she persuade her fellow campaigners to stick to peaceful means of protest if the prime minister was deliberately thwarting their attempts to use the correct parliamentary avenues? 'If this attitude on Mr Asquith's part was intended to provoke a renewed outburst of militantism, it certainly had the desired effect,' she wrote. 'Even the mildest and most pacific of suffragists felt that she had received from the prime minister a personal insult.'[20]

After the third Conciliation Bill failed, Fawcett was so exasperated and disgusted with the unreliable promises of the Liberal prime minister that she was prepared to separate from the party she had supported all her adult life and that her husband had backed until his death. Fawcett directed the many tens of thousands of women in the NUWSS to support Labour Party candidates in parliamentary elections. Switching support was an emotional wrench, but Fawcett was the ultimate pragmatist.

The Labour Party had been founded in 1900 and initially seemed warm towards the idea of women getting the vote. However, with the exception of individuals like Keir Hardie, the first working-class socialist MP, its enthusiasm quickly cooled. Just like the Liberal Party before them, support crumbled when Labour politicians realised that an avalanche of newly enfranchised middle-class women might be more likely to back right-wing parties at the ballot box.

When the First World War broke out, an already despondent Fawcett felt utterly miserable, believing the struggle for women's suffrage would be forgotten and she would never live to see the victories to which she had dedicated her life. Nonetheless, she was a patriot and she ordered her suffragist societies to back the war effort: 'We have another duty now. Let us show ourselves worthy of citizenship, whether our claim to it be recognised or not.'[21]

As men and boys were sucked towards the front line, women filled the jobs they had vacated. The number of women working in the civil service, the machine of government, increased from 65,000 in 1914 to 170,000 in 1918. Even the most fervent anti-feminists were unable to ignore the revolution transforming British society. Walter Long, the minister for local government who had consistently opposed giving women the vote, called Millicent Fawcett to a meeting at Grosvenor House on persuading more women to work in agriculture. She could scarcely believe her ears when Long started complaining that in some villages 'the women had become imbued with the idea that woman's place is home'. That idea, he added, 'must be met and combated'.[22] How things have changed, Fawcett thought.

When a shattered generation tried to pick up the pieces of a society blown apart by the war, the old rules no longer applied. Some believe the First World War was more important than any other factor in furthering the cause of female suffrage; others contend that it delayed what was already inevitable, thanks to the tireless campaigners. Whatever the truth, war created a society of suffragists. Once the horrors of the trenches were over, there was almost universal support for women, who had kept the country running, to vote, thereby becoming full citizens. 'The war revolutionised the industrial power of women,' Fawcett wrote. 'It found them serfs and left them free.'[23]

In January 1918 the Women's Suffrage Bill that Fawcett had helped negotiate passed through the House of Commons with a majority of sixty-three votes. 'It was the greatest moment of my life,' Fawcett wrote. 'We had won fairly and squarely, after a fight lasting fifty years. Henceforth, Women would be free citizens.'[24]

Fawcett had been present at the beginning of the organised movement for female suffrage and she was there to witness its moment of victory – she even voted in the election. But she had not finished yet. On 10 March 1918, she gave an interview to the *National News*: 'While I am delighted with the vote, I am by no means satisfied. A law which gives a boy the vote and withholds it from a woman until she is thirty cannot be said to be a fair one.'

When a bill was finally passed in 1928, giving women the same voting rights as men, a grey-haired old lady could be seen looking down on the proceedings from the public gallery. Millicent Fawcett lived to see the future she had dared to dream of as a bright-eyed teenager. The long battle that had given her energy and inspiration was finally over. She died within a year.

The Militants

'We women Suffragists have a great mission – the greatest mission the world has ever known. It is to free half the human race, and through that freedom to save the rest. And my last word to the Government: I incite this meeting to rebellion.'

– Emmeline Pankhurst

'The militants will rejoice when victory comes. And yet, mixed with their joy, will be regret that the most glorious chapter in women's history is closed, and the militant fight is over – over when so many have not yet known the exaltation, the rapture of battle.'

– Christabel Pankhurst

In the bustling centre of Manchester the Free Trade Hall is a two-storey building lovingly constructed from sandstone in the Italian palazzo style. Today the striking architecture is home to a luxury hotel, but when it was first built in 1853, the hall hosted concerts, public meetings and political debates. On the side of the building a red plaque reminds us that in 1819 it was also the site of a great tragedy, when hundreds of peaceful suffrage campaigners were attacked by soldiers as they demanded the right to vote. It seems fitting that eighty-six years after the Peterloo Massacre, it was on the same bloody spot that the suffragette movement was born.

The history of women winning the right to vote can be divided into two very distinct chapters: the patient, dogged suffragists, who pursued peaceful, constitutional methods, and the violent agitators who believed that smashed windows and burned-down buildings were more effective weapons than the pen. This is their exhilarating story.

There was no whiff of militancy when the Women's Social

and Political Union (WSPU) was first set up around Emmeline Pankhurst's kitchen table in 1903. A small group of nine women, including Emmeline's daughters, met at her red-brick Victorian villa in Nelson Street, Manchester. It was there that the famous 'Votes for Women' slogan was created – and unwittingly carved into Emmeline's wooden table where the group enthusiastically created placards. Christabel Pankhurst was twenty-three when the WSPU was created. She had marched with colourful banners and witnessed women sailing boats up the Thames to shout at MPs as they sipped wine on the riverside terrace of the House of Commons. She had watched as male politicians studiously ignored the group's polite letters requesting a meeting. Two years later, she had tired of waiting. With Annie Kenney, her closest ally, Christabel decided to take matters into her own hands. The WSPU might have been founded on Nelson Street, but it was at the Free Trade Hall that the suffragette movement was truly born.

On 13 October 1905 the beak-nosed Sir Edward Grey, a leading member of the Liberal Party who would become Foreign Secretary, made a speech in front of a packed audience at the Free Trade Hall, urging them to back the local party candidate at the upcoming election. A young Winston Churchill, seen as a rising star in the party, was running for the Manchester North West constituency. Oblivious to what was about to unfold, Sir Edward walked up on to the stage ready to make his address.

The building was busy, but Sir Edward would still have been able to make out the large white calico sheet that was unfurled in the audience as soon as he stepped out in front of the crowd. The banner was homemade. The young women clutching it had used black furniture stain and paintbrushes to write their message: 'Votes for Women!'

As Christabel Pankhurst raised it, Annie Kenney stood up and shouted: 'Will the Liberal government give votes to women?' Sir Edward did his best to carry on speaking, but the young suffragettes had not made the journey to Manchester to be ignored. They interrupted again.

Christabel later recalled: 'The effect was explosive! The meeting was aflame with excitement!'[1]

The two women made an unlikely pair. Christabel Pankhurst was a classically beautiful English rose from a privileged family. Annie Kenney had been sent to work in the Oldham cotton mills from the age of ten. She had a thin, wrinkled face framed by thick blonde hair, and was missing a finger, which had been torn off by a machine in the factory. Together the two young women shattered the illusion that the suffrage movement was of the upper and middle classes.

As the seated crowds looked round in amazement at the two women who would not stop shouting, the police moved in.

The *Manchester Guardian* recorded what happened: 'Superintendent Watson asked them to behave as ladies should, and not to create further disturbance. They were then at liberty to leave. Miss Pankhurst, however, turned and spat in the Superintendent's face.'[2]

That was the first truly militant act. Its violence marked a turning point from the well-behaved suffragists. Christabel played it down. 'It was not a real spit,' she later claimed, 'but only, shall we call it, a pout, a dry purse of the mouth.'[3]

Dry pout or wet spit, it had the desired effect. She and Kenney were charged with obstruction and assault. The court case that was to follow can only be described as a show trial. The canny Christabel, who would become the militant strategist behind the suffragettes, exploited it to her best advantage. She transformed the witness stand into a stage and the trial into a theatre.

As the two young women entered the court room, their allies hung the white calico banner over the dock rail just as they had unfurled it at the Free Trade Hall. 'We have not a vote, and so long as we have not votes we must be disorderly,' Christabel thundered, a confident and persuasive speaker. 'There is no other way whereby we can put forward our claims to political justice. When we have that, you will not see us in the police courts, but so long as we have not votes this will happen.'[4]

To maximise the publicity, Christabel and Annie refused to pay the fine of ten shillings and sixpence and were taken to Strangeways Prison. Emmeline, who could comfortably have covered the fine, was initially horrified at her daughter's decision. This was new territory for the WSPU. She hurried straight to the prison to try to persuade the head-strong Christabel: 'You have carried it far enough. Now I think you ought to let me pay your fines and take you home.' But Christabel had already recognised the public-relations potential of a jail term. 'If you pay my fine I will never go home again,' she replied.[5]

Emmeline left Strangeways impressed and inspired. Her daughter had convinced her that direct action was the most effective route to securing the vote. A week later, when Christabel was due to be released from Strangeways, she got up at four in the morning to travel from Ashton-under-Lyne to the prison to meet her. When Hannah Mitchell, a fellow suffragette who made the journey with her, tried to comfort Emmeline over her daughter's imprisonment, she brusquely replied: 'Never mind, we are making history.'[6]

A large crowd gathered to see the rebellious Christabel Pankhurst of the WSPU step out from the prison gates. Women from various suffrage groups across the country had travelled there to show their support. Christabel's headline-grabbing arrest had been calculated and executed perfectly. Hannah Mitchell later recalled: 'Twenty years of peaceful propaganda had not produced such an effect. Nor had fifty years of patient pleading, which had gone on before. The smouldering resentment in women's hearts burst into a flame of revolt.'[7]

The arrest of Christabel Pankhurst and Annie Kenney was a watershed in the history of women in politics. Until that point female writers, campaigners and suffragists had tried to argue, reason and persuade their way into Parliament. Now a generation of militants aimed for maximum disruption and attention, using methods that were decidedly unladylike: heckling in public meetings, willingly going to prison and, later, attacking property and empty buildings. 'The only limit that the Union puts to militancy is that human life shall be respected,' Christabel told her followers.[8] In other words, as long as you don't kill anyone, anything goes.

The emergence of the militant WSPU, with its motto 'Deeds not words', was down not to its founder, Emmeline Pankhurst, but her headstrong eldest daughter, Christabel, who was seen by many as the primary decision-maker and strategist. The militant phase of the battle for women's rights had begun.

Emmeline and Christabel Pankhurst were women of contradictions. They managed to be simultaneously magnetic, ruthless, brave, impulsive, feminine, domineering, deeply flawed and magnificent. Above all, they were natural leaders, who inspired blind loyalty in their followers. Many of the splits and tensions between the different groups of women's suffrage societies formed because of their demand for complete obedience and their conviction that they were always in the right.

Fellow suffragettes often referred to them in reverential tones. 'There has been no other woman like Emmeline Pankhurst,' gushed the feminist writer Rebecca West. 'She was beautiful. Her pale face, with its delicate square jaw and rounded temples, recalled the pansy by its shape and a kind of velvety bloom in the expression . . . One felt, as she lifted up her hoarse, sweet voice on the platform, that she was trembling like a reed, only the reed was of steel, and it was tremendous.'[9]

Christabel was arguably even more captivating than her mother. An electric speaker and dominating leader, she inspired a devotional loyalty in her followers that was almost sexual. From the moment she met her, the aristocratic suffragette Lady Constance Bulwer-Lytton – usually known as Lady Constance Lytton – was seduced. 'Christabel was the sunrise of the women's movement, I cannot describe her in any other way,' she wrote.[10]

*　　*　　*

Lady Constance Lytton was one of the most privileged members of the suffragette army: her father was an earl and viceroy of India, while her mother was a lady-in-waiting to Queen Victoria. She devoted the first forty years of her life to her family and, in particular, her mother, never marrying and living a private, secluded existence. When her godmother left her a legacy of a thousand pounds she decided to donate the money to the revival of morris dancing and, entirely by chance, met a group of suffragettes at the Esperance Guild, founded to help young dressmakers. The fight for women's rights was the focus she had been searching for, and she developed an almost obsessional affection for Christabel Pankhurst.

In October 1909 she was with her idol in Newcastle, where the Chancellor David Lloyd George was visiting. Determined to do her bit for the cause, she hurled a stone at a car she believed was carrying him. Imprisoned in Newcastle, she immediately refused to eat.

Hunger strikes had become a favourite weapon of the suffragettes, and the authorities struggled to deal with self-starving female prisoners. Marion Wallace Dunlop was the first to be forcibly fed in 1909, and that was the start of a brutal merry-go-round of tubes being shoved down noses and throats. Mouths were forced open with metal devices, often breaking teeth and ripping gums.

To Lady Constance's surprise, she was not force-fed like other suffragette prisoners and was released after just two days. A concerned doctor had performed a thorough medical examination on her, revealing a weak heart. She couldn't help but question whether her gentle treatment was because of her privileged background. The injustice stuck in her throat and she hatched an audacious plan to expose the double standards.

If you happened to be walking through the less salubrious shopping districts of Manchester in 1910, you might have witnessed a curious sight. A woman darting between stores cut a bizarre figure. Swamped by a long green coat, woollen scarf and tweed hat, the ill-fitting clothes looked cheap and ugly. A white silk neckerchief was tied around her throat and a pair of pince-nez spectacles perched upon her nose. In her gloved hands she clutched a purse and a net bag containing her personal papers. Perhaps most disfiguring of all, her hair was chopped short into resentful bristles and parted severely on either side of her face. Lady Constance Lytton had tried to persuade the hairdresser to bleach her hair, but she had point-blank refused, and the cheap dye she bought from a chemist proved ineffective.

'Before leaving Manchester I realised that my ugly disguise was a success,' Lady Constance recalls in her memoirs. 'I was an object of the greatest derision to street-boys, and street-girls could hardly keep their countenances while serving me.'[11]

She had decided to disguise herself as a working-class woman to try to expose the hypocrisy in the prison system. Now it was time to put her theory to the test.

Assuming the *alter ego* of Jane Warton, Lady Constance joined a suffragette demonstration outside Walton Prison in Liverpool to protest at the treatment of suffragettes inside. The prison was infamous for violently force-feeding activists, keeping them in irons and banning them from any communication with friends and family. To make sure she was arrested, she pelted the prison governor's house with large stones gathered from a garden earlier. It wasn't long before the police swooped. Along with two other suffragettes, Elsie Howie and a woman known only as Mrs Nugent, Lady Constance Lytton found herself locked in a cell.

At three in the morning, seven women were dragged from their cells and lined up along a wall. The policeman sitting at a desk called them forward one by one to give their names and ages. As Lady Constance stepped towards the officer to give her false name, her fellow prisoners broke out in titters at the sight of her cropped hair and ugly, cheap clothes. As she squinted through her new glasses, Jane Warton was a risible sight. Apparently feeling a wave of sympathy towards the pathetic figure, the policeman ticked the women off for mocking their fellow prisoner. Nobody suspected that the destitute working-class girl in front of them was in fact a wealthy aristocrat.

At the magistrates' court the next day, she was sentenced to two weeks in prison. Stripped and given a prison gown, she was taken to a cell alone. The aristocrat who had turned into Jane Warton now had another new identity – Prisoner 204. She made ink out of soap and dust and scrawled a message on the cell wall: 'Under a government which imprisons any unjustly, the true place for a just man (or woman) is also a prison.'

In Newcastle, the authorities had been so worried about Lady Constance Lytton's health that she had been released on medical grounds. In Liverpool, nobody had any concerns about Jane Warton. As soon as she went on hunger strike, she was taken to the force-feeding room and strapped into the chair. The violence of what happened next, and Lady Constance's subsequent account of it, shone an uncomfortable light on the experiences of dozens of Jane Wartons.

As she lay in the chair, refusing to speak or open her mouth, the doctor became increasingly irritated with her resistance. It might have explained his decision to use a steel gag to prise her teeth apart, rather than the wooden version that typically caused less pain and fewer cuts. As he did so, he told Lady Constance that if she continued to clamp her teeth together he would have to feed her through her nose. When the gag was finally forced between her teeth the doctor cranked her jaws open until her mouth was yawning wide and a large tube, about four foot long, was forced down her throat.

'I felt as though I were being killed. Absolute suffocation is the feeling,' she later recalled in a speech. 'You feel as though it would never stop. You cannot breathe, and yet you choke. It irritates the throat, it irritates the mucous membrane as it goes down, every second seems an hour, and you think they will never finish pushing it down.'[12]

Worse was yet to come. A mixture of milk, gruel, brandy, sugar, eggs and beef tea was poured down the tube. As the sticky slop gushed into her throat, Lady Constance doubled up to vomit. The wardresses pressed her head back and the doctor leaned on her knees.

'The horror of it was more than I can describe,' she remembered. 'I was sick over the doctor and wardresses, and it seemed a long time before they took the tube out. As the doctor left he gave me a slap on the cheek, not violently, but as it were, to express his contemptuous disapproval and he seemed to take for granted my distress was assumed.'[13]

Lady Constance was appalled. The doctor would never have dreamed of slapping her face if he had known her true identity. She was unable to move or clean herself. The wall by the bed was covered with vomit, her clothes were saturated with it. The wardresses, trying to help her sit up, apologetically admitted they could not get a change of clothes that night as the laundry was shut.

A few minutes later the room was filled again with noise. Next door the four-foot tube was being forced down the throat of Elsie Howey. When the ordeal was over, and everything was quiet again, Lady Constance had a sudden surge of energy. She started hammering on the wall, and shouting, 'No surrender!'

Weakly, another voice came back: 'No surrender!'

Elsie Howey was a rector's daughter, whose health never recovered after multiple force-feedings. The injuries to her throat remained raw for four months and she could barely speak. She died of chronic pyloric stenosis – a narrowing of the passage between the stomach and bowel preventing food from being digested – almost certainly related to force-feeding.

A public outcry erupted once Lady Constance Lytton's identity was known. Her friends and family were horrified to see her emaciated figure on leaving prison: she had lost nearly two stone and gained an erratically fluttering heart. A huge scandal ensued. When Sir Edward Troup of the Home Office wrote a letter to *The Times* in which he attempted to justify Lady Constance's treatment, her brother Victor was outraged. Writing directly to the home secretary, Herbert Gladstone, he blasted: 'My sister is unfortunately too ill to defend herself and I have therefore undertaken the task of vindicating both her sanity and her veracity.'[14]

On 19 February Gladstone was sacked as home secretary and replaced with Winston Churchill. Although privately dismissive of Lady Constance's claims, he was bright enough to understand the seriousness of the public outcry. From then on a medical officer had to sign a certificate to say that a suffragette had been medically examined before force-feeding could begin.

Lady Constance Lytton always insisted she had acted alone but the suffragette leaders were almost certainly aware of her plan. In a letter to the Liverpool organiser, who provided lodgings for Lady Constance, Christabel asked her 'not to tell a soul about our friend. It had better go on to the end. She is willing we know.'[15]

The aristocrat who sacrificed her health for the cause would not be the only willing soldier in the Pankhursts' militant campaign.

If Christabel's altercation with a policeman was a defining moment in the militant campaign, another turning point came in 1913 after the three Conciliation Bills had foundered in Parliament. Infuriated by the political class, the Pankhursts ordered a fresh round of violence to frighten them into submission.

In *The Times*, Pankhurst called on her followers to use 'all methods that are resorted to in time of war', including doing 'as much damage to their property as we can'. Although its leader had just put the WSPU on a war footing, she did stop short of telling her followers to kill anyone: 'One thing we will regard as sacred and that is human life.'[16]

Cloth that might once have been painted to make joyful banners was now stuffed into pillar boxes and set alight. A wave of acts took place that can only be described as terrorism. Suffragettes burned down several country houses, the stand at Ayr Racecourse, and a bomb even wrecked the house of Chancellor Lloyd George who had opposed the Conciliation Bill. It was the excuse he needed to withdraw his lukewarm support completely. The WSPU was now effectively an illegal organisation with its leaders on the run from the police. A warrant was issued for Christabel's arrest, and she fled to France under an assumed name.

It was in the 1913 wave of violence that the most famous sacrifice of the suffragette campaign was made. If there was one suffragette who was bolder, madder and more radical than any other, it was Emily Wilding Davison. Born into a middle-class Hertfordshire family, she was a devout Christian who loved the theatre and was a medal-winning swimmer – but she was sucked deep into the suffragette movement. Despite her devotion to the cause, she was seen as a loose cannon and never made it into the WSPU inner circle. Even the Pankhursts were sometimes shocked by her, unsure how to handle their most fanatical follower.

In 1909 she was sentenced to a month in prison after throwing rocks at a carriage carrying Lloyd George. One was wrapped in a piece of paper on which she had scrawled her personal motto: 'Freedom against tyrants is obedience to God.' Shut inside her cell, she barricaded the door with her bed while wardresses tried in vain to force it open with a crowbar, then resorted to blasting the room with jets of water from a fire hose. When the door finally gave way, the cell was six inches deep in water, which immediately flooded into the corridor. Bedraggled but defiant, Davison was given a hot bath and a hot-water bottle, then force-fed again.

This most uncontrollable of rebels lapped up the attention. In November 1911 she was sentenced to another six months in prison for thrusting a lit piece of linen, saturated in paraffin, through a pillar box. 'It is a great advertisement for the cause, isn't it?' she wrote gleefully to a friend. 'You know it is the Old Bailey at which I have to appear! That's rather fine, isn't it?'[17]

But Davison's story is also laced with darkness. It is hard to ignore a sense that a violent death was inevitable. When she was in prison in July 1912, she threw herself from a railing onto an iron staircase in protest at force-feeding. Knocked unconscious, she escaped serious injury. 'The idea in my mind was that one big tragedy might save many others,' she later explained.[18] It was not long before Davison achieved the big tragedy she wished for.

On 4 June 1913, thousands gathered at Epsom Downs in Surrey for horse-racing, beer and betting. King George V was in the stand, binoculars in hand, to watch the performance of his colt, Anmer. As the horses reached the halfway stage of Tattenham Corner, Anmer had fallen back into the chasing pack.

Emily Davison, who had never expressed an interest in racing before, was one of the onlookers clustered around the track. She had chosen her spot carefully. Because of the sharp bend, the horses crowded up against the railing as they thundered by at speed.

The Canadian suffragette Mary Richardson, famous for slashing *The Rokeby Venus* painting in the National Gallery, was also at Epsom and was surprised to see Emily standing alone next to the white-painted rails. 'She looked absorbed and yet far away from everybody else and seemed to have no interest in what was going on round her,' she later recalled. 'I shall always remember how beautifully calm her face was.' A minute before the race started, Richardson saw Davison raise a piece of paper before her eyes. 'I was watching her hand. It did not shake. Even when I heard the pounding of the horses' hoofs moving closer I saw she was still smiling.'[19]

According to another eye-witness, Davison darted under the railings as the King's horse Anmer approached the bend. 'She put up her hand, but whether it was to catch hold of the reins or to protect herself I do not know. It was all over in a few seconds. The horse knocked the woman over with very great force, and then stumbled and fell, pitching the jockey violently onto the ground. Both he and Miss Davison were bleeding profusely.'[20]

Anmer rolled over and galloped off to complete the race without his rider, suffering nothing more than slightly bruised shins. The jockey, Herbert Jones, lay completely still on the ground until the last horse passed over him. He then carefully got up and stumbled to safety, with a bruised face, fractured rib and mild concussion. He would always be haunted by the woman crushed under the hoofs of his horse.

Emily Davison did not get up. Her spine had been fractured at the base of her skull. Carefully sewn into her coat were the colours of the WSPU, purple, white and green, a visual testimony to the cause that she could no longer speak for. Four days later, on 8 June, she died in hospital at 4.50 p.m. Her fellow suffragettes had draped the cheerful WSPU banners around her bed, but nobody kept a vigil beside her. Her death was witnessed only by the hospital staff.

Did Davison intend to die for the cause? The jockey believed she was just trying to slow the horse down by grabbing the reins, so she could affix a suffragette banner to him. Sylvia Pankhurst – another of Emmeline's daughters – agreed: 'She had concerted a Derby protest without tragedy – a mere waving of the purple-white-and-green at Tattenham Corner, which, by its suddenness, it was hoped, would stop the race.'[21]

In her pocket she had had a return rail ticket. It is hard, though, to forget Davison hurling herself down the iron staircase and dreaming of a 'big tragedy'. If she did not actively seek death, she was happy to brush it by.

The newspapers were alarmed by the new breed of violent female militant. 'She nearly killed a jockey as well as herself and she brought down a valuable horse,' said *The Times*. 'Reckless fanaticism,' it added, is not 'a qualification for the franchise.'[22] For the increasingly violent and angry suffragette movement, though, Davison was transformed in death from reckless outrider to fearless freedom fighter. The movement's lone wolf was now clasped tight. A resplendent militant procession was organised to mark her funeral, with crowds lining the streets of London to watch her coffin go by. Emily Davison was more useful to the movement as a dead martyr than a living suffragette, inspiring other young women in a year when militancy was at its most fierce.

The suffragette journal *Votes for Women* described the day in June 1913:

Waiting there in the sun, in that gay scene, among the heedless crowd, she had in her soul the thought, the vision of wronged women. That thought she held to her; that vision she kept before her. Thus inspired, she threw herself into the fierce current of the race. So greatly did she care for her freedom that she died for it.

In January 1913, just days after Emmeline Pankhurst had called on her followers to damage property and use all means apart from murder to further the suffragette cause, an unfamiliar face appeared at the WSPU headquarters.

Long-haired and strikingly beautiful, Lilian Ida Lenton told the women who greeted her: 'I didn't want to break any more windows but that I did want to burn some buildings,' so long as 'it did not endanger human life other than our own'.[23] Introduced to another keen new recruit, she was soon travelling the country lugging heavy cases of petrol and paraffin.

The life of Lilian Lenton reads like a nail-biting thriller but remarkably little has been written about her. In death Emily Davison earned her place in the suffragette canon, but many other militants sacrificed their health and happiness for the cause only to be all but forgotten by the generations they had fought for. Like Annie Kenney, Lenton was one of many working-class suffragettes who had a strong sense of self-worth and the conviction that they should be treated as full citizens.

Lenton grew up in Leicester, a quickly expanding industrial town of shoemakers and hosiers. Her father worked as a joiner and carpenter to support his wife, Mahalah, and five children. Rather than learning to make stockings or hunting for a suitable husband, Lilian trained as a dancer. When she heard Emmeline Pankhurst speak in her home town, though, she decided on a different path. 'I made up my mind that night that as soon as I was twenty-one and my own boss, I would go through these dancing exams and then volunteer,' she later explained.[24]

It wasn't long before Lenton was carrying out audacious arson attacks, aiming to create a state of affairs so intolerable that politicians would be forced to give women the vote. 'Whenever I was out of prison my object was to burn two buildings a week,' she said. 'No one could ignore arson, nor could they ignore young women who went about saying what I said – that whenever we saw an empty building we would burn it. And, as I say, after that I did burn an empty building whenever I saw one.'[25]

Ten days after Emmeline Pankhurst had called on suffragettes to damage property, Lilian Lenton made her way to Kew Gardens, a botanical paradise in west London founded in 1840. The WSPU had introduced her to Gertrude Harding, a Canadian suffragette, who was also keen to get involved. Together they smashed the glass orchid houses and ripped up plants by the roots.

Less than two weeks later, Lilian returned to Kew Gardens with an even more audacious plan. She was accompanied by Olive Wharry, a middle-class Londoner, who became a close conspirator despite their different backgrounds. A little after three in the morning an employee noticed a light coming from the refreshment pavilions. To his alarm flickering flames were soon piercing the night sky and he could see two forms in the darkness. Sounding the alarm, he grabbed a hose to try to put out the fire – but it was too late. The building and its contents were destroyed, causing nine hundred pounds' worth of damage.

In the chaos after the explosion, Lenton and Wharry bolted to the nearest railway station, followed by constables. They were seen throwing away two sturdy leather bags as they ran, which were quickly picked up by the police. One contained a hammer, a saw, rags stinking of paraffin and some paper smelling strongly of tar. The other bag was empty. The inflammables it had contained had been used. The evidence was incontrovertible (Lilian had even given her real name at the station). The two suffragettes were sent to Holloway Prison, where they began a hunger strike.

Lenton starved herself for two days before the force-feeding started. Strapped into the chair, her head dragged sharply backwards by her hair, the doctors had some difficulty inserting the tube and had to push it up her nose. The thick rubber was forced not into her oesophagus but into her windpipe. As food poured into her left lung, the young woman started to choke violently. Two hours later Lilian Lenton had collapsed in her cell and nearly died from septic pneumonia.

In Parliament there was little sympathy: one MP suggested she should have been left to die, another that she be deported. Only Keir Hardie, the pro-suffrage Labour MP, commented that the problem would be solved if women were given the vote. Sensing a public storm, the home secretary, Reginald McKenna, tried to claim that Lenton hadn't been force-fed but had made herself ill by refusing food. When Home Office papers were released and the truth was revealed, there was an instant outcry.

To avoid more embarrassment, the government rushed through legislation that would become known as the Cat and Mouse Act. It allowed hunger strikers to be released on temporary licence on health grounds, only to be arrested again once they had recovered. Lenton, like many other suffragettes, became one of the mice running in a wheel of constant arrests.

A few weeks after the scandal, the militant suffragette Mary Richardson travelled to Birmingham under a false name, accompanied by a young woman calling herself Lilian Mitchell. It is impossible to know for sure, but there has been speculation that she was in fact Lilian Lenton. The two women had arranged to stay at the family home of a suffragette sympathiser, who was conveniently out of town. They were looked after by the woman's businessman husband, who was happily oblivious to the real reason he had acquired two temporary lodgers.

In the middle of the night, Lilian was woken by a loud hissing coming from the wardrobe in the room where they were staying. She knew there was no time to waste. Shaking Mary awake, Lilian told her that the homemade bomb they had named 'Black Jennie' and stashed in the cupboard was making strange noises. They pulled on clothes and shoes, then gingerly approached the wardrobe and opened the door.

Richardson describes what happened next: 'I looked at Jennie in alarm. She was certainly spluttering and hissing. I felt that my last moment had come, and the thing would explode the moment I touched it. To pick up that black bag with the homemade time bomb inside terrified me. I took the strings of the bag carefully in my fingers and lifted.'[26]

'Don't drop her whatever you do!' warned Lilian, as the spluttering increased.[27]

Carrying their deadly luggage, the two women walked to Birmingham's new railway station. Taking care not to drop the bomb, they left it at the ticket office as they scrambled back to safety.

At three in the morning, Jennie exploded.

The next day, at breakfast, Lilian and Mary were the picture of innocence when their host cried, 'Those blasted women!' as he read of their exploit in the morning newspaper.[28]

Lilian Lenton was becoming famous for her daring escapades and great escapes. In exasperation, Leeds Police filed a report to the Home Office about the dangerous suffragette known as the 'tiny, wily, elusive Pimpernel'.[29] In June the police managed to lock her up but only because she handed herself in after another woman was blamed for an arson attack in Blaby, Leicestershire. After refusing food again, she was released under the Cat and Mouse Act and went to stay in Leeds with one of the founders of the Men's Political Union for Women's Enfranchisement, Frank Rutter. This time, the authorities were determined not to lose her and stationed police outside the house. By then, they had a photograph taken covertly of Lenton standing in a prison yard, reaching up to touch her long, dishevelled hair. Her five-foot frame is dwarfed under a mannish coat.

What happened next sounds more like fiction than reality. As the detectives sat watching the house, determined not to let that dangerous woman elude them again, a van pulled up in front of the door. A boy, who had been sitting on the tail-board of the vehicle, got up and went inside. After just a few moments the lad reappeared, munching an apple, and resumed his seat at the back of the vehicle. It pulled away from the house and drove down the road.

The detectives continued their watch, but by then it was too late. Lilian Lenton had already gone. She escaped to France on a private yacht.[30]

On 28 March 1917 some women got the vote. This advance is often painted as an unequivocal victory but in reality those who qualified were over thirty, householders, the wives of householders, occupied properties with an annual rent of more than five pounds or were university graduates. Lenton was a respectable girl from Leicestershire who became an outlaw and ruined her health to campaign for a change in the law that she did not initially benefit from. 'Personally, I didn't vote for a long time, because I hadn't either a husband or furniture, although I was over thirty,' she told an interviewer.[31] Working-class women, such as Lenton, were still locked out of democracy.

The Pioneers

'Dress suitably in short skirts and strong boots, leave your jewels and gold wands in the bank, and buy a revolver.'

         – Countess Constance Markievicz

'Pioneers may be picturesque figures, but they are often rather lonely ones.'

         – Lady Astor

In March 1919, a woman was walking in disguise under the round face of Big Ben. She did not know her way around Westminster's honeycomb of wood-panelled corridors and spiral staircases, but she was determined not to draw attention to herself or betray her true identity. The figure scuttled across New Palace Yard, an open space in front of Parliament where criminals were once displayed in the stocks, and passed through the Members' Entrance. There, just around the corner, was the Members' Cloakroom. To this day, every elected MP is allocated a peg on which to hang their coat, arranged alphabetically, and the woman quickly searched for her own. Under the coat hook, she would have found a purple ribbon dangling from a coat hanger on which to hang her sword. Today the only swords you may find attached to the ribbons would be of the wooden or plastic variety, put there as a joke by irreverent MPs. Countess Constance Markievicz would have been unlikely to hang a sword under her allotted peg. A pistol was her weapon of choice.

For someone so determined to be unseen, it seems a strange risk to enter the House of Commons to visit the cloakroom. But the countess was an extraordinary woman in an unprecedented situation. She was rumoured to have smuggled herself into the Houses of Parliament like a burglar, but she had every right to be there: she was the MP for Dublin St Patrick and the first ever woman to be elected in the UK. She was also an Irish revolutionary who scorned the Parliament at Westminster and refused to take her seat. But, legend has it, she could not resist the chance to sneak into the House of Commons to steal a glance at her own coat peg, neatly labelled with her name. The countess had told friends that she took pleasure in knowing the peg was there, patiently waiting for a coat to hang from it, while its owner was locked up in Holloway Prison. Perhaps when she was released, she was unable to resist the opportunity to see written proof that the first woman had been elected to Parliament. She was a devoted Republican – but she was also a suffragette.

In February 1918, the historic event that generations had fought for finally took place: women (or, at least, some women) were given the right to vote. The Representation of the People Act was given royal assent after gaining an overwhelming majority in the House of Commons. Almost without anyone realising, a second piece of legislation slipped through at the same time. The Parliament (Qualification of Women) Act 1918 was an apparent afterthought but it was to have an unprecedented impact on Westminster's stuffy corridors because it allowed women to run for election. Perhaps because of the distraction of the Representation of the People Act, it slipped through with remarkably little resistance.

However, when the first flurry of female candidates stood for Parliament in the 1918 election, the suffragette script went horribly wrong. It was not the rugged, battle-hardened survivors of the Cat and Mouse Act who were to become the new female champions in Westminster – if not for want of trying. Experienced campaigners who had devoted their lives to the cause put themselves forward at the ballot box, including some famous names.

Freshly triumphant, Christabel Pankhurst stood as a candidate for the Women's Party in Smethwick, a newly created constituency near Birmingham. She campaigned on a nationalistic platform with slogans including 'Make Germany Pay'. When she narrowly lost by 775 votes to a Labour Party candidate, she initially refused to accept defeat and demanded a recount. For the warrior of the WSPU, the first punch of failure was difficult to accept. Afterwards, the Pankhursts left centre stage, allowing a new band of parliamentary actresses to take their place in the spotlight.

Another candidate who would have been quietly confident of success was Mary Macarthur, an experienced and well-known trade unionist who stood for the Labour Party in Stourbridge, Worcester. She, too, failed to take the seat by less than a thousand votes. Macarthur was known by her maiden name in trade-union circles, but the returning officer insisted that her married name must appear on the ballot paper, which might have put her at a disadvantage.

Seventeen women stood for election in 1918 and, one by one, nearly all fell. After the results were counted and verified, the lone female MP was an Irish prisoner, who refused to take her seat in Parliament. A year later, the first woman to take her seat was a society beauty who had shown little interest in the suffragist cause and was elected because of her husband. That was not how the story was supposed to end.

Little in Markievicz's early life would have predicted her violent future. She was born into an idyllic and privileged life in 1868, the daughter of the philanthropist and explorer Sir Henry Gore-Booth, who lived at the resplendent neo-classical Lissadell estate in County Sligo. Wealthy, beautiful and Protestant, the young Constance Gore-Booth could have chosen a life of privilege. Instead she decided to become a soldier. When she came of age in 1897, she was presented at court in London, but then this strong-willed Irish woman abandoned the script. She fell in love with a penniless Polish count and married him in 1900. A year later they had a daughter, whom they offloaded on Constance's mother, and moved back to Ireland.

When they moved back to Ireland, Constance became

increasingly passionate about nationalist politics. The couple soon separated and Count Casimir Markievicz set off for the Balkans to be a war reporter. While her husband decided to report on conflict, Constance chose to fight in it, shrugging off the privileged future that awaited her. She turned up to her first Sinn Fein meeting wearing a diamond tiara and satin gown after attending a ball at Dublin Castle.

In 1907 Markievicz joined the militant women's organisation Daughters of Ireland – Inghinidhe na hÉireann – a radical group that fought for independence. Shortly afterwards she signed up to the Irish Citizens Army, where her shooting and horse-riding skills were put to good use. A publicity shot from 1915 shows her in full military uniform, holding a gun.

The countess had a strong feminist identity and was involved in the Irish suffrage movement in her twenties. In 1909 she advised students in Dublin: 'Don't trust to your "feminine charm" and your capacity for getting on the soft side of men, but take up your responsibilities and be prepared to go your own way depending for safety on your own courage . . . A consciousness of their own dignity and worth should be encouraged in women. They should be urged to get away from wrong ideals and false standards of womanhood, to escape from their domestic ruts, their feminine pens.'[1]

As war loomed, the self-determination the Irish had been promised was suddenly put on the back-burner. Irish, English, Scottish and Welsh men were fighting – and dying – together in the trenches, but in Dublin tensions were growing. The Irish Citizens Army and Cumann na mBan – the League of Women – were preparing for battle, and Markievicz was embedded in both. When the 1916 Easter Rising erupted against British rule in Ireland, the countess was at the centre of the resistance. A group of Irish nationalists staged a rebellion in the centre of Dublin, seizing key locations in the city and proclaiming outside the General Post Office that Ireland was an independent republic. Initially the British military response was slow, but when additional soldiers were drafted in, fierce street battles took place in the centre of Dublin and heavy shelling destroyed many of its buildings.

As a lieutenant in the Citizens Army, the countess was second in command of the rebel forces and would have been an eye-catching figure in her military uniform of a green Irish Citizens Army coat complete with an ostrich-feathered hat. She was fighting on the front line at St Stephen's Green, a public space in the middle of Dublin. Contemporary reports describe her as toying with a large automatic gun, and bearing so many weapons 'that the casual onlooker might readily be pardoned for mistaking her for the representative of an enterprising firm of small arms manufacturers'.[2] She commandeered vehicles, supervised first aid for the injured and blew the lock off a door in a building. An eye-witness account from a district nurse caused major controversy over what Markievicz might or might not have done. Geraldine Fitzgerald was working at a nurses' home based at St Stephen's Green when she saw Sinn Fein soldiers digging trenches and carrying rifles. She recorded in her diary that she saw 'a lady in a green uniform the same as the men were wearing'; the feathers in her hat 'were the only feminine feature in her appearance'. The woman was holding a revolver in one hand and a cigarette in the other while she gave orders to the men. Geraldine Fitzgerald continued:

> We recognised her as the Countess de Markievicz – such a specimen of womanhood. We had only been looking out a few minutes when we saw a policeman walking down the footpath . . . he had only gone a short way when we heard a shot and then saw him fall forward on his face. The Countess ran triumphantly into the Green saying 'I got him' and some of the rebels took her by the hand and seemed to congratulate her.[3]

Michael Lahiff, an unarmed police constable, was sent to hospital and died half an hour later. Confusion surrounds the event and the identity of his killer remains unresolved a hundred years later. The countess vehemently denied shooting a policeman. However, several months later, she told her sister that she might have hit one in the arm as he jumped.

A shoot-out between the Irish Citizens Army and the British Army ensued. Alongside her fellow fighters, Markievicz stayed barricaded in at the Royal College of Surgeons, eating porridge, saying prayers and singing. When she eventually surrendered, with green shoes to match her green military uniform, she walked up to the officer, saluted, took out her revolver and kissed it affectionately before handing it over.

The bloody revolt lasted five days. A total of 132 British soldiers and police died, along with 64 Irish Republican fighters and nearly 250 civilians.

Afterwards 3,500 people were arrested – more than double the number who had been involved in the Rising. Many of those who had taken part were court-martialled for treason, 90 were sentenced to death and 15 actually shot. Markievicz was a commander of the rebel forces and consequently sentenced to death by shooting. She had refused to be limited by her sex but in the end that was what saved her: she escaped with a prison sentence because she was a woman (and would eventually be freed under the general amnesty). Locked up in solitary confinement, listening to the sound of gunshots as her comrades were executed, she told the officer who brought the news of her reprieve: 'I do wish your lot had the decency to shoot me.'⁴

The Easter Rising originally achieved only limited public support, but the iron fist used to flatten those involved hardened Irish opinion and turned the dead into martyrs. As a result, Sinn Fein went from having no parliamentary seats in 1910 to seventy-three in 1918. In 1921, a treaty was signed to create the Irish Free State, which came into effect in 1922 and founded the modern Republic of Ireland. That growing tide of support swept the first woman to electoral victory.

Countess Constance Markievicz was in prison when she discovered, on 28 December 1918, that she had become the MP for Dublin St Patrick. It was a strange sort of victory. The first woman to smash through Westminster's ancient ceiling and win an election was someone who had once written: 'A good nationalist should look upon slugs in a garden much in the same way as she looks on the English in Ireland, and only regret that she cannot crush the Nation's enemies with the same ease as she can the garden's.'[5]

Along with the seventy-two other Sinn Fein MPs, the countess refused to take her seat. The first female MP never spoke in a debate, voted on legislation or tabled an amendment, and there is some question whether she ever set foot inside the Palace of Westminster. The official summons was addressed to her cell in Holloway Prison, a key battleground of the women's movement where so many suffragette prisoners had been forcibly fed. It is fitting somehow that the first woman to be elected as a Westminster MP celebrated her victory in that north London jail.

Almost exactly a year later, a very different woman shimmied into Westminster. The jagged coastline and historic soil of Ireland's County Sligo had produced the first elected female MP, but the bracing American air of southern Virginia would blow the second to Parliament.

Lady Astor, the first female MP to take her seat in the House of Commons, was a southern belle who had risen to the upper echelons of British high society. Well-connected, with a razor-sharp wit, she was famous for hosting exclusive parties at her palatial county pile for the 'Cliveden set' of fashionable gentry and high-profile politicians. The American dynamo was already uncomfortably close to the upper-class establishment who had resisted the advancement of women. Now she was determined to direct a Virginian hurricane into its stuffy corners.

Nancy Astor had inherited her sharp elbows from her father, a tobacco auctioneer who worked his way up from poverty to amass a small fortune to bestow on his five beautiful and gifted daughters. By the age of twenty-four she was divorced from her alcoholic first husband, observing in her typically wry manner: 'I married beneath me, all women do.'[6] Within a few years, she had moved to England and found a new partner. She met Viscount Waldorf Astor, one of the richest men in the world, on a ship crossing the Atlantic, and when they married in 1906 Nancy gained a title, along with the lavish Cliveden estate in Buckinghamshire. Soon she had five children of her own.

Waldorf Astor was the Conservative MP for Plymouth Sutton, and when he was elevated to the House of Lords in 1919 his wife slipped almost seamlessly into his vacated seat. For the women who had faced prison, force-feeding and even death for the cause, it must have seemed a remarkably easy route to power. Nancy Astor might have been the first woman to take her seat in the House of Commons, but she had not been involved in the fight for the vote and gave her husband the credit for her election. 'My entrance into the House of Commons was not, as some thought, in the nature of a revolution. It was simply evolution,' she later wrote. 'My husband was the one who started me off on this downward career – from home to the House. If I have helped the cause of women, he is the one to thank – not me.'[7]

Not all of Lady Astor's friends were so relaxed. J. M. Barrie, the creator of Peter Pan, who had enjoyed her generous hospitality at Cliveden, sent a furious letter: 'I hear of your presumptuous ambitions at Plymouth. How any woman can dare to stand up against a man I don't understand. What can you know about politics? These things require a man's brains, a man's knowledge.'[8]

The prospect of a woman canvassing for votes in the constituency brought its own challenges. Plymouth was a commercial shipping port that could not have been further away from the opulence of Lady Astor's Cliveden retreat in Buckinghamshire. She was given a naval officer as an escort as she went from door to door meeting voters. On one occasion she was greeted by a young girl, who said her mother had instructed her to tell any lady turning up at the door with a sailor that they could use the upstairs room and leave ten bob (shillings).

When the by-election result was announced on Saturday, 28

November, Lady Astor had stormed to victory by more than 5,000 votes. A huge crowd was waiting outside Plymouth's Guildhall to find out who was to be the new MP when the windows on the balcony were flung open and Lady Astor stepped out. The look on her face told it all. The cheers and shouts drowned any doubt that Plymouth Sutton was not ready for a female MP.

The media seemed unsure how to cope with the light-hearted lady who took a cold bath every day, loved cartwheeling and seemed remarkably relaxed, considering the historic significance of her election. 'Lady Astor is laughing her way into Parliament,' proclaimed the *Evening Standard*, while *The Times* declared: 'She is treating the whole affair as a huge joke.'[9]

Unlike Constance de Markievicz, Nancy Astor wasted little time in getting to Westminster. As the train from Plymouth pulled into London's Paddington station, word of her victory had already spread and a crowd had gathered. A small band of suffragettes was waiting patiently for her on the platform to bear witness to the historic moment they had sacrificed so much to bring about. The wealthy, elegant lady who emerged from the carriage was not the woman they had expected to be Britain's first sitting female MP, but one elderly suffragette came forward to give her a badge and take her hand. Just a few years earlier, that woman had been locked up in Holloway Prison, pinned down as rubber tubes containing milky sludge were forced into her stomach. She had tears in her eyes as she stepped towards Astor, saying her victory had made everything worthwhile.

Lady Astor wore the sense of history lightly, but she was said to be deeply touched by the moment. Suddenly, a man in the crowd shouted, 'I never voted for you!'

She didn't miss a beat: 'Thank Heaven for that!'[10]

Dressed simply in a tailored black skirt and jacket, Lady Astor took her seat in Parliament for the first time on Monday, 1 December. She completed the look with a white blouse, white kid gloves, a black hat and a white gardenia. The Chamber was full, with 707 MPs squeezing onto the green benches and crowding behind the speaker's chair, keen to witness the arrival of the first lady Member. The Strangers' Gallery – set aside for the public – was packed with women, and there were even two female journalists in the reporters' area, from a news agency and a London paper, who had pleaded with the serjeant-at-arms for admission. It was the first time they had been allowed into the Press Gallery; the arrival of a female MP was already opening new doors for women.

Lady Astor stood at the bar of the House, flanked by the lanky former prime minister Arthur Balfour and the pocket-sized incumbent Lloyd George. With her chaperones, she marched five steps towards the mace, paused, took another five steps forward and bowed to the speaker before taking the oath and signing the roll. The ritual of a new Member taking their seat was familiar; everything else was uncannily different.

Lady Astor might have enjoyed a gilded entry into the House of Commons, but once she was there, things quickly became difficult and she often cut a lonely figure on the green benches. She got her first taste of what was in store when she made her first address, her maiden speech, to Parliament in February. Sir John Rees, the Unionist MP for Nottingham East, knew Lady Astor would be speaking directly after him so decided to set her up with a crude double-entendre, staring straight at her as he said: 'I do not doubt that a rod is in pickle for me when I sit down, but I will accept the chastisement with resignation and am indeed ready to kiss the rod.'[11]

If he had intended to put her off, he failed. She told Sir John that she would consider his proposal if he would support her pro-temperance position on pub opening hours. 'I know that it was very difficult for some Honourable Members to receive the first lady MP into the House,' she continued. 'It was almost as difficult for some of them as it was for the lady MP herself to come in. Honourable Members, however, should not be frightened of what Plymouth sends out into the world . . . I would like to say that I am quite certain that the women of the whole world will not forget that it was the fighting men of Devon who dared to send the first woman to represent women in the Mother of Parliaments.'[12]

The marriage of a vastly wealthy American divorcee with the dockers and seamen of Plymouth was an unlikely match. But Nancy Astor saw something rebellious and romantic in her constituents, who had waved off the first English settlers to sail to Virginia, and they embraced their new MP far more warmly than many of the supposedly enlightened men in the House of Commons. She later admitted how difficult her voyage of faith had been: 'Some of the Honourable Members looked upon me more as a pirate than a Pilgrim! A woman in the House of Commons! It was almost enough to have broken up the House. I don't blame them, but it was as hard on the woman as it was on them. Pioneers may be picturesque figures, but they are often rather lonely ones.'[13]

As men from opposing parties united in their discomfort at her election, the Member for Plymouth Sutton soon learned to avoid the bars and smoking rooms that were Parliament's social hub. One influential figure that she would perhaps have expected to stand up for her was Winston Churchill. The Liberal MP was a frequent guest at Cliveden, where he soaked up the Astors' hospitality with vigour, but he was so disgusted by the idea of a woman being elected to the House of Commons' gentlemen's club that he refused to speak to her for two years. One of his most famous put-downs is believed to have been addressed to Astor after she allegedly accused him of being 'disgustingly drunk'. 'My dear,' he is claimed to have replied, 'you are ugly and, what's more, you are disgustingly ugly. But tomorrow I shall be sober and you will still be disgustingly ugly.'[14] Churchill's acerbic wit is often applauded, laughed over and included in books of the 'greatest ever' quotations. If that was directed at the one woman among hundreds of men, it is hard to laugh with him.

Astor, however, gave as good as she got. When she finally

cornered her old friend and demanded to know why he was blanking her, he replied: 'I find a woman's intrusion into the House of Commons as embarrassing as if she burst into my bathroom when I had nothing to defend myself, not even a sponge.'

She quipped back: 'You are not handsome enough to have worries of that kind.'[15]

She also had to negotiate her way through Westminster's maze of traditions and protocols. There was a furious fluster over whether the Member for Plymouth Sutton should wear a hat and, if she did, whether it should stay on her head at all times. *The Times* spluttered: 'Will the appearance of a woman in the House of Commons lead to any embarrassments as to seats, procedure and etiquette? Where is Lady Astor to sit? No doubt she will wear her hat in the House, as she would do in a church or chapel. And, if she wears the hat, should she remove it when she rises to speak, as male MPs are bound to do?'[16]

Thanks to the paraphernalia of hatpins and veils, it was not so simple for a woman to remove her hat to make a speech, so the speaker granted her special dispensation to keep it on when she stood up. Other seemingly insurmountable problems ranged from the question of whether she should bow or curtsy to the Chair and which lavatory she should use.

While male MPs enjoyed the dining room, smoking room, tea room and riverside terraces, Lady Astor was allotted a tiny room overlooking the river and a dressing room attached to it, with washing facilities. She was known for her vivacious energy and networking skills, but in Parliament she restricted herself to her own little corner.

Nancy Astor was a stickler for proper dressing and took seriously her role in deciding what was appropriate for female MPs to wear in the House. She saw her decisions as setting a precedent for other women to follow, which helps explain her declaration that 'I shall wear nothing that the poorest woman elected to the House could not wear.'[17] For two decades she stuck to the parliamentary uniform she had adopted on her very first day. She paid short shrift to women who failed to live up to her high standards of dress. Shirley Williams, who would go on to become one of the best-known politicians of the twentieth century, remembers being introduced to Lady Astor by her father when she was a scruffy teenager. When her father proudly said that his daughter wanted to become an MP, Astor replied: 'Not with that hair!'[18]

Lady Astor devoted herself to social reforms, including temperance, raising the school-leaving age and the abolition of the death penalty for pregnant women. It was 'Lady Astor's Bill' that raised the legal drinking age from fourteen to eighteen. Her second speech was in support of an amendment to the Representation of the People Act that would give women the vote at twenty-one.

She was convinced that better nursery schooling was a key route out of poverty and ill health, setting up several nurseries in Plymouth and helping to establish a training school for nursery-school teachers. Passionate about creating better housing for poor families, she argued that building homes was as important as building battleships. In 1925 she introduced a bill that would have made men who bought sex – not just female prostitutes – liable to prosecution. She also successfully argued that people committing sexual assault should not be able to claim they had reasonable cause to believe the victim was over the age of consent.

Many of the causes she pushed in Parliament would have made positive changes to the lives of women, and Astor believed she had different legislative priorities because she was a female MP: 'When I got into the House of Commons I realised that as for certain problems, such as moral questions which are of vital interest to women, no political party cared sufficiently or realised how much women cared. As a result, Liberal and Unionist and Labour men often put such questions in their programme, but more often they sat down when the time came to stand up and fight for them.'[19] Low pay for teachers was one example, she said. 'Do you believe that if women had been voting as long as men that we should have allowed almost the most important people in the country to be underpaid?'[20]

When the second female MP took her seat in the House of Commons in 1921, Lady Astor gave her a warm welcome. After two years on her own, she was relieved, perhaps, to see another woman in Parliament – even if she was from a different party. Margaret Wintringham, the Liberal MP for Louth, took over her husband's seat after he had a heart attack in the House of Commons library just a year after being elected as an MP. She was so consumed by grief that she refused to make speeches during the election campaign. Perhaps the sympathy vote worked in her favour: she won by 723.

The Yorkshire woman born as 'Maggie Longbottom' was a very different character from the Virginian socialite, but the two swiftly became close political and personal friends and even toured mining communities in Wales together. Wintringham's first speech in Parliament was an intervention on the economy and taxes – she admitted to feeling 'rather like a new girl at school'. After two years the House of Commons was used to the idea of female MPs so she received a warm welcome from her colleagues. Sir Park Goff, the Conservative MP for Cleveland, said: 'With her width of practical knowledge and wealth of experience we all hope her interventions in Debate will be frequent in the future. We are very proud to welcome the Honourable Member as the first British-born lady Member to enter the Mother of Parliaments.'[21]

The MP for Louth was a former teacher, active in the Women's Institute and determined to elevate housework to the status of a skilled and important job. She campaigned for equal pay, rail carriages reserved for female passengers and for women to get the vote at twenty-one. She lost her seat in the 1924 election, when the Liberal Party was annihilated at the polls, but remained a close friend of Nancy Astor and a frequent visitor to Cliveden.

The first women MPs were by no means perfect. Lady Astor was accused of hypocrisy when she opposed the relaxation of the divorce laws in 1920, even though she had hidden her first marriage to protect her second husband's political career. Her enemies nicknamed her 'Lady Dis-Astor' and there were many stories of her disregarding parliamentary etiquette by pulling faces, whistling, tugging people's coat-tails to make them give way and forgetting to speak through the Chair. Although not the first MP to be guilty of being a windbag, she often spoke for too long and irritated other politicians with her regular interruptions.

More seriously, she backed Neville Chamberlain's potentially disastrous policy of appeasement towards Hitler. In 1936, after the German invasion of the Rhineland, she even held a dinner party at Cliveden where she played musical chairs with Joachim von Ribbentrop, the Nazi ambassador. Later, however, when the bombs began to fall on Plymouth during the Blitz, she and her husband stayed there until it had been almost crushed. Afterwards, they ploughed money into having it rebuilt.

More than anything, Lady Astor was an individualist. She refused to play the role of token female and proved beyond doubt that women could make effective and intelligent MPs. Her own constituents – the toughest jury of all – were certainly convinced. She was re-elected in 1922, 1923, 1924 and 1929 in the face of tough opposition from the Liberals and Labour.

Astor wore her responsibility lightly, but a letter from her close friend George Bernard Shaw, sent during the time of her re-election battle, gives perhaps the most illuminating glimpse into what life must have been like for the first woman in Westminster. He advised: 'Tell them you are making enemies all the time because you can't suffer fools gladly and are up against 600 of them every working night of your life, and that under God your refuge is Plymouth, and if Plymouth turns you down it will shut the gates of mercy on mankind. In short, dear Nancy, let yourself rip, and wear all your pearls: prudence is not your game; and if you ride hard enough for a fall you won't get it.'[22]

Plymouth did not turn her down: she was elected there seven times. When the aristocratic American finally left the political stage, the dockers and sailors chose another woman as their representative at Westminster.

The Class Warriors

'In connection with the political work of our country we can take the experience of the workman's wife and daughter, educated in the university of experience, who have had to face the hardships, ugliness and suffering which surrounds so much of our social conditions to-day. They have the experience that very few people who have passed through universities have. We want to bring into our political life and into the general pool of experience that kind of education.'[1]

– Margaret Bondfield

'I am not a lady – I am a Member of Parliament.'[2]

– Ellen Wilkinson

'I will fight for what I believe in until I drop dead. That's what keeps you alive.'[3]

– Barbara Castle

Suddenly the banging started. The teenage girls packed closely together in the dormitory could barely see through the darkness but they knew where the sound was coming from – the windows that opened onto the street. It wasn't the first time the panes had been rattled and thumped as someone tried to force them open. During Race Week more than 10,000 people would travel to Brighton racecourse, thanks to the easy rail journey from London. After a long day's drinking, groups of men would begin knocking on the ground-floor windows, then try to pull them open and reach the girls inside. After a struggle, the windows were finally shut and bolted.

The women lying together in the darkness were not the kind of working girls the men had been hoping for. They were employees of W. Hetherington's, a large drapery shop in the seaside town of

Brighton. At the end of the nineteenth century the 'living-in' system was commonplace, where employers provided their workers with board and lodging in return for a hefty slice out of their wages.

One of the girls lying in silent fear as the windows shook was Margaret Bondfield. The early life of the first female government minister could not have been more different from that of Lady Astor, the first woman MP. Originally from Chard, in Somerset, Bondfield had travelled a long way for her job. Her father was a factory foreman who struggled to support eleven children – a situation made even more difficult when he lost his job. As soon as she reached the age of fourteen Bondfield left school and moved to Brighton to find a post in a shop, which she saw as the readiest available work. A junior position at W. Hetherington's was a rude awakening to the realities of the living-in system.

Work for a junior shop-girl started at 7.30 a.m. sharp and finished at 8 p.m. After their working day was over, there would be a sudden rush to the public baths where they were permitted to wash themselves for fifteen minutes after closing time. Then it was back to sleep in the dormitory, where they huddled under the covers in the freezing winter and sweltered in the summer.

Looking back on her life as an adult, Bondfield recalled: 'Overcrowded, unsanitary conditions, poor and insufficient food were the main characteristics of this system, with an undertone of violence to the young boy and girl "up from the country". In some houses both unnatural and natural vices found a breeding ground.'[4]

By her twenty-first birthday, Bondfield had saved five pounds and moved to London to live with her brother, Frank. Finding work, however, was far more difficult than she had imagined. In 1894 huge queues snaking around employment offices were a common sight. In a single day, Bondfield visited every shop on Oxford Street asking for a job, often being told she was too short. To some employers, Bondfield's appearance – small and dumpy, with a round red face – was wrong for the shop floor. After stretching her five pounds out for three months, she was finally given a job, working seventy-five hours a week in return for twenty-five pounds a year. The Victorians had invented late-night shopping, with gas light and cheap labour, and Bondfield would be sent down Oxford Street to see if their competitors had closed before she could finally finish for the day.

The sudden explosion of female shop assistants meant that by 1907 at least a million women were working for low wages in this largely unregulated industry. It was Bondfield's experience as a shop girl that politicised her and she became active within the trade-union movement. For the new breed of class warriors, trade unionism was a new and growing route to political power.

Bondfield joined the National Union of Shop Assistants, Warehousemen and Clerks after reading about it in a newspaper wrapped around a portion of fish and chips. It was one of the many unions set up in the 1890s after the exhilarating victory of the Bryant & May match girls' strike. Female membership, however, was low and women workers not a priority. Many union leaders believed a man should be paid a fair wage so he could provide for his family so that, ideally, working-class women need not go out to work.

Bondfield started dropping leaflets behind counters and tried to sign up fellow shop girls to her cause, with mixed success. One furious grocer, she later remembered, ripped up one of her leaflets, stamped on it and shouted: 'Union indeed! Go home and mend your stockings!'[5]

By her mid-twenties, Bondfield was the assistant secretary of the National Union of Shop Assistants, Warehousemen and Clerks, chief woman officer for the National Union of General and Municipal Workers and had started working with the Women's Trade Union League to improve conditions for female workers. Trade unionism was her first and lasting love. She was the first female delegate to be sent to the Trades Union Congress, and twenty-four years later, in 1923, became its first woman chair.

In the early twentieth century, class was becoming an

increasingly political concern and campaigners won some significant successes. The 1904 Shop Hours Act limited legal working hours, and in 1907 steps were taken to end the living-in system. The new wave of class warriors had begun to influence political decision-making, improving the lives of millions of working people. Westminster would never be quite the same.

When the 1918 Representation of the People Act was finally inked onto the traditional vellum used for recording new laws, it was a revolution. The Act is most famous for giving women of over thirty the vote, but it also enfranchised every adult male regardless of class. As the ink dried, 14 million people were about to become full citizens and the proportion of the adult population qualified to vote went from 28 per cent to 78 per cent. Working-class men who had left friends, limbs and their former selves in the trenches of the First World War now had a political voice in the country they had fought for.

The Labour Party, which grew out of the socialist and trade-union movements, was the immediate benefactor from the sudden wave of working-class voters. At the 1923 general election the party gained power for the first time and sent 191 MPs to Westminster – including three women. Margaret Bondfield was elected as the Labour MP for Northampton, with a majority of at least 4,000, among a small vanguard of female class warriors to break into Parliament.

Dorothy Jewson, a former school teacher and suffragette, was elected to represent Norwich, while Arabella Susan Lawrence, who was wealthy, had a cut-glass accent and wore a pince-nez, to the London constituency of East Ham North. Arabella, or Susan as she preferred to be called, had gone to prison as a local councillor for refusing to levy a Poor Rate, making herself a heroine of the left. Once the First World War was over she called for women to leave their jobs and free up vacancies for working-class men returning from the front line. She was far from alone in this. By 1921, a million people were unemployed and women had retreated to traditionally female jobs: 33 per cent worked in domestic service, 12 per cent in the textile industries, 11 per cent in clothing and 4 per cent in teaching. The ground hard-won by women during the war was shrinking, expectations were changing and equal pay was still a distant dream. In the areas where female employment was relatively high, there was a lack of urgency to improve conditions because women's work was seen as temporary. Lauded during the war for doing their bit, women employees were now expected to scuttle back home. It seems particularly fitting, therefore, that eight years later the first female cabinet minister was the minister for labour.

Margaret Bondfield deserved a holiday more than most. After months of election campaigning in Wallsend, a town nestled on the banks of the River Tyne close to Hadrian's Wall, she was exhausted. She needed time to recuperate ahead of months of juggling her trade-union duties with her responsibilities as one of Britain's small band of female MPs.

As she returned from her break, Bondfield must have been puzzled by the sight of the newly appointed foreign secretary, Arthur Henderson, waiting for her at Victoria station holding a telegram. They knew each other well and Henderson was a keen supporter of women's emancipation. He must have been unable to resist the idea of delivering the message to Bondfield personally, before she had had a chance to unpack her suitcases.

Inside the telegram was a message from the new prime minister, Ramsay MacDonald. Labour had won 288 seats in the general election of May 1929, making it the largest party but just short of a majority. MacDonald wanted to see the MP for Wallsend as soon as possible. In fact, he had been trying to find her for days to appoint her as the first ever female cabinet minister and privy councillor, serving as minister of labour. A few days later, she was sworn in by King George V at Windsor. Traditionally the ceremony took place in silence. However, when she knelt on the King's footstool the monarch told her that he was delighted to have the opportunity to swear in the first woman.

Bondfield's appointment could not have come at a more difficult time. The Great Depression was named so for a reason. A stock-market crash sent the global economy tumbling, and Britain was not immune. Unemployment soared and growth slumped. Bondfield presided over the Unemployment Insurance Fund, which rapidly ran out of money due to the unexpected increase in pay-outs. It led to one of the most difficult decisions of her career, which she made reluctantly. When the 1931 Anomalies Act was introduced, it excluded 180,000 married women from unemployment benefit, even though they had paid their contributions when they were at work. Wives were penalised in a way single women and men were not. The move condemned tens of thousands of women to poverty, and many in the trade-union movement never forgave Bondfield for her part in it.

The perceived betrayal would have hurt her deeply. She was passionate about working conditions for women, and had campaigned for key reforms, including a minimum wage, health insurance for employees, maternity benefits and better conditions for working children. First and foremost, she was a trade unionist.

If anyone understood the pain of political compromise, it was the firecracker who was one of Bondfield's fellow class warriors. Ellen Wilkinson came to Westminster a year after the first trickle of Labour women, in the 1924 election that saw the party tumble from power after just a year of running a minority government. 'Red Ellen' was nicknamed for her short, thick shock of auburn hair and her stridently left-wing views. She was a trade unionist, feminist and former Communist Party member, who also loved theatre, fashion and Elizabeth Arden makeup.

She made an instant impact. Until that point, the handful of female MPs had mainly stuck to the few rooms designated for women, but Wilkinson viewed no area as off limits. When a policeman was shocked to see a lady try to enter the smoking room, that bastion of parliamentary masculinity, he refused her access. Wilkinson marched in anyway: 'I am not a lady – I am a Member of Parliament.'[6] As part of the Kitchen Committee, in charge of refreshment facilities at the House of Commons, she fought for women to be allowed into the Strangers' Dining Room where male MPs frequently lunched and networked. The serjeant-at-arms recommended that the request be refused because the dining room was very busy, there was no women's lavatory nearby and, in his view, many MPs preferred an all-male environment to entertain their guests. The speaker, however, sided with the electric new MP.

Wilkinson made an impact outside Westminster too. The global depression of the 1930s hit industrial towns particularly hard and, in 1935, the closure of the shipbuilding yard in her Jarrow constituency caused a crippling 70 per cent unemployment rate. More than 11,000 people signed a petition demanding that a new steelworks should open to bring jobs to the town. It was carried to Westminster in an oak box by 200 unemployed local men – and one woman. The famous Jarrow march of 1936 was led by the redoubtable local MP and a stray dog called Paddy. Everything was done to ensure the procession was respectable: it began with a church service, drinking was banned and the marchers walked and sang for three hundred peaceful miles from the North-East to London.

Wilkinson presented the petition to the House of Commons but she was unable to force the government to act or to persuade the prime minister even to meet the marchers.

It was nearly ten years later that Wilkinson gained real political power: in 1945 she was appointed education minister – only the second woman to rise to a ministerial role. Like Margaret Bondfield before her, the fiery Red Ellen of the Jarrow march was forced to temper her revolutionary spirit. She was responsible for pushing through the 1944 Education Act that promised free universal education, but some within the Labour movement wanted to see a comprehensive-school system without the eleven-plus exam. Under fire from the Conservatives and her own side, Wilkinson battled to push through the reforms. Despite the controversy, she believed passionately in education for all children and fought the idea that literature and humanities should be reserved for the middle and upper classes. 'Can't Shakespeare mean more than a scrubbing brush? Can't enough of a foreign language be taught to open the windows on the world a bit wider?' she questioned, adding: 'I learned French verbs saying them as I scrubbed the floors at home.'[7]

Her conviction that children of all classes could benefit from a rounded education was why Wilkinson battled to raise the school-leaving age to fifteen, fighting to convince a sceptical cabinet. When her colleagues began to waver and the Treasury proposed delaying the plan, she argued during an explosive cabinet meeting in 1947 that education was always the first casualty when a government was in trouble: 'Just because I made the country believe the government meant to keep its word,' she told the men sitting around the long, wooden table, 'the phased programme is now ready enough to do its job: we shall never get the same intensity of effort to a date again, and those to suffer most by deferment will be precisely those working-class children whose education has already been so seriously interrupted by the war.'[8] It was only after she threatened to resign that the majority of the cabinet, including the prime minister, gave in and promised to support her.

One person who stubbornly refused to back the isolated education minister as the cabinet circled around her was the round-spectacled deputy prime minister. For Wilkinson, that was the cruellest betrayal of all. She had been having an affair with the married Herbert Morrison, who was a brilliant tactician, a formidable politician but a hard-hearted lover.

A photo exists of Ellen Wilkinson opening south London's Old Vic Theatre School on 25 January 1947. It was bitterly cold, and the face staring out of the picture looks exhausted. It would have been easy for her to slip into the warmth of the building, but she stayed outside to make sure the photographer got the best shot. A few days later, she was admitted to St Mary's Hospital in Paddington. Accounts of her illness differ, some suggesting it was exacerbated by her catching pneumonia at the theatre school ceremony. Herbert Morrison sent neither flowers nor a message. She died on 6 February 1947. In April the school-leaving age was raised to fifteen.

In the post-war election of 1945, Winston Churchill was defeated by Clement Attlee's Labour Party. The Attlee government is rightly seen as one of the most radically reformist in British history but the impact of female politicians and political thinkers is often underestimated. Many within the Labour movement get misty-eyed at the thought of the National Health Service pioneered by Aneurin Bevan, the former miner, who became minister for health in 1945. But in 1909, when he was twelve, the reformist thinker Beatrice Webb introduced the idea of a 'Public Medical Service' in her report for the Poor Law Royal Commission.

The idea for child benefit was pioneered by Eleanor Rathbone, who was born into a philanthropic family of ship-owners in Liverpool and later became an independent MP. Rathbone strongly believed in giving women the independence to support their families, remarking: 'After all, the rearing of families is not a sort of masculine hobby, like tobacco smoking or pigeon flying,' so politicians should not rely on 'the clumsy device of paying men wage-earners more than women'.[9] Her solution was a system of family allowances, which were, crucially, paid to the mother rather than the father. The concept was included in the Beveridge Report of 1942, which laid the foundations of the welfare state. Many believe that document was the chief reason for the Labour Party's dramatic success in the 1945 election. However, Westminster didn't wait for a change of government to implement family allowances because nearly everyone agreed with Rathbone's idea.

Twenty-four women won seats in 1945, with twenty-one in the Labour Party. They included 'Battling Bessie' Braddock, who pushed for mental health and prison reform, Edith Summerskill, who became minister of food and a campaigner on equal pay, birth control and maternity services, and Jennie Lee, a future minister for the arts, who later helped to set up the Open University. The minister Douglas Jay gave a flavour of what the new women MPs were up against when he said: 'Housewives as a whole cannot be trusted to buy all the right things, where nutrition and health are concerned. This is really no more than an extension of the principle according to which the housewife herself would not trust a child of four to elect the week's purchases. For in the case of nutrition and health, just as in the case for education, the gentleman from Whitehall really does know better what is good for people than the people know themselves.'[10]

There was one star among the 1945 intake who shone particularly sharply. Like Ellen Wilkinson, Barbara Castle was red-headed, stridently socialist and battled against a hostile, male-dominated cabinet. Labour's 'Red Queen' was central to twentieth-century politics and – for many – should have been her party's first female leader.

The Labour Party faithful packing out the conference hall imperceptibly shifted forward in their seats. The annual party meetings have a reputation for being of interest only to aficionados, more about raising money and hot-air oratory than the birth of a revolution. As the constituency Labour Party delegate from St Pancras borough council walked up to the podium in 1943, there was no indication that anything unusual was about to happen. But as the elfin-featured figure began to speak there was no sound of programmes rustling or sandwiches being munched. The audience felt that punch in the throat and stirring in the belly that comes only with a truly exceptional political speech.

Barbara Betts was angry. She accused the leadership of preparing to delay the Beveridge Report, the all-important blueprint that laid the foundations of the welfare state. For a generation that had been scarred by two world wars, it was part of the better future for which they had sacrificed so much. Labour supporters were fed up with being told to keep quiet until after the war and – in the words of the tiny but forceful speaker – being offered 'jam yesterday, jam tomorrow but never jam today!'

Almost overnight, the thirty-two-year-old redhead was the new darling of the left. Barbara Betts had never spoken at conference before but Labour Party politics were in her blood: her father Frank was a passionate socialist, who penned left-wing articles under a pseudonym because he was a tax inspector. She had excelled at Bradford Grammar School and struggled through Oxford University, leaving with a third-class degree and a sense of intellectual inferiority. But under the conference hall's spotlight, she felt no nerves at all.

As he listened to Betts's passionate rallying call, the night editor of the *Daily Mirror*, Ted Castle, was so bowled over that he put the story on the front page. Admiration soon turned to love. Ted and Barbara married in 1944 and remained together, despite some difficult times, for thirty-four years.

After the exhilaration of that speech, Barbara Castle was hooked on politics. Now she just had to find a way of getting to Parliament as an MP, which was no easy task. In the early 1940s, local constituency parties were wary of selecting women candidates, whether because of personal prejudices or a fear that women were simply unelectable. Castle tackled the problem with the single-minded determination that characterised her entire career. When she saw the list of candidates drawn up to fight her local constituency, Blackburn, she didn't feel disappointment – but anger. Every name on the list was a man's. According to Shirley Williams, who was also a Labour MP, Castle told the female members of the local party that it was 'appalling' to have an all-male shortlist, adding: 'I suggest we tell them we'll stop making the tea, bringing buns and washing up after the meetings.

If they don't want any women MPs they can't have any women tea-makers either!'

The prospect of doing their own washing-up proved too much, and the men quickly agreed to put a woman's name on the list. That name was Barbara Castle's – but only after she had dropped her maiden name at the insistence of the local agent, who told her the constituency didn't like career women. 'I only got my start in Parliament through positive discrimination,' she later said, adding: 'You do need to give women a kick-start.'[11] Castle went on to win the selection and a year later was propelled to Westminster when the party won a landslide. She represented Blackburn until her retirement from the House of Commons in 1979.

Once in Parliament, Barbara Castle was seen as dynamic, determined, charming, single-minded and a troublesome left-winger. To much mocking in the House of Commons, she successfully lobbied to flush out sexism in public toilets, where women had to pay while men got away without having 'to spend a penny'. The charge was finally scrapped in the Public Lavatories (Turnstiles) Act 1963.

Castle carried out a similar revolution in the House of Commons. Women MPs had been irritated for some time that, while the men had a handy lavatory in the corridor behind the speaker's chair, the Ladies was a long walk from the Chamber, a significant inconvenience during votes or long debates. Castle was fed up with crossing her legs while spending long hours on the front bench. Her polite request for a female loo was hit by a wall of excuses from the House of Commons authorities: they lined up numerous experts who declared that the plumbing made installation impossible. Castle was not the kind of woman to give up easily. Eventually, after much haranguing, the beleaguered authorities admitted it was perfectly possible. The new lavatory was christened 'Barbara's Castle'.

The darling of the party conference had little chance of promotion in Clement Attlee's new government, and allied herself with giants of the left, including Michael Foot and Aneurin Bevan. She was in the House of Commons for nineteen years before her friend and colleague Harold Wilson became prime minister and, in 1964, presented her with a chance to serve on the political front line.

As minister for overseas development, Castle was the fourth woman to hold a cabinet post and had the chance to shape the newly created department. With typical self-confidence, she ordered her staff to pick up a copy of a pamphlet she had previously written on foreign aid and treat it as a guide. Within a year, the fledgling department's future – and budget – was secured.

If overseas aid was safe ground, Castle's next move, in 1965, was onto far more treacherous footing. Harold Wilson ordered her to Transport and Industry, declaring, in the words of a popular petrol advert, 'I want a tiger in my tank.'[12] Castle tried to argue that she was a poor fit because she could not drive, but Wilson was having none of it.

Barbara Castle pushed through a revolution in road safety that saved thousands of lives. The new secretary of state introduced the breathalyser, extended the 70 m.p.h. speed limit trial and made it a legal requirement for all new cars to have seatbelts. When she arrived in the department, eight thousand people a year were dying on the roads and the numbers were on a seemingly unstoppable ascendancy. In the first year after the new measures were introduced, the number of deaths fell by 1,200. By the end of the century, deaths had fallen to half the total in 1945 even though many more cars and lorries were on the roads.

Castle's glittering time in Transport was dulled by some ugly sexism. Misogynistic threats became a common occurrence, with letters promising: 'We'll get you yet, you old cow.'[13] BBC interviewers also struggled to come to terms with a female minister, as this exchange from 1967 shows:

INTERVIEWER: Minister, this is a rotten idea, you're really spoiling my fun as a motorist, so, Minister, what's the idea behind it?

CASTLE: The idea is to save your life, not mine. I don't drive. You do. And I know that if you drink when you drive you've got a multiple chance of being killed or seriously injured so I am ready to risk unpopularity to save you perhaps from yourself.

INTERVIEWER: But you're going to stop me having a lot of fun in the process, aren't you?

CASTLE: No, not at all. Go out, have your Saturday-night drinks with your pals but make sure somebody drives you home.

INTERVIEWER: You're only a woman, you don't drive, what do you know about it?[14]

It was her first taste of the ugly side of political life, but standing up to the powerful motoring lobby was child's play in comparison to her next ministerial move.

On Thursday, 4 April 1968, Barbara Castle was on the night sleeper from London to her Blackburn constituency. MPs frequently voted well into the night and it was 11.15 p.m. when she finally boarded the train home. Once in the carriage she undressed and got into bed with a glass of hot milk and a hot-water bottle. Suddenly there was a tap at the door. Pushing it ajar, the station master handed over a scrap of paper instructing her to call Whitehall 4433. Without a second thought, Castle tucked her nightie into her knickers, pulled on a skirt and coat and walked out onto the cold platform in bare legs to find the nearest telephone. The conversation she was about to have with Prime Minister Harold Wilson was to change the course of her career – and perhaps deprive the Labour Party of the best leader it never had.

Wilson told his friend she was to be the new secretary of state for employment and productivity. At the time the perilously fragile economy was frequently hit by unofficial wildcat strikes. Wilson's matey beer-and-sandwiches approach had failed, so now he wanted a tougher line. The left-wing Castle was an unlikely scourge of the unions but her diary the following day shows she knew what was expected:

> Well, I am in the thick of it now, for better or for worse – probably worse. I am under no illusions that I may be committing political suicide. I have at last moved from the periphery of the whirlwind into its very heart . . . If I go down in the disaster as well I may, at least I shall become an adult before I die.[15]

The woman who had stood up to the motorists now had to find a way of dealing with the equally masculine trade-union movement. In 1967 2,117 disputes had led to the loss of 2.7 million working days; by 1969 that had risen to 3,116 disputes losing 6.8 million days. Castle's response, the White Paper 'In Place of Strife', proposed pre-strike ballots, a twenty-eight-day pause before strikes took place and powers for the government to impose settlements for unofficial strikes as a last resort. There were also measures to try to improve employment rights, including safeguards against unfair dismissal and the right to join a trade union. 'All I asked,' she later wrote, 'was the unions should co-operate in avoiding unnecessary strikes.'[16] In comparison to what was to come under the iron fist of Margaret Thatcher, Barbara Castle's reforms look timid – but the trade unions were furious at what they saw as an attack on rights they had fought for over many decades. Vic Feather, the TUC general secretary, was a friend of Castle and had known her father. He was to lead the movement against her, dismissing her as 'a lass he knew when she was still in dirty knickers'.[17]

As the resistance grew, Castle's support in cabinet was crumbling. With an eye on a future leadership contest, her arch nemesis James Callaghan broke ranks to publicly undermine her and side with the trade unions. Just as with Ellen Wilkinson before her, the men around the table turned their backs. Harold Wilson and Barbara Castle were forced into a humiliating defeat. Eventually, she was even abandoned by the prime minister, who said, in an aside to a civil servant: 'Poor Barbara. She hangs around like someone with a stillborn child. She can't believe it's dead.'[18]

Wilson was praised for finding a compromise and his reputation quickly recovered. Castle's never did, and any hope of her becoming Labour's first female leader was lost. Alienated from her friends on the left, she felt stabbed in the back by her colleagues.

Hindsight is a wonderful thing. Failing to get a grip on wildcat strikes eventually led to the 1978/9 'winter of discontent' when more than a million public-sector workers went on strike, rubbish piled up on the streets, schools closed and the dead remained unburied. Union leaders and Labour ministers who had refused to back 'In Place of Strife' had made Margaret Thatcher's revolution almost inevitable.

Some blame must be apportioned to Castle's refusal or inability to build alliances with her colleagues. She was more likely to be found poring over her ministerial red boxes in her offices than drinking beer or sipping tea in the House of Commons' bars and tea rooms. She doodled when others were talking in cabinet and once fell asleep during a meeting.

Yet there is also a more sinister undercurrent running through her relationships with party colleagues. One colleague accused her of 'screeching' in cabinet meetings: 'She went on like a mechanical drill until your nerves couldn't stand it any more.' Labour MPs would make snide comments, claiming Harold Wilson was her henpecked husband and she only had to 'waggle that bottom of hers and she gets all her own way'.[19]

Harold Wilson – who referred to her as his 'little minister' – may also have held her back. After Labour lost the 1970 election, Castle let him know she was planning to stand against Roy Jenkins as deputy leader of the party. Wilson told her sharply not to, and that if she did she wouldn't get ten votes. Upset, Castle insisted she would stand anyway. The man she saw as her closest political friend then told her that if she ran for the deputy leadership he would resign. When the race opened, Castle's name was not there.[20] She was also sometimes the butt of Wilson's jokes to political aides and colleagues. Once he claimed to have changed his private number to stop Barbara calling him all the time. On another occasion he described her as 'behaving like a bitch. We gave her everything she asked for last year. She is just an old woman in a hurry; no sense at all.'[21]

Despite her devastating fall from grace Barbara Castle was yet to pull off what is considered her greatest achievement. Side-lined, cabinet backing or not, she was a woman who still had work to do.

In 1968, at the rather unglamorous sounding Department for Employment and Productivity, a revolution was brewed over tea. The cameras clicked to capture women laughing as they perched on their chairs, cups and saucers precariously balanced on their laps, cigarette packets nestling against the ashtrays on the little round tables in front of them. The room was a riot of colourful sixties dresses and heavily backcombed hair. In the press photographs that appeared in the next day's newspapers, the women look as though they were attending a Women's Institute get-together. In fact that political meeting was to transform the future for millions of British workers and take on the most powerful business and political establishments. The women in that room were stitching up what would become the most radical legacy of the then Labour government.

Barbara Castle had been speaking passionately but ineffectively for years about women's wages but now, as the minister in charge of employment, she could do something about it. When she heard that 183 female workers had walked out in protest at their treatment by the car manufacturer Ford, she invited them for a cup of tea in her office. They were sewing machinists at the Dagenham factory in east London, making seats for the shiny Cortinas and Zephyrs that rolled off the production line and onto Britain's driveways. When the company reclassified the women's work as 'unskilled' – putting it on the same level as that of the young boys who swept the floors – the subsequent strike nearly stopped production at all of Ford's UK factories.

Castle made sure the media were present to capture her personal intervention. She spoke to each woman in turn, then donated ten pounds to their hardship fund. After ordering the cameramen and reporters to leave the room, she opened her drinks cabinet and poured everyone a glass of whisky.

That meeting was the beginning of Castle's battle to legislate for equal pay. She faced significant hostility from her own side, many of whom worried that equal pay would simply drag down the wages of male workers. This time, though, she wasn't backing down.

The 1970 Equal Pay Act was implemented in 1975 and it had an immediate impact. In 1970, before its introduction, women's hourly wages were on average 63.1 per cent of men's. By 1977 they had shot up to 75.5 per cent.

Castle saw women's rights as part of her vision for a fairer society and flinched at being pigeonholed as someone only interested in 'women's issues'. 'It is hard for anyone, male or female, to fulfil themselves if they are poor, ill housed, ill-educated and struggling with ill health,' she later wrote.[22] 'Real equality,' she argued, is about 'the mundane things, like how do I get enough to live on, do I or do I not have children, who will help me to bring them up.'[23]

In 1974, when the Conservative prime minister Edward Heath called an early election and lost, Labour unexpectedly stumbled into power again. Barbara Castle had another chance to make a difference in cabinet and bulldoze more significant reform through Parliament as secretary of state for health and social services. During her first year in the job she announced that family planning – contraception – would be free on the NHS for anyone who needed it, regardless of whether they were married, without any prescription charge. A year later she steered through the 1975 Child Benefit Act, which gave some working-class women the first dependable income they had ever known, and introduced new allowances to help single women and those who gave up their jobs to care for disabled relatives. She also revolutionised the pension system for women who had seen their nest egg whittled away by years of caring for children or elderly relatives, and introduced the State Earnings Related Pension Scheme (SERPS) for those who did not belong to a private pension scheme.

For those who knew her, Barbara Castle was, above all, someone who could not be neatly packaged into a political box.

Clare Short, the former Labour MP and cabinet minister, remembered: 'She wasn't a stereotype. She was on the left but she brought in "In Place of Strife". She was a feminist but wanted to look good and for men to like her. She was a brave, creative, able woman right up until she died. I think the country yearns for more independently minded people like Barbara in politics, who tell the truth as they see it.'

An old university friend remembered her at Oxford 'creaming her face and hands at night and wearing gloves, drinking fruit juice, eating rusks and reading some obscure economics handbook all at the same time'.[24] Even as a leading politician, Castle had her hair done every day, hung up evening gowns in her office and covered her chair in the cabinet room with cretonne to make sure she didn't ladder her stockings or tights on the wood. When she first arrived in Parliament, she shaved a few years off her date of birth in her *Who's Who* entry. She was only too aware that, for women in politics, appearance mattered.

When he took over from Harold Wilson as prime minister in 1976, James Callaghan sacked her. He told her she had to go in order to make way for younger people. At the time, she was sixty-five and he was sixty-four. The most restrained moment of her life, she later said, was when she stopped herself replying: 'Then why not start with yourself?'[25]

The Ceiling Smashers Part 1

'What has women's lib ever done for me?'

— Margaret Thatcher

'It would have been all right if I had gone into what they would regard as one of the traditional professions. All right if I had followed Florence Nightingale.'

— Margaret Thatcher

Inside the Lady Members' Room, the leader of the Conservative Party was ironing her husband's shirts. That was not an unusual sight. Margaret Thatcher took her marriage to Denis extremely seriously; ensuring he had a steady supply of neatly folded shirts and clean socks was part of being a good wife. It was a habit she continued throughout her premiership. When she entered Number 10 as prime minister, she balked at the taxpayer funding an ironing board costing nineteen pounds and decided to pay for her own cheaper model.

As she pressed the hot iron across the cotton, a second MP burst into the room. Thatcher was always immaculately turned out but the new arrival was somewhat dishevelled. Shirley Williams was a young Labour MP with a bright future; at that moment, though, it didn't feel like it. She threw herself down on the patterned sofa in the corner of the room.

It was 1974 and she had recently been appointed to the cabinet as prices and consumer protection minister in Harold Wilson's Labour government. Inflation was high and she was under pressure to get it back under control, particularly from the trade unions. The beleaguered new minister had just experienced a mauling in the House of Commons Chamber. 'The Tories were in a mood to be particularly aggressive – not least because I was a woman as well. They didn't like that at all. I was like Saint

Sebastian – shot at by everyone,' Williams said. 'I was wrung out. I went to the Lady Members' Room, where Mrs Thatcher was doing the ironing, as she frequently did. The ironing board was used almost entirely by Mrs Thatcher.'

As a rising star in the Labour Party, Williams was not expecting any sympathy from the woman who was then shadow environment Secretary but Thatcher struck up a conversation. 'You did all right,' she said.

'You thought it was okay?'

'Yes, it was all right. You did all right.' There was a pause, before Thatcher continued: 'After all, we can't let them get the better of us.'

Received wisdom is that Margaret Thatcher's loyalty and sympathy was directed to the Conservative Party tribe and not to the female one. That intimate moment in the Lady Members' Room suggests it might not always have been the case. Williams continued: 'One of the things Mrs Thatcher once said to me was: "Men treat politics as a game. Women treat it as something so serious one couldn't see it as a game." Everything about Margaret Thatcher suggested exactly that. It's perfectly true, the idea of politics as a game is frequently discovered, particularly among those MPs whose whole families had been in politics – the Butlers, the Halifaxes, the earls of Hertfordshire. But Mrs Thatcher took it extremely seriously, and most women do.'

The first female prime minister famously asked: 'What has women's lib ever done for me?'[1] When she stood on the steps of Downing Street for the first time, she was asked what Emmeline Pankhurst would have thought of her victory. Thatcher ducked the question and spoke of her father. She would have scorned the idea of a book dedicated to the history of women in politics – particularly when she discovered herself in a chapter entitled 'The Ceiling Smashers'.

Or would she?

* * *

Margaret Thatcher was iron-willed, girlish, plain-talking and argumentative, a political outsider who reached the innermost sanctuaries of Westminster and a revolutionary leader with a vision to change the soul of Britain. Endless columns, biographies and speeches have been made about her but she remains mercurial and hard to pin down. Along with Clement Attlee, she was one of the twentieth century's most radical prime ministers, who smashed the political consensus and rebuilt the country in a very different shape. Thatcher believed in the strong moral values of marriage, neighbourliness, savings and hard work. But under her leadership, Thatcherism also came to stand for materialism, wealth, capitalism and – above all – the individual.

She privatised swathes of industry, from British Steel to the water authority, British Telecom to British Gas, a policy she said was 'reclaiming territory for freedom',[2] and created a new era of share ownership. Almost two million people bought their council homes at a discount as a result of her Right to Buy scheme. She went into furious battle with miners striking over pit closures, branding them 'the enemy within', and when she tried to bulldoze through the poll tax it was her own premiership that crumbled in the rubble. For her critics, she was a hard-nosed prime minister, who expressed little support for those people experiencing genuine hardship as a result of her policies. The woman who posed for pictures driving a tank, scarf whipping around her neck in the wind, led her country to a patriotic victory in the Falklands War and played a pivotal role in ending the Cold War by charming the US President Ronald Reagan and the Soviet leader Mikhail Gorbachev. When Soviet journalists dubbed her the 'Iron Lady', they didn't realise she would help raise the Iron Curtain.

Throughout her premiership Thatcher played down her gender. 'It never occurred to me that I was a woman prime minister,' she claimed in her memoirs.[3] Even coming from the Iron Lady, that is hard to believe.

Born in 1925, Margaret Hilda Roberts grew up above her family's greengrocery in Grantham, Lincolnshire, in an apartment with no inside lavatory or running hot water. Her upbringing was characterised by the Methodist values of serious, sober virtues and a strong work ethic. She won a scholarship to grammar school and studied at Somerville College, Oxford, one of the university's first female colleges, which was an incubator for politicians, including the Indian prime minister Indira Gandhi. Unlike the many history and politics graduates who pack Parliament's green benches, Thatcher studied chemistry. Before becoming the MP for Finchley she was a research chemist in Colchester, qualified and practised as a tax barrister and became a mother to twins.

In her late twenties, when she was looking for a suitable constituency, Thatcher wrote an article for the *Sunday Graphic* under the attention-grabbing headline 'Wake Up Women'. It was a passionate argument that women shouldn't have to choose between their family and a career – even if they wanted to run for Westminster's top jobs. 'Should a woman arise equal to the task,' she wrote, 'I say let her have an equal chance with the men for the leading Cabinet posts. Why not a woman Chancellor – or Foreign Secretary?'[4] That was a radical argument in 1952, when Ellen Wilkinson and Margaret Bondfield had been the only two female cabinet ministers – and, of course, Thatcher would set her sights even higher. First, though, she had to be selected for a winnable seat – no easy task in the 1950s, particularly with a husband and children in tow.

The early impression Thatcher made on the Conservative Party was positive but there were early concerns about the fact that she was married. John Hare, the Conservative Party vice-chairman, wrote of the keen young candidate:

> She is a remarkable young woman who is not to be deterred from pursuing a political career in spite of her recent marriage and the possibility of producing and bringing up a family. Miss Beryl Cook [the regional agent] describes her as the best woman candidate she has ever known. I would also agree, as in our short interview she struck me as being a woman of immense

personality and charm with a brain quite clearly above the average. I did my best to warn her of the horrors of life in the House of Commons especially in so far as this life affects the home. Nothing I said deterred her.[5]

Thatcher enjoyed some initial success when she fought the unwinnable seat of Dartford in 1950. The local party was under no illusions about its chances of taking the seat from Labour so decided to make a bit of a splash and guarantee some press coverage by picking a young female candidate. She caught the eye of one local member in particular, a successful businessman called Denis, who spent the campaign driving her around in his Jaguar. A year later, they were married. Denis was a long way from the henpecked husband of cruel satirists, but was a highly successful executive who bankrolled his wife's career and retired very rich.

The local association at Dartford were prepared to take a risk on a female candidate when they had nothing to lose, but Thatcher's battle to find a constituency that might actually propel her to Westminster was far tougher. She applied unsuccessfully to Canterbury, Orpington, Beckenham, Hemel Hempstead and Maidstone. None of the men who beat her to the candidacies enjoyed an exceptional parliamentary career. She also had to field endless questions about how she could balance the demands of being an MP with her responsibilities to her husband and children.

In Maidstone Thatcher was the clear front runner against two relatively lightweight candidates and she began to feel quietly confident of winning the seat. However, according to the report by the deputy Central Office area agent John Entwistle, there was one hurdle she failed to clear: 'She was asked about her ability to cope as a Member,' he wrote, 'having in mind the fact that she had a husband and a small family, and I do not think her reply did her a lot of good. She spoke of having an excellent nanny and said that as a Member she would have the mornings free.'[6] No equivalent question was asked of her rivals John Wells, who had four children under ten, or Captain Litchfield, who had two.

Thatcher had come to expect it. In her autobiography, she wrote:

> With my family commitments, would I have time enough for the constituency? Did I realise how much being a Member of Parliament would keep me away from home? Did I really think that I could fulfil my duties as a mother with young children to look after and as an MP?
>
> I felt that Selection Committees had every right to ask me these questions. I explained our family circumstances and that I already had the help of a first-class nanny. I also used to describe how I had found it possible to be a professional woman and a mother by organising my time properly. What I resented, however, was that beneath some of the criticism I detected a feeling that the House of Commons was not really the right place for a woman anyway. Perhaps some of the men at Selection Committees entertained this prejudice, but I found then and later that it was the women who came nearest to expressing it openly . . . I was hurt and disappointed by these experiences. They were, after all, an attack on me not just as a candidate but as a wife and mother. But I refused to be put off by them.[7]

Initially things weren't looking good for the determined young candidate in Finchley, a safe Conservative constituency in north London. The outgoing MP, an overbearing Old Etonian, Sir John Crowder, couldn't believe his ears when he heard the latest about the selection process, complaining to the party chairman that the Conservative Central Office was trying to rig the selection and give the local party a choice between 'a bloody Jew and a bloody woman'.[8] Things didn't improve when the other three shortlisted candidates brought their wives along to the selection meeting to sit prettily in the front row. Denis was away on a business trip to South Africa, so Margaret went alone. She managed to scrape through by just three votes, no mean feat for a thirty-two-year-old mother of twins in 1958. The headline in the *Evening Standard* was: 'Tories Choose Beauty'.⁹

A year later she was elected to Parliament on an increased majority of almost 3,500 votes. It was the third successive election victory for Harold Macmillan's Conservative Party. However, just twenty-five of the 630 MPs who won seats in the 1959 election were women. Heads kept turning for the new MP for Finchley, and the girl from Grantham continued to progress. When she was appointed as a parliamentary under-secretary to the minister for pensions in 1961 she was not only the youngest ever woman to be given a front-bench job but the first of the 1959 intake to be promoted, regardless of sex.

Initially even her new boss thought it was down to positive discrimination. John Boyd-Carpenter, the minister of pensions, admitted: 'I thought, frankly, when Harold Macmillan appointed her that it was just a little bit of a gimmick on his part. Here was a good-looking young woman and he was obviously, I thought, trying to brighten up the image of his government.'¹⁰

Just as Thatcher's career seemed on the rise, the political wheel turned the Conservatives out of power in 1964 and Harold Wilson's Labour Party formed a government. The new Conservative Party leader, Edward Heath, was no great champion of women's rights. Shirley Williams remembered him blanking her at a dinner party and asking the man sitting on her left: 'Does Ted Heath not speak to women?'¹¹

In the swinging sixties, however, even Heath couldn't get away for long without having what was known as the 'statutory woman' on his front-bench team. By 1966 his shadow cabinet team was still an all-male affair and pressure was mounting for that to change. Margaret Thatcher, however, was not the type of female politician he was looking for. When her name was suggested, Heath went quiet for some time before replying: 'Yes. Willie [Whitelaw] agrees she's much the most able, but he says once she's there we'll never be able to get rid of her. So we both think it's got to be Mervyn Pike.'¹²

Mervyn Pike – named after her father's best friend who was killed in action – was the Conservative MP for Melton who had a career in manufacturing before entering Parliament in 1956. In her more junior role on the shadow Treasury team, Thatcher sensed she was neither valued nor listened to. In her autobiography she wrote: 'For Ted and perhaps others I was principally there as the statutory woman whose main task was to explain what "women" – Kiri Te Kanawa, Barbara Cartland, Esther Rantzen, Stella Rimington and all the rest of our uniform, undifferentiated sex – were likely to think and want on troublesome issues.'[13] For Thatcher, the champion of the individual, this was nonsense. She never self-identified as feminist but her conviction that women were as different and diverse as men, rather than constrained by stifling stereotyping, is feminist in a sense.

In 1970 Heath unexpectedly won the general election and faced the uncomfortable issue of what to do with his most troublesome female MP now that he had to form a government. Margaret Thatcher was given what was considered the female-friendly role of education, thus becoming only the second female secretary of state after Florence Horsbrugh, who had been the education secretary in Winston Churchill's government. Heath parked her right at the end of his cabinet table, where it was impossible for her to catch his eye if she got up to try to speak. There followed a difficult few years for Thatcher. She was dubbed 'the most unpopular woman in Britain' by the *Sun* newspaper after she scrapped free milk for schoolchildren and she was relieved when she moved to the role of deputy shadow chancellor, 'Margaret Thatcher milk snatcher' ringing in her ears. Education may have been seen as a better fit for a woman than the Treasury, but Thatcher was no stereotypical woman. In her new role she shone in the House of Commons rough-and-tumble against Labour, and her moment in the sun could not have come at a better time.

Heath lost the 1974 general election and his support among Conservative MPs soon crumbled. It was only a matter of time before a challenger emerged through the rubble. Margaret

Thatcher's name was rarely mentioned by the men scheming in the smoking rooms, bars and tea rooms of the House of Commons. Slowly but surely, though, some of the leading male contenders started dropping out of the race.

Keith Joseph, the leading candidate of the right, never recovered after making an ill-advised speech lamenting the rising number of children born to women who, he claimed, were unfit to have them. Smooth-talking Edward du Cann decided not to launch his own bid because his wife hated the idea and his business was going through a rocky patch. The experienced Willie Whitelaw loyally refused to stand while Heath was still in the race.

Even Norman Tebbit, who was to become a key member of Thatcher's cabinet, admitted: 'If there had been a man with the same qualities as her I would have gone for him because it would have just been easier. But quite clearly, she was the best man among the candidates.'[14]

Thatcher knew Heath would be furious to hear she was planning to run against him for the leadership. When she went to his office to break the news, she found him sitting angrily at his desk. 'I must tell you,' she explained, 'that I have decided to stand for the leadership.'

'He looked at me coldly,' she later remembered, 'turned his back, shrugged his shoulders, and said: "If you must." I slipped out of the room.'[15]

A few weeks later a sticker appeared on the party chairman's door at Conservative Central Office. It cheekily read: 'Put a woman on top for a change.' The youthful culprit, Lord Forsyth, was involved in her leadership campaign. 'I thought, She will never speak to me again, but typically, she pretended not to understand the double entendre.'[16]

When Margaret Thatcher won the 1975 leadership contest in the second round and sent the wounded Edward Heath bitterly limping off, nobody could quite believe what had just happened. The Conservative Party woke up, blinking and bleary-eyed, to the realisation they had just elected a woman to the leadership. Geoffrey Howe, who was to become her first chancellor, remembered: 'She really only made an impact on us in the party when she was, to our surprise, elected leader. Put simply, nobody thought a woman could win – and then suddenly, there she was. I remember when she appeared for the first time at the meeting of the 1922 committee, this frail little woman in the middle of an all-male gathering, but rather proud of herself. And all of us surprised to find ourselves forming a quasi-Elizabethan court around her.'[17]

At that time nobody had any idea how radical the new Conservative Party leader would be – apart from one person. Margaret Thatcher herself regarded her victory as 'a shattering blow . . . to the Conservative establishment. I had no sympathy for them. They had fought me unscrupulously all the way.'[18]

The Labour Party, struggling through an economic recession, party splits and an uncompromising trade-union movement, could not quite believe its luck. Margaret Thatcher was seen as a weak opponent who could be pummelled in a general election. Lord Gilbert, who was then a middle-ranking minister in Harold Wilson's government, later recalled: 'I remember rejoicing with my noble friend Lord Barnett, who was leading for the government. He was chief secretary and I was financial secretary to the Treasury on that occasion. We rejoiced and said, "That's marvellous. The Tories will never win a seat north of Watford from now on." It just shows how wrong and stupid one can be.'[19]

Not everyone in the Labour Party was quite so gleeful at their new female opponent. Harold Wilson, then Labour prime minister, nervously poured himself a generous glass of whisky.[20] Barbara Castle wrote Thatcher a heartfelt message of congratulations. She recognised a fellow fighter who did not slot neatly into the male networks of the House of Commons. Being an ambitious female politician in the 1970s was a lonely road.

*   *   *

Margaret Thatcher didn't win the 1979 election: Labour lost it. James Callaghan's sickly government had struggled with high unemployment and the infamous 'winter of discontent'. The first ever female prime minister was elected with a majority of forty-four. Before that time no woman had held any of the top four government positions: prime minister, chancellor, foreign secretary or home secretary. Now, and for the next eleven years, the highest glass ceiling was shattered.

Despite Thatcher's success, remarkably few other women scrambled up the rungs behind her. The 1979 election saw the smallest number of women elected as MPs since 1951. Just nineteen won seats, compared to twenty-seven in the previous parliament, making up 3 per cent of the total. Representation was going backwards: when Thatcher had become MP for Finchley in 1959, there had been twenty-five women. The dream of a steadily increasing stream of females simply wasn't happening.

During her time as prime minister, Thatcher appointed just one woman to her cabinet: Baroness Young, leader of the House of Lords from 1981 until 1983. She appeared reluctant to support or promote women, although in 1979 she had eight women MPs to choose from. Throughout her time as prime minister, she showed little interest in helping ambitious women up the parliamentary ladder.

There is no mention of female MPs such as Edwina Currie, Virginia Bottomley or Gillian Shephard in her autobiography. Lynda Chalker, seen by many as one of the great female talents of the time, never reached her potential in Thatcher's government. She had also battled to be selected as MP for Wallasey in 1974, failing to be chosen for several seats previously. 'Now we come to the subject of what I would refer to as pillow talk,' said the chair of a selection committee in East Anglia. Chalker's heart sank. Her first husband had recently left her and she was coping with a divorce. 'As soon as they heard that, it was not going to happen,' she said. At the time, she replied: 'It has nothing to do with my ability as a candidate – and I suspect it applies to other people in this room too.'

'It was probably why I didn't get it,' she says, laughing.

Chalker was effective in her stints at Social Security, Transport and the Foreign Office, where she was minister for Africa for more than eleven years. Despite her promise, she was never promoted further. Chalker admits that this was partly because she was a woman and partly because she talked back to Thatcher; 'She encouraged people who were putting the issues the way she wanted them. I wasn't afraid to say my bit.'

Even those MPs who were in awe of their prime minister bumped their heads on a glass ceiling they might have assumed had disappeared.

Edwina Currie was elected in 1983 and promoted to the junior position of parliamentary under-secretary for health under Margaret Thatcher: 'She was tremendous. She had won elections in the teeth of opposition and demonstrated she was a better man than most of the men and that she was more in tune with the spirit of much of the UK.' Currie was not, however, to be promoted further. 'It didn't dawn on us until really quite late in Margaret's reign that we were not going to get into cabinet, she was going to appoint dim but beautiful men. Good-looking men were her weakness . . . attractive yes-men who were actually not very good at their job.'

Currie adds: 'My own theory is that she always felt like a fraud who was going to be found out. There was that deep-seated inse-curity that women often feel. When she was asked whether she would appoint Ted Heath to the cabinet, she said, "Ted would sit opposite me and look at me in the way a woman would." Quite a bizarre thing to say. I think what she meant was, He thinks I'm a fraud, he's right. He would look at me with contempt and any other woman would be the same.'

Ann Widdecombe, elected MP for Maidstone in 1987, was a loyalist who fought hard on Thatcher's behalf when the rest of the parliamentary party was turning against her. After she became a minister in John Major's government, she stood by Thatcher in the voting lobby. 'She didn't say thank you and she didn't say congratulations, and I actually would have taken a bet that if you'd said to her, "Margaret, who's that MP?" she might have had difficulty.' Widdecombe quickly adds: 'If I had been in her shoes and I was trying to turn the country around and get the unions under control and end the Cold War, a few little minor things like that, I don't really think I would have bothered too much about outreach towards women.'

Not everyone, however, accepts the idea that the first female prime minister failed to help other women. Baroness Trumpington was the one woman Thatcher sent to the House of Lords in the 1980 Honours List. 'I owe Margaret Thatcher everything,' she remembers. When her boss was unable to attend a cabinet meeting, Trumpington had to go in his place in order to recommend a professor for a government job: 'In terror I said it three times.' When the meeting was over, Thatcher came up to her and patted her shoulder, then said: 'I'll see that your professor gets the job.' Trumpington adds: 'That was the way in which we operated. It was either death to the end or eternal friendship.'[21]

Perhaps the most telling incident happened in 1979, just before Margaret Thatcher became prime minister. The party was holding a candidates' dinner ahead of the election to allow the overwhelmingly male group of hopefuls to meet the Conservative leader. It was a female guest, however, who caught Thatcher's eye. Cheryl Gillan was only there because her friend was unable to accompany the Conservative candidate David Shaw and she had stepped in as his last minute plus-one.

Out of the blue, after chatting for a little while, Thatcher piped up: 'We need women like you. Have you thought of being an MP?'

The young woman had never even considered it. 'It was that night that I thought I'd have a go,' she says. Gillan was to become a high-profile Conservative MP and a future cabinet minister. 'I was always quite surprised when people said [Thatcher] didn't encourage other women, because I never had that experience myself.'

When it came to her policy decisions, Margaret Thatcher did little specifically to further women's rights. She abolished the universal maternity grant in 1986, a twenty-five-pound payment to help with the costs of having a baby, and made it harder for women to qualify for maternity leave. The 1989 Education Act made it tougher to get a nursery place as local authorities were no longer required to provide care for three- to five-year-olds.

For Margaret Thatcher, weakness was the ultimate insult. When she was first elected leader, she told the radio interviewer Jimmy Young: 'If you want someone weak you don't want me. There are plenty of others to choose from.'[22] Her view did not change. After she left office, she said in an interview: 'The prime minister should be intimidating. There's not much point being a weak, floppy thing in the chair.'[23]

When Argentina invaded the Falklands Islands, she decided to fight back. The 1982 war was defining for Margaret Thatcher and when 300,000 people turned out to the victory parade it was clear the Conservatives had won the political battle. Before the invasion Labour was ahead in the polls and Tory MPs were actively conspiring against their female leader. In the aftermath of the victory, Thatcher was so confident of her popularity that she called an early election for June 1983 and was rewarded with an increased majority of 144 seats. Labour, in contrast, recorded their worst performance since 1918. As a result, Thatcher's position was virtually unchallengeable.

After the rush of victory came the ultimate blow. A year later Thatcher experienced one of the most devastating moments of her life. In the early hours of the morning on 12 October 1984, the IRA set off a bomb in Brighton's Grand Hotel, the venue for the Conservative Party conference. Five people were killed, including Sir Anthony Berry MP, while Norman Tebbit was badly injured and his wife left paralysed. The windows in Thatcher's room were blown straight through but she escaped unharmed. At her insistence, the conference opened the next morning promptly at nine thirty. She delivered her hastily redrafted speech that afternoon with a quiet determination: 'The fact that we are gathered here now, shocked but composed and determined, is a sign not only that this attack has failed, but that all attempts to destroy democracy by terrorism will fail.'

Thatcher was the Conservative Party's most successful election machine, yet the cosy male networks of the House of Commons remained impenetrable even by her. She was only grudgingly allowed membership to London's Carlton Club, frequented by Conservative politicians, when she became leader of the Conservative Party. Women still felt like intruders in the House of Commons smoking room, where many late-night plots and deals were made. Thatcher usually avoided Parliament's boozy bars, while poor facilities existed for women MPs. The Lady Members' Room, where she had done her ironing, was often crowded, leading some female MPs to work on benches in corridors, pen and paper balanced carefully on their laps.

Spurred on by her loyal parliamentary private secretary Ian Gow, who acted as an adviser, she tried to reach out to her colleagues with mixed success. The Conservative MP Julian Critchley remembers enjoying lunch with a group of men in the Members' Dining Room: 'Suddenly you look up and the first thing you see is the sight of Ian Gow with the sunlight glinting from his spectacles, and you know that this is the harbinger of trouble. And then in she would come and everyone would stop talking and she'd look at you and say, "Julian, what are your views on the money supply?"'[24]

Although Thatcher commanded respect and sometimes loyalty among her political acquaintances, she had few friends. Westminster alliances were built through public schools, cricket teams and drinking buddies and Thatcher often cut a lonely figure.

*　　*　　*

Like Barbara Castle before her, Margaret Thatcher knew that image mattered for a woman trying to reach the dizziest of political heights. Although the wildly popular *Spitting Image* portrayed her as a puppet wearing a man's suit and voiced by a male actor, she embraced – and exploited – her femininity. Thatcher employed a TV producer to help with her clothes and voice, and a playwright, Ronald Millar, to add sparkle to her speeches. He was responsible for some of her most memorable phrases, including her steely response to colleagues nervous about her policies: 'U-turn if you want to. The lady's not for turning.' Before her first party conference speech as prime minister, he sensed her nerves and tried to calm her down: 'Piece of cake, Prime Minister.'

Her reply was: 'No, not now, thank you, dear.'[25]

As her language tightened and toughened, her image softened. In the 1979 election her team set up a photo shoot at a farm where Thatcher could cuddle a lamb in front of the cameras. When she turned up, though, she inexplicably made a beeline to a rather heavier calf, grabbed hold of it and declared to the watching journalists that its name would be 'Victory'. Unknown to Thatcher, the calf had been battling an illness. When the cameras stopped flashing and the entourage had left, the best vets were immediately called in to try to make sure that 'Victory' did not drop dead before the election.

Thatcher underwent voice training and bought a new wardrobe in the drive to blunt the edges of her image. As her power grew so did her shoulders, with a new range of Aquascutum suit jackets and skirts (she never wore trousers). Nigel Lawson, her chancellor from 1983 to 1989, explained: 'She was convinced that her authority . . . would be diminished if she was not impeccably turned out at all times. She was probably right.'[26]

For the more genteel members of British society, the makeover was outrageous. The Oxford philosopher Lady Warnock hated her 'elocution accent' and found the way in which she dressed 'not exactly vulgar, just low', while the theatre director Jonathan

Miller despised her 'odious suburban gentility', which catered to the 'worst elements in commuter idiocy'.[27] It wasn't just her sex that made Thatcher an outsider: her class left her shut out of the cosy political establishment too.

Her accent may have been studiously coached, but her language remained that of the Grantham shop: 'Each woman who runs a house is a manager and an organiser,' she claimed.[28]

To view Margaret Thatcher as a woman who played the role of a man is a fundamental misreading of her premiership. Conservative MPs saw their prime minister as a series of female stereotypes, including battle-hardened Boudicca, scornful headmistress, harassed housewife, concerned mother and girlish flirt. She played up to each of them.

Barbara Castle recognised in her 'a combination men fear most: a brain as good as most of theirs plus a mastery of the arts of femininity'[29] (it takes one to know one).

'I like being made a fuss of by a lot of chaps,' Thatcher once said, and it showed.[30] She enjoyed male flattery and graciously accepted any attempts at traditional gallantry. On her death, the tribute of MPs such as Sir Gerald Howarth would have pleased her:

None of us can forget Margaret Thatcher's extraordinary elegance. I remember coming to the Chamber at about 4 o'clock in the morning during an all-night sitting – none of you lot know what an all-night sitting is about, but we used to have them regularly. It was 4 o'clock in the morning, people had had a bit to drink and, for us chaps, there was a bit of stubble and it was really pretty unpleasant. I was sitting on the Front Bench wondering when this purgatory was going to end, and then there was a frisson at the back of the Chair. All of a sudden, in walked the Prime Minister, not a hair out of place, handbag there, smiling. We sort of slid up the Bench and looked at the Prime Minister, saying, 'Here I am.' She was an inspiration to

us all and she inspired huge loyalty. When I asked Bob King-
ston, her personal protection officer, what it was like working
for her, he said, 'I would catch bullets between my teeth to save
that woman.'[31]

Margaret Thatcher knew the power of a little light flirting,
but she was equally adept at playing the role of concerned
mother. During her first Christmas as prime minister, she asked
Michael Jopling, her minister for agriculture, if he knew of any
Conservatives who would be alone over the festive period
because of death or divorce: she wanted to ask them to stay at
Chequers.[32]

Fresh from the exhilaration of the 1979 election victory, the
ambitious Conservative Robert Armstrong could not help the
rush of excitement when he received a call from the Number 10
switchboard informing him that the new prime minister would
like to see him. Surely, he hoped, Margaret Thatcher intended to
give him a job in her first cabinet. He rapped the lion knocker at
10 Downing Street, was greeted at the door and whisked upstairs
to her study. As Armstrong walked in, the prime minister glanced
up from her desk and said: 'Robert, you're looking very tired.'
Caught off guard, he stammered something about being up late
the previous night. Without missing a beat, Thatcher informed
him she wanted to appoint him as the new cabinet secretary. A
delighted, if somewhat confused, new cabinet secretary bounced
down the stairs and admitted to the senior civil servant who was
showing him out: 'It was a bit odd that she started by saying,
"Robert, you look very tired."'

He replied: 'Oh, don't worry about that – she's saying that to
everybody this morning.'[33]

The clucking concern was also an exercise in control and power.
For the woman who famously got by on just four hours a night,
sleep was a weapon. The Conservative MP George Walden
explained: 'What she was saying when she commented on how
terrible you looked was that you were a man and she was a woman,

you were a junior and she was prime minister, and yet unlike you she was never tired.'[34]

In her role as stern headmistress, cabinet ministers would frequently experience verbal thrashings from their leader, and with chancellor Geoffrey Howe in particular her behaviour verged on bullying. Thatcher began one meeting by announcing in front of embarrassed officials: 'I know what you are going to say Geoffrey, and the answer is no.' At the start of another, she said: 'Your paper is twaddle, complete and utter twaddle.'[35]

Housewife was another role that Thatcher took extremely seriously. No matter how late her engagements ran into the night she would try to get back to Downing Street to cook Denis his breakfast, even though she survived on an apple and a vitamin pill. Her speech writer Ronnie Millar remembers when she dragged Denis away from a party, saying: 'If you want me to poach your egg, come now!'[36]

Margaret Thatcher may not have identified with the feminist movement, but she believed that women could have it all – career, marriage and children. She completed her applications to sit the bar examinations while she was still in the maternity ward. In 1954, long before she was prime minister, she defended working mothers: 'What is the effect on the family when the mother goes out to work each day? If she has a powerful and dominant personality her personal influence is there the whole time . . . From my own experience I feel there is much to be said for being away from the family for part of the day. When looking after them without a break it is sometimes difficult not to get a little impatient . . . whereas, having been out, every moment spent with them is a pleasure.'[37]

Inevitably, when juggling family responsibilities with being prime minister, balls were dropped. Carol Thatcher has said her mother 'had total tunnel vision when it came to work'. She remembers watching a pop-music show on television with her brother while Thatcher was doing constituency paperwork in the same room. Worried the loud noise was distracting, Carol asked if her mother wanted her to turn down the volume. 'No,' the reply came: she hadn't even realised the TV was on.[38] Perhaps most poignantly, in 1995 Thatcher said to the Conservative MP Sir Michael Spicer: 'If I had my time again, I wouldn't go into politics because of what it does to your family.'[39]

Like all political careers, Margaret Thatcher's ended in pain and disappointment. Her poll ratings nose-dived after rows over the poll tax, high interest rates and Europe, but it was her own party that pulled the trigger on her career. After the devastating resignation speech of Geoffrey Howe, her support crumbled. She took it as a very personal betrayal: 'I was sick at heart . . . What grieved me was the desertion of those I had always considered friends and allies and the weasel words whereby they had transmuted their betrayal into frank advice and concern for my fate.'[40] Always an outsider, Thatcher's suit of armour was her ability to win elections. Once that was in doubt, the knife was plunged in.

Margaret Thatcher only occasionally allowed us a glimpse into how it felt to be the first female prime minister, speaking at the despatch box to a House of Commons in which fewer than one in ten MPs were women, walking into the bars and seeing the men shift round in their seats to stare. She admitted: 'The House of Commons is still very much male dominated, and there is something about them, a sort of "little women" thing. It would have been all right if I had gone into what they would regard as one of the traditional professions. All right if I had followed Florence Nightingale.'[41] There was no blueprint for how a female prime minister should act. Her husband Denis described her as 'Florence Nightingale with a blowtorch'.[42]

Perhaps more than any other prime minister, Margaret Thatcher inspired the full spectrum of responses from sexist abuse to legitimate criticism to unadulterated love. Democracy, however, was her greatest weapon against her critics: she was elected three times. When she won her third successive election victory on 11 June 1987, it was the first time a prime minister had done so since 1826. Never again could it be said that women were unelectable.

The Fighters

'We were like a little coven of witches.'

– Shirley Williams

'Yes, you were patronised and there was sexism, but a young woman MP had far bigger chances of promotion than a young man of the same vintage or qualifications.'

– Margaret Beckett

'It felt like the barriers were coming down and it was up to women to show they were good enough. That now sounds to us terribly prejudiced, but then sounded to my generation like an open gate.'

– Edwina Currie

'Everybody moans, everybody looks for reasons why it's difficult to be a woman MP – it isn't!'

– Ann Widdecombe

In the early hours of the morning, a small cluster of women had gathered in the Lady Members' Room. The late-night vote had spilled over into the early hours of the morning, and the debate was still going on in the Chamber. In the 1980s 'family-friendly hours' were not even under discussion – going home at 10 p.m. was considered an early night. But the women taking a breather from the lengthy debate would not have been likely to moan about that. The female MPs in Parliament in the sixties, seventies and eighties were the political survivors – tough, determined and dismissive of special treatment.

As the eight or nine women chatted to pass the time, one told a story about a senior male MP who had made a pass at her, even though he was in a position of influence. Then another woman piped up: 'Hang on a minute, something similar happened to me.' It soon became apparent there was no woman in the room that the man in question hadn't chatted up. One Labour MP recounted a story in which the man had attempted to persuade her into bed by saying that he had 'fifteen minutes to spare'. Nowadays that would be grounds for a serious complaint to the Whips Office and inevitable disciplinary action. At the time, however, the room simply erupted in laughter, with some clutching their stomachs and others wiping tears from their eyes. They found it hilarious.

Parliament in the twentieth century was a nest of drinking, flirting and bad behaviour and there are plenty of similar stories. Unwelcome fingers wandered in the division lobby, the two corridors running to the left and right of the Chamber where MPs register their vote by choosing the 'aye' or 'no' side. The area can be extremely busy, with men and women packed together as if they were on a bus. In the 1960s, one Honourable Member was taking full advantage. Women found they were being pinched – quite hard – on the bottom, arm or leg.

Shirley Williams, the young Labour MP for Hitchin, had had enough. 'We were fed up about it,' she remembers. 'We were Members of Parliament, we were elected, why should we be treated as feminine fodder?' There were only twenty-nine female MPs, so it was easy to get together and work out a strategy. 'We decided that the next time there was a three-line whip and the lobbies were packed, we would all wear our sharpest stiletto heels. Few things hurt more than stiletto heels driven into the foot.'

The following day, Williams was sipping coffee when a male MP in his sixties hobbled into the tea room. He immediately found himself circled by women, clucking in mock-concern: 'Oh, what's happened to you? How awful! It looks as though your foot has been really badly hurt. What on earth has led to this? Have you been in a car accident?'

After a pause, the man in question spluttered: 'Gout!'

The groping mysteriously stopped and no more was said about

it. Fifty years later, Williams still believes, 'The response was very effective.' She would not have done anything differently.

Shirley Williams was used to being in a minority. Before she entered Parliament, she worked at the *Financial Times*, where she was told: 'You may not be any good, but at least you're cheap.'[1] She was banned from writing editorials because she was a woman. In 1964, at just thirty-four, she was elected as the Labour MP for Hitchin, gaining the highest swing of any constituency in the country.

'We were like a little coven of witches,' she says, of the twenty-nine women who had won seats. 'On the whole we were quite close and there wasn't a lot of cattiness. Women from different parties pulled together and we were reluctant to bite into one another. The attitude of the men, however, could be quite patronising.'

About three months after being elected, Shirley heard the bells jangling through the Palace of Westminster to alert MPs to a vote. Thanks to a prior speaking engagement, she had no idea what the subject matter was but, luckily, she bumped into her 'pair', the Conservative MP Sir Bernard Braine. In the 'pairing system' two MPs from opposing parties agree not to vote if the other can't make it due to unavoidable circumstances, thereby cancelling each other out. 'He was a very gallant, sweet old gentleman who sat for Canvey Island and was obviously quite pleased to have a young, female pair.'

Williams bounded up to him and said: 'Bernard, the bells are ringing, there must be a vote!'

He replied, 'There is.'

'Come on, tell me what it's about.'

'I don't think you need to know.'

'Well, I think I ought to vote,' Williams said, growing irritated, 'but I do need to know what it's about.'

'No, I think really not. You don't need to know at all.'

'Bernard, please! You're my pair! Please tell me.'

He leaned forward, patted Williams on the head, and said: 'Don't you trouble your pretty little head about it.'

The vote was about the legalisation of adult homosexuality. 'Bernard was trying to protect me from ugly things like sex,' Williams says. 'He was very, very gallant. But his gallantry overcame his democracy. He was a sweet man but of the old school. It just shows you how huge the gap was.'

The Parliament of the 1960s was a baffling place for a woman in her thirties, seemingly untouched by the cultural revolution raging outside its Gothic walls. Women had been sitting as MPs for more than forty years, but the parliamentary facilities were still catching up. There were no signs above doors banning female MPs from the oak-panelled dining rooms or bars but women venturing into the tight-knit networks were made to feel like strangers. A veteran MP was horrified to see a Labour colleague walk into the smoking room with Williams at his side, and hissed: 'This is obscene!'

Wherever possible, women were kept separate: the chintzy Lady Members' Room was their territory. Even their coat pegs were placed in a different area of the cloakroom, thoughtfully positioned at the front so the men could gallantly help them put on their coats. The number of lavatories failed to keep pace with even the derisory number of women MPs.

The segregation continued in London's gentlemen's clubs, where male MPs built powerful alliances and debated policy ideas over wine and dinner. The Conservatives met in the resplendent clubs of St James's and Pall Mall, the Liberals used the palatial Reform Club while Labour intellectuals formed the XYZ Club above a pub in the City. Women, however, were barred and the Reform Club remained all-male until 1981. When the club hosted a meeting in the late 1960s for scientists and politicians to discuss genetic factors in health care, Shirley Williams, who was junior science minister at the time, was forced to scuttle through the basement and into a goods lift to avoid polluting the all-male club. The trade unions that formed the backbone of the Labour

Party were also heavily masculine. The general secretary of the teaching union, the NASUWT, introduced Shirley Williams to conference when she was education secretary by saying there were 'man brains' and 'women brains' and as women brains went she had quite a good one. Typically, she swallowed her irritation and said nothing.[2]

Once tipped to be the UK's first female prime minister, Williams was quickly promoted by both Harold Wilson and later James Callaghan. Two years after her election, she was sent to the Ministry of Labour when the department was wrestling with a wave of strikes and a splintering relationship with the trade unions. In May 1966 the minister in charge, Ray Gunter, was on sick leave when the National Union of Seamen called a strike, leaving exports piling up at the ports. It fell to Williams to attend cabinet and take the governmental lead – but the department's most senior civil servant refused to speak to her. Sir James Dunnett, the permanent secretary, was a 'gruff and short-fused civil servant of the old school', who had firmly opposed the idea of a woman in his department. At a time of national crisis, he would offer advice only to the prime minister and simply cut Williams out. It fell to the embarrassed deputy secretary Denis Barnes to convey messages between them.

Despite the difficulties, Williams skipped through a variety of government roles, leafing through pornographic magazines carefully wrapped in brown paper as Home Office minister in 1969, trying to determine whether any should be banned, and spending twenty-four hours as an undercover inmate in Holloway Prison to see what conditions were really like, telling her fellow jailbirds that she had been 'on the game'. She battled rising inflation as secretary of state for prices and consumer protection in 1974 but her greatest achievements, she feels, were in the Department for Education, where she pushed for more nursery schools and oversaw the growth of comprehensives. 'The huge beneficiaries were, of course, girls. The number of young women going to university leaped as a result.'

But Shirley Williams's gilded route to power was about to take a sudden handbrake turn. In the 1970s Labour was a fractured and factional party, split between the hard left and those (like Williams) keen to occupy the centre ground. For the militants and left-wingers, the Labour government ministers were a sell-out. 'The abuse from the far left was awful,' Williams recalls. 'I remember walking into party conference and lines of people shouting and spitting and calling me a traitor.'

When Margaret Thatcher was swept to power in 1979, Shirley Williams lost her seat. Disillusioned with what she saw as the hard left's attempt to infiltrate Labour, she embarked on a breathtaking mission to form a new centre-left political party. David Owen, Roy Jenkins and Bill Rodgers made up the rest of the 'Gang of Four', who founded the Social Democratic Party. After taking the ultimate political risk, her confidence ran out. Williams stepped aside to let Roy Jenkins contest the 1981 election in Warrington and didn't run for the leadership of the fledgling party – even though her government experience, media skills and popularity with the public arguably made her a far superior choice to her male colleagues, who had no such qualms with putting themselves forward. 'I readily conceded, both publicly and privately, that Roy was a greater person than I was,' she admits, adding: 'I doubt whether that would have mattered so much to me if I had then had the love and support of a spouse like Dick Neustadt, who believed in me more than I believed in myself.'[3]

She married Neustadt, an American political scholar, in 1987. Her first husband, the dashing Sir Bernard Williams, had left her for another woman when she was shadow home secretary in 1971. For much of her time in Parliament she was a single mother, divorced and raising a young daughter. Bernard Williams had struggled to handle his wife's blossoming career. At parties, other men would try deliberately to humiliate him, stretching out their hands and asking: 'This must be Mr Shirley Williams, I presume?'

'With the benefit of hindsight, I see now that I underestimated how difficult it was for an ambitious and brilliant young man to have a wife equally strongly committed to a career, still rare in the 1960s,' Williams reflects.[4]

If being a woman in Westminster was a rarity in the seventies, being a mother – especially a single one – was even lonelier. 'Like many women of my generation and the generation before mine, I thought of myself as not quite good enough for the very highest positions in politics,' Williams says. 'Few people write about the partners of political leaders but they are indispensable. It is still easier for an able male politician to find such a person than for a woman, though thankfully that is beginning to alter.'[5]

In the sixties and seventies, while a few determined fighters like Shirley Williams and Barbara Castle climbed the rungs of the ministerial ladder, the number of female MPs was stagnating. In 1964, when Williams first entered Parliament, she was one of twenty-nine women and the number of female MPs didn't pass that total for more than twenty years, until it limbered up to forty-one in 1987 – still just 6.3 per cent of the total. Few women were putting themselves forward for election, and those who did were stumbling. As a result, the survivors were strong-minded and frequently exceptional MPs.

In October 1974 Margaret Beckett, the candidate for Lincoln, won a seat. In a career spanning more than fifty years, she was to become the first female foreign secretary, the first female acting leader of the Labour Party and only the second woman after Margaret Thatcher to hold one of the top four jobs.

Born in Ashton-under-Lyne, Margaret Jackson never set out to become an MP. Her father was a Bevin Boy during the war, working in the coal mines because a bout of rheumatic fever blocked him from joining the army. After long hours down the pit, his health broke down and he caught pneumonia. A proud man, he refused to see his friends because he couldn't bear them to witness his weakened and pathetic state. He died aged just forty-nine, his heart irretrievably damaged, after spending a decade in and out of hospital. 'He was always a semi-invalid,' Beckett remembers.

'He couldn't exert himself in any great way, which he hated because he had been very fit and a water-polo player. But we were extraordinarily lucky because my mother was a trained teacher.'

With her husband bed-bound, Winifred Jackson went back to the profession she had given up when she was married. Without her teaching qualification, the family would have been destitute. It was a lesson that was not lost on her three girls. 'It was taken for granted in our household that women study and women go out to work,' Margaret explains. 'We knew that even if you marry you can't rely on being supported by someone else.' The Jackson sisters studied hard and Margaret did an engineering apprentice-ship – but politics soon beckoned. 'What I could see from my own family life was that a lot of people had considerable problems through no fault of their own, things they couldn't do anything about, and there wasn't enough of a safety net.' When she was twenty-one she signed up to the local Labour Party, and after her first ward meeting she was hooked.

After a spell working in a laboratory in Manchester, she joined the party's research unit. Working on industrial policy in its London office brought her into close contact with high-flying politicians, including Tony Benn, hero of the left and future cabinet minister. When Labour won the election, he asked the young researcher to be the head of his political office, but it was too late. Margaret Jackson had caught the political bug and now aspired to higher things.

In Lincoln, something unusual was happening: the constituency Labour Party had decided it was in need of a female candidate. The local chairman, Leo Beckett, was desperate for someone who could overturn the daunting majority won at the last election by the independent MP Dick Taverne, a smart young lawyer. He felt the only way to wrestle the seat back was to choose someone alto-gether different. He also sensed Taverne would struggle to handle a female rival. It was serendipitous that Margaret Jackson decided to apply.

Sitting on the train home after the selection meeting in 1973, she thought: That seemed to go quite well. I wonder if I'm in with a chance. A second thought slipped in: If I do get it, will I be any good?

Was that a stereotypically female moment of self-doubt? 'More than likely. I didn't think of that then, but now it seems incredibly familiar.'

Not only did the working-class girl from Ashton-under-Lyne win the seat in 1974, she fell in love with the man who had believed in her from the start. Margaret Jackson married Leo Beckett, who never doubted her abilities and would later manage her parliamentary office. The sight of Margaret and Leo grabbing a bite to eat in the canteen after a long day at work was a familiar sight in the Houses of Parliament. 'It's worked out all right,' Beckett says of her marriage, with typical under-statement.

Margaret Beckett's first years in Westminster had none of the glitz of expectancy that Shirley Williams's did. Her rise was steady but inexorable. A total of eighteen Labour women won seats at the 1974 election, including Helene Hayman and Ann Taylor. For Sir Bernard Braine it was all too much. 'Bernard Braine couldn't tell the difference between us, and we don't look at all alike,' Beckett says. 'He congratulated Ann when Helene had her baby and he congratulated Helene when I got made a minister. He was completely incapable of remembering which of us was which.'

After her experience of running Manchester University's electro-microscopic laboratory, that was nothing. 'A lot of people were patronising towards women MPs but I was used to it so it didn't impinge on me half as much as it did on colleagues. There were more women in Parliament than I was accustomed to having around me, so it didn't come as a shock to me. It was the water I swam in. When you work in a factory of 24,000 people, and you're one of a handful of women, they're much blunter than MPs.

'And there was another side to the coin. Because there were so few women, a young woman MP had got far bigger chances of promotion than a young man of the same vintage or qualifications. There were advantages.'

In 1975, just a year after she had entered Parliament, Beckett was promoted to the Whips' Office. The Labour prime minister, Harold Wilson, was known to be a champion of women, giving jobs to Barbara Castle and Shirley Williams before her, but not everyone was happy to see another woman on the ascendant.

One female Labour MP asked: 'So, who have you been sleeping with?'

Rattled, Beckett responded: 'Nobody. Perhaps that's why I've been promoted.'

A year later, when she was elevated again to the Department of Education, a jovial, intoxicated Conservative MP said to her: 'You're doing very well, my dear girl. But don't worry, we'll bring you down in the end.'

Will you indeed, she thought. That's a very helpful warning, thank you very much!

Beckett moved seamlessly through the cabinet ranks, from spokeswoman on social security to shadow chief secretary to the Treasury, and after the 1992 general election she was elected deputy leader – the first woman to hold that job. Two years later, tragedy forced her into another historic first. John Smith, the leader of the Labour Party, died of a heart attack on 12 May 1994 and Margaret Beckett found herself acting leader. 'I hope I never live through a period as difficult as that again. I was a leader without a deputy and on the brink of the nationwide European elections.'

Not everyone in the Labour Party was as supportive as has been widely assumed. Some members of John Smith's immediate staff were unhelpful and appeared resentful towards their new boss. Meanwhile, hostile Labour MPs were forming into camps. While some grieved, others saw political opportunity. Nobody openly campaigned against Beckett's leadership as she tried to steady the ship, but jealousy and bitterness towards her grew from some of the circling opportunists.

The morning after John Smith died, the shadow secretary for trade and industry, Robin Cook, telephoned her. 'We've agreed that the only sensible thing is for you to stay on as leader,' he pronounced.

Keen not to antagonise anyone, she replied: 'That's kind of you, Robin.'

It had nothing to do with him: Margaret Beckett was the acting leader of the Labour Party whether Cook liked it or not. However, the conversation made clear that there had been discussions about whether to push her out and engineer a leadership election. John Smith wasn't even in his coffin. Whatever the truth, forces within the party were clearly unhappy that Margaret Beckett was in the top job.

Two months later, when the leadership race was called, Beckett launched her own candidacy. 'Although I was getting quite a bit of hostility from MPs, out in the country I had a great reaction. I remember walking into an airport terminal and people breaking out into spontaneous applause. When I attended the D Day commemorations I was mobbed by veterans. But the parliamentary party didn't want to hear that I was popular with the public because they had a different candidate.'

Tony Blair, the ambitious young shadow home secretary, was also in the race. 'Tony Blair was a brilliant candidate, very charismatic, but not very experienced, which is one of the reasons I ran against him. I knew I wasn't popular enough in the party but I thought it might be my duty.' Beckett also believes her sex might have counted against her. 'Thatcher poisoned the water as far as Labour was concerned. People just didn't want another woman. And in my case it was another Margaret, which didn't help.' In one of her campaign speeches, Beckett joked that if she became prime minister, the Conservatives would be marching past Downing Street shouting: 'Maggie, Maggie, Maggie, out, out, out!'

When the results were announced, Tony Blair won with 57 per cent of the vote. Margaret Beckett finished in third place, behind

John Prescott. She also lost out in the fight for the deputy leadership.

Beckett went on to have a distinguished cabinet career under Tony Blair's leadership, becoming the first female foreign secretary in 2006. However, when asked about her greatest achievement, she goes back to 1997 when, as secretary of state for trade and industry, she pushed through plans for a national minimum wage. Beckett says: 'I know the minimum wage was my greatest achievement because absolutely everyone tries to take the credit for it – without mentioning me. Tony Blair says how proud he was of achieving it, Gordon Brown does too. Nobody mentions either me or Ian McCartney [a minister in her department], even though we made sure it got through politically.'

A decade after the minimum wage was introduced, a reception in Downing Street was arranged to celebrate the legislation. A friend of Beckett's happened to be working at Number 10 and glanced at the guest list in amazement. 'Hang on, you haven't got Margaret Beckett or Ian McCartney down, or any of the people on the committee,' he said. 'In fact, the more I look at it, none of the people on this list had anything to do with the minimum wage legislation.'

Margaret Beckett says: 'They didn't add us to the list. They cancelled the reception.'

Like her fellow female fighters of the seventies and eighties, Margaret Beckett's political adolescence was shaped by Thatcherism. In 1983, when the Conservative prime minister was at the peak of her powers, an extraordinary cast of characters entered the House of Commons, including three future Labour leaders: Tony Blair, Gordon Brown and Jeremy Corbyn. Strong-minded and self-reliant female MPs, including Edwina Currie and Clare Short, joined the ranks while Shirley Williams, by then standing for the SDP, lost her seat. Just twenty-three female MPs were elected. The UK had an all-powerful female prime minister but there were now fewer women in Parliament than there had been in 1945, just 3.5 per cent of the total. The women who survived the 1983 election, however, did not moan about it. Female MPs of both parties took a leaf out of Margaret Thatcher's handbook on individualism, self-reliance and sheer bloody determination.

Edwina Currie – effervescent and a little bit bonkers – felt part of a tidal wave of opportunity when she entered Parliament. 'It felt like the barriers were coming down and it was up to women to show they were good enough. That now sounds to us terribly prejudiced, but sounded to my generation like an open gate – we were no longer barred from things, the opportunity was there if we were good enough, and of course many of us were more than good enough – haha!'

Currie grew up in a Liverpool that 'was sliding downhill fast', with the docks and manufacturing industry in decline. Her parents were Orthodox Jews who ran a tailoring business. She was always interested in politics. 'How could this great city with wonderful public buildings just die? I thought, There's something political going on here.'

Currie's life was a whirlwind from the start. She sold spangled tights and sequined dresses to local prostitutes in her first job working in a shop, won a scholarship to Oxford University and subsequently lived in a London bedsit where she was so broke she couldn't afford a winter coat. Asked what her greatest achievement is, she doesn't miss a beat. 'Getting into Oxford was the thing that made a huge difference. Once I got that scholarship, I could look anyone in the eye. At university I met the kind of people who were being trained to go into Parliament and I thought, I'm as smart as them. That was when I knew I wanted to go into politics.

'At that stage you don't realise what an immense mountain you're setting out to climb and the fact you don't realise it is the oxygen tank on your back.'

After university Currie trained as an accountant, joined Birmingham City Council and fell in love. Her parents refused to come to the wedding because Ray Currie was not Jewish. Her father never spoke to Edwina again, even when his two grand-daughters were born. How did she balance raising a family with her political career? 'That's a very prejudicial question. Do you ask that of the men?' she replies. Speaking about her second husband John Jones, who she married in 2001, she says: 'The first thing is I've never done housework, ever. I'm deliberately bad at it. I didn't want to be like my mother. I still do not own a cooking recipe. My husband does all the cooking and he's very good at it – every woman should have one – and I've always had some-body looking after the house.'

Currie also called on the 'big family' of the Conservative Party for help. 'My invention, of which I am quite proud, was Rent-a-Granny. When the children were about three or four, I passed a message around the local Conservative branch saying I'm looking for someone who is missing their own grandchildren and can take my daughters home and have tea with them, teach them manners and how to sit at the table properly. A lovely lady came forward and did so for about four years. I created an extended family so there was always somebody else I could call on.'

Currie had built up a formidable CV before putting herself forward as a candidate. She had served on Birmingham City Council from the age of twenty-eight, with a baby tucked under either arm, regularly promoted until she was in charge of a £200 million budget. She had spoken at party conference, written angry letters to newspapers and was a fixture on TV and local radio. However, when she applied for the candidacy at Stratford-upon-Avon – where she had spoken at several local party dinners – she wasn't even called for interview. Shocked, she wrote to the chair-man to ask why. He replied that there were no circumstances under which they would choose a woman and, anyway, they wanted someone of 'cabinet quality'.

Currie went on to win the selection for South Derbyshire and entered Parliament at the 1983 election. She decided to visit the House of Commons a few days before the flood of MPs returned after the recess. 'It was a hot summer's day so I had on a little summer dress, some sandals, no tights. I came into the lobby and there was a little old lady standing there – I can't be sure who it was. It was someone who had been an MP.'

The woman, dressed smartly and wearing a pillbox hat, turned to Edwina and asked: 'Are you one of the new lady members?'

'Yes, I am. I'm the MP for South Derbyshire,' she replied.

'Well, you're improperly dressed. We lady members decided many years ago, when you're on duty in the House you wear a black suit with a white shirt, black tie or scarf, if you wish, black stockings, black shoes and a hat.' Nancy Astor's uniform had clearly survived.

'I looked at her and said, "I'm awfully sorry but I only ever dress like that when I go to funerals,"' Edwina Currie remembers. 'She was disgusted.'

After being the chair of Birmingham City Council, Currie was used to possessing authority and commanding respect. As one of only a handful of women MPs, she was often mistaken for a secretary. When asked whom she worked for, Currie learned to reply tartly: 'The people of South Derbyshire. Who are *you* working for?'

'When you're in the House of Commons, you're a backbencher, you're a newcomer, you're nobody, you're a newbie and you're a *girl*,' she explains. 'It's very exasperating, very frustrating.' Currie, however, has always been thick-skinned. 'You need to remember I'm Scouse. I'm Liverpool. If you can look after yourself walking down Lime Street, believe me, you can look after yourself in the House of Commons.'

Edwina Currie's anonymity, unsurprisingly, did not last long. Within three years of being elected, Margaret Thatcher made her a junior health minister. One of her most lasting achievements was bringing in breast and cervical cancer screening for women, saving many thousands of lives. To convince a sceptical prime minister to stump up the money, Currie argued that, without the programme, working-age women would die and no longer pay taxes. She deployed a similar economic argument to convince the initially reluctant Thatcher to get behind an HIV awareness campaign in the spring of 1986. Once it was signed off, Currie launched herself into it, sending leaflets to every household and even going on television to demonstrate how to put on a condom.

When health workers revealed that teenagers with HIV were reluctant to come forward because gay sex was illegal until the age of twenty-one, Currie had found her next political mission. Changing the law while Margaret Thatcher was prime minister was out of the question, but as soon as John Major won the 1992 election she led a group of MPs in a campaign to lower the homosexual age of consent. 'The men asked me to push it forward in Parliament because it was much easier for a woman to do so,' Currie says. 'You have no idea what the atmosphere was like against gays – it was horrendous. I had friends and colleagues who were blackmailed, people who committed suicide, and some of my gay friends had lavender marriages. If a man had argued for the law to be changed, people would have thought he was a homosexual.'

Even so, newspapers sent reporters to South Derbyshire to find out if any of Edwina Currie's constituents thought she was a lesbian. Determined to get cross-party support, Currie met with the Labour leader, Neil Kinnock. She had been warned that he was unlikely to support the campaign because he was Welsh, working class and had sons. 'We met in secret over rock buns at St Ermin's Hotel, and I told him, "If you believe in equality, this is equality. The law should treat everyone the same." And, bless his cotton socks, he supported it.'

In February 1994, Edwina Currie's amendment to lower the homosexual age of consent to sixteen was narrowly defeated, but resulted in the legal age being reduced to eighteen. Equality between heterosexual and homosexual sex came six years later, in 2000. There are pubs in Brighton where gay men still buy her drinks, she says proudly.

*   *   *

It was her own sex life, though, that Edwina Currie will be most remembered for. Between 1984 and 1988, she had an affair with John Major. On the surface he seemed an unlikely lover for the outspoken, sexually exuberant Currie. Major tucked his shirt into his underpants, ate peas with nearly every meal and loved cricket, but for Edwina, he was her 'sexy beast'. In the early days Currie was a backbencher and he was a government whip, but as he scrambled up the career ladder the affair became a liability.

When he was made chief secretary to the Treasury, Major abruptly ended the dalliance. In 1990, he unexpectedly won the Conservative leadership election. The cabinet he formed was the first for a quarter of a century that had no women in it. Edwina Currie was furious at her former lover. To make things worse, he defended his choices by saying he had appointed on merit – in other words, the women just weren't up to it. For the survivors of the eighties, tough, uncomplaining, determined, it was a betrayal. Edwina Currie, Emma Nicholson and Teresa Gorman were among the women bitterly disappointed. 'If we'd had tomatoes in our hands, we'd have pelted him with them,' Currie says. 'If he was appointing on merit, there were plenty of women in the party who were a lot smarter than he was.'

When he won the election two years later, John Major offered Edwina Currie a position working under Kenneth Clarke at the Home Office. It was a job Edwina felt she could not do: 'Isn't there anything else?'

'No,' the reply came. 'You were very difficult to contact.'

'I thought, That's a lie. I could have been contacted for two days. I said, "I'm sorry but I don't want to do that."

'John Major said: '"You can't refuse!"

'"Why can't I refuse?"

'"We've already put out the press release."

'"Well, Prime Minister, that's just too bad."'

Currie was furious. 'He put Jonathan Aitken in Defence who was too close to the Saudis. He gave a job to Neil Hamilton, who is mainly motivated by money. I was angrier than I've ever been.

He could have created a ministry of all the talents, and he didn't. I was devastated at that time and I didn't understand what was going on. It was only much later I realised you had to be ingratiating to get a job.'

Edwina Currie waited patiently for her revenge, but when she published her intimate diaries in 2002 the effect was devastating. John Major, the man who, as prime minister, lectured everyone else to go 'Back to Basics', was a cheat. For Currie, unceremoniously dumped by her lover as he climbed the career ladder, Back to Basics was 'absolute humbug'.

Westminster was left reeling. 'Edwina recreated John Major,' Shirley Williams says. 'A number of women suddenly looked at him and thought, He's rather fetching. Nobody thought that before – he was considered a grey suit and nothing inside.'

Currie herself is unrepentant. 'The apotheosis of John Major claims that he was a good, wonderful man and he was just dealt bad luck. Well, it wasn't bad luck that he had idiots in his government. It was him. I was pleased when he was elected leader and pleased when we won the election of 'ninety-two, but then he let it slip through his hands like sand and he is actually quite a weak personality. And I know him better than anybody.'

Sitting in the corner of the Carlton Club, which only permitted women to become full members in 2008, Ann Widdecombe scoffs at the idea that John Major held women back.

'It's quite true that John Major's first cabinet had no women, and that was the source of much press commentary,' she says. 'Now, to me that didn't matter because John was picking a cabinet on merit and trying to take the best. John was above all a meritocrat – he hadn't been born into any sort of privilege.'

Widdecombe bristles at the idea of special treatment for women. Like her fellow fighters, she's proud to have got where she did without extra help and denies her sex held her back in any way. 'I never really understood why people think it's an issue,' she says. 'From the moment I decided I was going into politics, I never saw it as an advantage or a disadvantage. If you look for problems it becomes self-fulfilling prophecy and you find them.'

Widdecombe's battle to be selected as an MP was fraught with difficulties. She did more than a hundred interviews across three different elections before she was chosen for a winnable seat. In the seventies and eighties there were no all-women shortlists or A-lists of candidates to help women enter Parliament. Fighting to be selected for the 1979 election, Widdecombe was frequently asked whether she was planning to get married. 'Now, to me that was a perfectly fair question.' Her experience in the Sunderland selection meeting, however, was too much even for her. 'You look very small and frail,' complained one of the female members of the local party, then sketched a triangle on a piece of paper, which was supposed to resemble Ann Widdecombe's frame. 'Are you sure you're up to it?' Although Widdecombe stood at five foot one and weighed just six stone twelve at the time, frail is not an adjective you would use to describe her.

'It was nearly always the women,' she says. 'Either they resented the fact that women suddenly had opportunities they hadn't or they thought quite genuinely women should be at home. Being single was an advantage, because nobody could say I ought to be at home because of the children.'

Later in 1979 she was chosen to fight the seat of Burnley. Just before calling Widdecombe back into the room to tell her the good news, one of the men said: 'Hang on, we've selected a woman. Is this constituency ready?'

Another voice piped up: 'Well, next door they've had Barbara Castle for years.'

'That's what they always say,' Widdecombe says, looking back. 'Is this constituency ready – not "I've got doubts."'

Ann Widdecombe is not the only female MP who struggled to win a seat before going on to have an accomplished Westminster career. Cheryl Gillan, the Conservative MP for Chesham and Amersham, worked as a highly successful marketing executive before entering the House of Commons. When fighting for selection in the early 1990s, she was frequently asked whether she intended to have children. 'It's none of your business,' came the well-rehearsed reply. 'That's a private discussion between myself and my husband.'

She was also asked – on more than one occasion – what her husband thought of her becoming an MP. 'I always gave a civilised answer, but inside that really rankled. I am not a chattel. I make my own decisions. They would never ask that question of a man.'

Gillan's constituents also had to get used to the idea that their new MP was female. She had only just installed herself in her parliamentary office when she answered the telephone to hear a man asking: 'Hello, can I please speak to the MP?'

Gillan replied: 'Yes, can I help you?'

Louder this time: 'I want to speak to my MP!'

'Yes, and can I help you?'

'Don't be silly – put me through to Charles Gillan!'

'I'm terribly sorry, my name is Cheryl Gillan. I am your MP and you are my constituent.'

Two years after she entered Parliament, Cheryl Gillan was promoted by John Major and rejects the claim that he did not promote women. Like her fellow fighters, she takes pride in the fact she didn't have a leg-up. 'Angela Knight, Angela Browning and I were all the 1992 intake and we all made it in. I shouldn't say this, but I think we were quite good! Don't forget, we were women who had made it through without any help at all. In a funny sort of way, that gave us a much higher degree of resilience.' Gillan adds: 'If you go out looking for sexism you will find it. You can either wear it as a great big chip on both shoulders, or you can just get on with it and deal with it. There are a couple of my parliamentary colleagues who just can't help themselves. They've got misogynist written right across their foreheads and think they're superior beings. Sometimes you can't help but manipulate and tease them a little – and they don't even realise.'

Ann Widdecombe's long fight for selection made the final

victory all the sweeter when she entered the House of Commons in 1987 as the MP for Maidstone. 'It was wonderful. I always said, "I'll believe I'm there when I feel the green benches under my posterior." I sat on the green bench and I thought, I'm here. I've made it. There was quite a camaraderie among women because there weren't that many of us.'

After three years in Parliament, Widdecombe was made parliamentary under-secretary for social security. Following in the footsteps of John Major and Margaret Thatcher, she was convinced that the junior role would lead to greater things. The following year she was moved to look after pensions and, for the first time, felt she was making a difference.

'I developed an enormous interest in pensions. You name it, it was happening in pensions at the time. There was the Good Report into occupational pensions. The mis-selling of private pensions was just beginning to be understood. We were being told by Europe that we had to equalise the state pension age. So I had a really wonderful productive, interesting, useful time.'

All too quickly, however, she was moved to the Department of Employment and felt a square peg in a round hole. 'It was just not the same. There was a lot of politically correct stuff in Employment, a lot of talk about the glass ceiling which I don't believe in.'

Moving to the Home Office in 1995 was even more difficult – although for different reasons. She fell out badly with Michael Howard, then home secretary. When he ran for the Conservative leadership in 1997 she skewered his hopes by saying he had 'something of the night' about him. 'Do I regret it? Absolutely not. Never have.'

The one time during our interview Widdecombe's tough shell appears to have been penetrated is in discussion of the false claims that she forced female prisoners to be chained during childbirth. A Home Office survey had pinpointed that a disproportionate number of women were escaping when travelling between prison and hospital because, unlike male prisoners, they weren't handcuffed. As a result it was decided all prisoners should be secured until medical treatment started.

'Of course, if pregnant women had to keep the cuffs on until delivery was imminent that would have been barbarous,' Widdecombe says, 'so the rule was as soon as labour was confirmed you would take off the cuffs.'

The trouble came when Channel 4 filmed a prisoner from Holloway going to hospital to give birth. When she went for a cigarette in the general area, she was pictured cuffed to a male prison officer on a long chain. 'Almost within a week people thought the policy was to chain women up in childbirth. Horrendous. My biggest problem was Labour's female MPs were gunning for me. They were talking to the press and saying that because I didn't have children, I wouldn't understand. It was pretty nasty.'

Widdecombe became one of the most high-profile female MPs of the twentieth century, responsible for the equalisation of the state pension age and the disability working allowance, rising to shadow secretary of state for health and shadow home secretary in 1999. When she became an unlikely star of the BBC reality show *Strictly Come Dancing* after leaving Parliament, the judges despaired. Len Goodman compared her to 'haemorrhoids' while Craig Revel Horwood said she was a 'dancing hippo' and a 'Dalek in drag'.

This was water off a duck's back for a woman who had battled her way through Parliament without complaint. Anyway, she was used to insults. When the Labour MP Paul Flynn nicknamed her Doris Karloff after the actor Boris, famous for portraying Frankenstein's monster, it quickly caught on.

Ann Widdecombe started answering her office phone with a defiant: 'Hello, Doris speaking!'

In July 1983 Alan Clark, the deliciously indiscreet diarist and junior minister, was addressing the House of Commons about equal pay legislation. MPs were voting late and Clark did not start speaking until 10 p.m., after an evening spent drinking wine at a friend's house. 'We "tasted" first a bottle of '61 Palmer, then "for comparison" a bottle of '75 Palmer then, switching back to '61, a really delicious Pichon Longueville,' he recorded in his diary. 'By 9.40 I was muzzy.'[6] Jumping into his chauffeur-driven car to make his way to the House of Commons, he smoked a cigar and flicked through the speech written by his civil servants. Staring at the convoluted words in front of him, he knew he was in trouble.

As he stood up in the Chamber, Alan Clark's words started to slip away from him. Out of the corner of his eye, he saw an unfamiliar woman on the opposition benches, dark-haired with a Brummie accent, shoot up out of her seat to make a point of order.

Clare Short had been elected as the Labour MP for Birmingham Ladywood just a month before. Admitting that she knew you could not accuse a fellow MP of being drunk, she continued: 'I seriously put it to you that the minister is incapable . . . It is disrespectful to the House and to the office that he holds that he should come here in this condition.'

The House of Commons erupted. Bellows and shouts came from similarly well-refreshed MPs who had been filling Parliament's bars as they waited for the vote. Rather than censuring the drunk minister, the deputy speaker forced the new MP to withdraw her accusation. 'If I am allowed to withdraw when the House understands that I meant what I said, I withdraw,' came the response.

Alan Clark had no idea who the fiery young MP was when she stood up to admonish him, but after that scandalous evening Westminster's bars were ringing with the name of Clare Short. 'Parliament can be quite an aggressive, rude place,' Short remembers. 'I always was that slightly stroppy girl, so I just launched myself into it.'

Clare Short grew up in an Irish family in Birmingham with seven brothers and sisters. After studying political science and joining the local Labour Party in Chapeltown, she took exams to join the civil service 'and have a look at the British establishment at work'.

'I was passionate about policy but knew I didn't want to be neutral for ever. After meeting lots of politicians, I thought, I can do this. If I hadn't seen them in action I wouldn't have thought people like me could become an MP.'

After failing to win a few unlikely selections – not untypical for male MPs as well as female – she was elected to represent Birmingham Ladywood in 1983. 'It was my dream to represent the streets where I went to primary school, where my granny lived, where my parents lived. It was a real privilege.' Clare Short rose to become the first international development secretary in 1997 after Tony Blair's landslide election victory. Her parliamentary career would end in a gut-wrenching battle over the Iraq War, when she quit the front bench, resigned the Labour whip and eventually stood down as an MP.

When she first entered Parliament in 1983, as one of ten Labour women MPs, she caused quite a stir by making frequent points of order. Astonishingly, at the time MPs had to put on a top hat if they wanted to interrupt the speaker during a debate. They had to reach under the serjeant-at-arms' chair, pull out a collapsible hat and wear it until they had finished speaking. Then they tossed it, like a frisbee, to the next MP who wanted to speak. When Short had to put it on, some of the male members found the burlesque nature of the event all too much. 'They responded as though it was a scene from *Cabaret*. It was just mad,' she remembers. 'I never felt it was vicious, though. It was just badly behaving men being silly. It was public-school culture and I looked down on them rather than feeling threatened by them.'

Things became even more raucous in the Chamber when Short campaigned to ban topless page-three models from the *Sun* news-paper. 'The men behaved outrageously. They couldn't control themselves if you said the word "breast". If you had a debate and mentioned screening for cervical cancer some of them would giggle. There was a complete immaturity and inability to deal with such issues or see women as equals.'

She was not the only woman who was the target of rowdy behaviour. One Conservative MP in particular was targeted because her voice would rise when she was nervous. As she addressed the House with a high-pitched squeak the mimics would soon start up until the green benches were full of a chorus of mockery. As the votes went on well into the night, the raucous atmosphere in Westminster's bars and dining rooms spilled into the Chamber. In the Thatcher years, working gruelling hours was a sign of commitment and the average time the House of Commons finished for the night was well after midnight. Votes would frequently be held in the early hours of the morning. Once, in April 1984, the Conservative MP Jill Knight went through the voting lobby at 3.15 a.m. wearing her fur coat in order to be first in the taxi queue home.

The female fighters of the eighties and nineties are quick to point out that men had it just as tough. One recalls the example of Roy Jenkins, who left Labour for the SDP and was targeted in the early 1980s by the left-wing Labour MP Dennis Skinner. Whenever Jenkins got up to speak, Skinner would purposefully sit very close to him and mutter, just loudly enough for Jenkins to hear, 'Your flies are undone.' At the time Roy Jenkins was in his seventies. Resisting the urge to glance down was almost impossible.

Clare Short claims some of her male colleagues found it far tougher to cope than she did. 'Often male MPs were very nervous before speaking in the Chamber, particularly former miners. They would be drinking whisky in the bars to give them courage, so I took on this quiet role of advising some of the men who were finding it difficult. The place can be intimidating and really hurtful and cruel, but that doesn't only extend to women. It extends to anyone who hasn't been in such a place before and finds it difficult to operate in that culture.'

Ann Widdecombe received her share of insults flung across the floor of the House. Once when she was speaking, a front-bench Labour MP shouted: 'Hurry up, your broomstick's being clamped!'

Quick as a flash, she replied: 'Well, before my broomstick's clamped, let me try and cast a spell.'

'I didn't have that because I was a woman,' she says. 'There were comments about Ken Clarke's Hush Puppies, and William Hague's baldness, and someone else's roly-polyness, but somehow we only focus when it's a woman getting it.'

Widdecombe enjoyed the clubby culture of the House of Commons and was a regular fixture in the smoking room when votes went on into the night. Did she ever struggle with abuse in the Chamber? 'You need to be looking for it to find it, and if you're looking for it they'll give it to you,' she says, refusing to accept that women get a tougher time.

The female fighters broke into Parliament without any special treatment, coping with long hours, bottom-pinching and isolation in an environment where there were vastly more men than women. Ever since Lady Astor had become the first woman elected in 1918, women had never made up more than 10 per cent of MPs. In the 1997 election that would suddenly change.

Not everyone would be impressed by the new breed of female MP. Asked if they need to toughen up, Widdecombe says: 'Oh, they all do. Wimps. Everybody moans, everybody looks for reasons why it's difficult to be a woman MP. It isn't!'

The Ceiling Smashers Part 2

*'If you're in politics it's a tough life and you've got to tough it
out.'*

– Betty Boothroyd

*'I'm not a bra-burning liberator. I'm not sure if I'm a feminist, I
never know where I stand on it. I'm an egalitarian. I think if
you want to make the grade you can make it.'*

– Betty Boothroyd

It was ladies' finals day at Wimbledon and the guests milling
around the hospitality box with glasses of champagne were
getting restless. They could smell the slices of cold salmon and
warm, crispy-skinned chicken underneath the silver cloches, but
the buffet lunch was still not being served. Glancing nervously at
the guest of honour, they waited for her to give the green light so
they could start tucking in.

Baroness Thatcher, however, was a stickler for the appropriate
traditions. Understandably, the other guests might have regarded
the former prime minister as the most important person in the
room that day. Margaret Thatcher did not. There was another
name on the guest list, that of someone she respected deeply –
and she was not going to allow the meal to start until the speaker
of the House of Commons had arrived.

'It was only a buffet lunch, not a grand sit-down meal,' Baroness
Boothroyd remembers, with her infectious giggle. 'I thought it
was very funny. Baroness Thatcher was always polite – she was a
traditionalist and she recognised the status. Yes, I appreciated
that about her.'

In 1992, thirteen years after Thatcher had shattered the glass
ceiling to become the first female prime minister, the Labour MP
Betty Boothroyd smashed through another. The speaker of the

House of Commons is the embodiment of Parliament and bears the weight of its history. Modern historians consider Robert Walpole to have been the first prime minister in 1721, but the post of speaker stretches back to the fourteenth century. Responsible for chairing debates and required to be politically impartial, the speaker is the highest authority in the House of Commons. No wonder Margaret Thatcher refused to start lunch until Betty Boothroyd had arrived.

Betty Boothroyd was born into a happy working-class family in Dewsbury, Yorkshire, the only child of two textile workers. As a restlessly ambitious girl she would wash her neighbour's steps for a few pennies, rubbing the black edges with a white pebble she had got from the beach in Bridlington. She loved to dance and her doting mother saved up to buy her lessons. 'When I was sixteen or seventeen I thought I was going to take the West End by storm,' she remembers. Boothroyd entertained servicemen with her splits and high kicks across Yorkshire as part of the war effort, then joined the Tiller Girls and moved to London. Life was tougher than she had hoped. After a physically exhausting day's work, she would scrub off the stage makeup – called 'leg white' – and scour the stage for sequins that had fallen off the dresses.

The ambitious young dancer's career did not hit the dizzy heights she had hoped for. After dancing at the Palladium for six pounds a week, she was sent to the pantomime in Luton, 'which I thought was rather like the theatrical equivalent of being transferred to Siberia'. A foot infection gave her the excuse she needed to return home, 'chastened but wiser'.[1] Back in Dewsbury, she spread her political wings.

It was Boothroyd's mother who broadened her horizons beyond the former mill town in Yorkshire. A member of the Labour Party, Mary Boothroyd would take her daughter to hear political speeches in Leeds, packing home-made jam sandwiches that she hoped she could swap for Spam. Soaking up speeches from Labour Party giants, including Clement Attlee and Aneurin Bevan, young

Betty was soon hooked on the thrill of political promises. 'I wanted to make jobs for my father, who was unemployed a good deal of the time,' Boothroyd says. 'I wanted my mother to have better pay because she worked five and a half days a week as a weaver, and came home at night and did all the scrubbing and the baking and the rest of it. I wanted to give people a better life, that's all.'

It wasn't long before Boothroyd managed to get a job working in Parliament as a secretary to two MPs, Barbara Castle and Geoffrey de Freitas, 'gregarious intellectuals in a party where sober suits and tribal loyalties still held sway'.[2] The Labour Party secretaries worked together in a large, ill-equipped office in Westminster Hall, Parliament's oldest and most commanding building where dead monarchs lie in state looked down upon by statues of famous parliamentarians. The women worked hard and there was a great sense of camaraderie; Barbara Castle would treat Boothroyd to egg and chips when she worked late.

Many of the secretaries harboured political ambitions of their own. Jo Richardson, for instance, worked alongside Boothroyd and was a firm friend. It was twenty-three years before she finally became the MP for Barking in 1974. It was similarly difficult for Boothroyd to find a winnable seat.

Desperate to get on the B-list of approved party candidates – she wasn't brazen enough to expect to reach the A-list – Boothroyd turned to Barbara Castle for support. She had already been nominated to make the list by some constituency parties, and asked Castle if she would speak to Len Williams, at the time Labour's national agent. Boothroyd assumed her mentor had supported her inclusion on the B-list. Months later she realised she had not. Castle blamed Williams, saying he 'wouldn't have it and I didn't want to push it'.[3]

A furious Boothroyd went to see Williams, who told her she 'hadn't enough age on her shoulders'.

'I thought, what a bloody thing to say to me,' remembers Boothroyd. 'I was mature. I had a lot of experience. Those on the

Tory benches were a damn sight younger than the Labour Party members were then.'

Most painful was the sense that the woman she had spent years working for had not reached out a hand to help. 'Barbara never helped me become a candidate,' Boothroyd says. 'When I needed that lift she wasn't there. I don't know whether she hadn't the time or the inclination, but I wanted a step up and it wasn't there.'

The bruising experience merely convinced her to try all the harder. When the selection for South East Leicester came up in 1956, Betty Boothroyd was chosen as the Labour candidate. 'There were not a lot of people who wanted to have a go at a twenty thousand Tory majority, but I did. I was so damn determined, I thought, Damn you and Len Williams and all the rest. I'll get there myself.'

It was to be her first taste of the political spotlight. Beneath the headline 'Yorkshire Lass of 26 Chosen to Oppose Tory', the *Leicester Evening Mail* wrote: 'A parliamentary candidate's vital statistics are usually the last general election figures, but Miss Boothroyd has others that are also worth quoting: 38–28–40.'[4]

Boothroyd spent the next seventeen years fighting unsuccessful elections, supporting herself by working as a House of Commons secretary. She lost Peterborough in 1959, failed to be selected in Huddersfield in 1962 and Plymouth Sutton in 1965, then fought and lost in Nelson and Colne in 1968. 'I don't think that I was not selected because I was a woman,' Boothroyd continues. 'Because I'm unmarried they can't say, "Who is going to look after the kids? Who is going to iron the shirts for your husband?" I never believe in packing anything in. I am the sort of person who picks myself up and goes on. As someone who never went to university or never really had any advantages like that, I just thought it was wonderful that things were coming my way.'

When she lost the election in Rossendale in 1970, Boothroyd decided she had one last attempt in her. The chance came sooner than she expected when, later that year, a by-election was called in West Bromwich, an industrial town on the edge of the Black Country. 'We took to each other from the start.'[5]

Not everyone, however, was impressed when she put her name in for the candidate selection. One woman stood up at a party meeting to tell Boothroyd directly she couldn't count on her vote. 'You're unmarried, you don't know what it's like to raise children or make ends meet in the family home,' she said. 'You've had an easy life, you don't know how tough it is to get married and bring up children and peel potatoes and do the shopping. Nobody is going to vote for you.'

'Because I'm unmarried and I haven't had any of those problems,' Boothroyd replied, 'I'll have more time to look after the likes of you.'

Betty Boothroyd can't suppress a smile at the memory of her quick-witted response. 'I was very pleased about that.' She won the selection.

On election night, Boothroyd was despondent. In the hotel room, she told her mother in tears she was convinced she had lost yet again. '"Don't worry, love. You're still my daughter," came the reply. That's the sort of things mums say – she couldn't care less. Proud of me whatever I did.'

The next morning, her mother was to witness the moment her daughter became an MP. Boothroyd had won the 1970 by-election by a comfortable 8,000 votes with a 9 per cent swing to Labour.

Having worked in the House of Commons since the mid-1950s, Boothroyd didn't find Parliament overwhelming when she first entered as an MP. She was well known about the place already – some of the policemen had even sent her telegrams wishing her well on polling day. 'You may be disappointed in what I have to say,' she tells me, 'but I didn't think it was a men's club, or a boys' club, because I had grown up with it. I was privileged to be there and I found it a great honour.'

Four years later, Boothroyd got her first promotion when she became a junior whip. The chief whip told her she was known for

Queen Mary II, the first and only joint monarch, and the first woman to have serious influence on modern parliament.

Queen Victoria was opposed to women's suffrage but still, unwittingly, broke down barriers for women.

As one of the first women to make use of the printing press, Elinor James was able to upset the establishment with her political pamphlets.

Defiant and refusing to be constrained by society's expectations, Mary Wollstonecraft was the most radical British feminist of her time.

Josephine Butler Centenary

Josephine Butler Centenary

A

PUBLIC MEETING

WILL BE HELD IN

THE COUNCIL HOUSE,

TREATY RD., HOUNSLOW,

ON

Thursday, May 3rd,

At 8 p.m.,

IN COMMEMORATION OF

JOSEPHINE BUTLER,

" The Most Distinguished Woman of the Nineteenth Century."

SPEAKER :

MRS. MURIEL MATTERS PORTER.

ADMISSION FREE.

Caroline Norton and Josephine Butler achieved political reform that impacted on the lives of hundreds of thousands, if not millions, of people. Despite being banned from voting or sitting in Parliament, they managed to change the law.

Annie Besant campaigned for the rights of the 'factory girls' working in dangerous conditions at the Bryant & May match factory.

A radical suffragist campaigner, Mary Fildes was attacked at the Peterloo Massacre, which only fuelled her passion for the cause of Chartism.

Millicent Garret Fawcett arguably did more in the fight for votes for women than anybody else, devoting her life to the cause.

Emmeline Pankhurst, founder of the Women's Social and Political Union, and her daughter Christabel, who made the movement militant.

Countess Constance Markievicz, MP for Dublin St Patrick, the first ever woman to be elected in the UK. She was also an Irish revolutionary who scorned the Parliament at Westminster and refused to take her seat.

Lady Astor, the first female MP to take her seat in the House of Commons.

'Red' Ellen Wilkinson, a trade unionist, feminist and former Communist Party member, she made an instant impact as an MP.

Margaret Bondfield pictured here as the first female cabinet minister.

Barbara Castle was stridently socialist and battled against a hostile, male-dominated cabinet. She was central to twentieth-century politics and – for many – should have been her party's first female leader.

Like Queen Victoria, Margaret Thatcher did not identify herself as a feminist, famously asking, 'What has women's lib ever done for me?'

Shirley Williams was elected, at just thirty-four years-old. She battled sexism in the House of Commons and was a single mother for much of her time in Parliament.

Ann Widdecombe became one of the most high-profile female MPs of the twentieth century, responsible for the equalisation of the state pension age and the disability working allowance.

Betty Boothroyd is a legendary House of Commons character who smashed one of the final glass ceilings for women in Parliament. Objective, humorous and commanding, she became one of Parliament's most distinguished speakers.

The infamous 'Blair's Babes' photograph, ninety-six newly elected women cluster around the triumphant new prime minister,

Yvette Cooper and Harriet Harman campaigning in the 2015
General Election outside the much-maligned pink bus.

Kezia Dugdale, Nicola Sturgeon and Ruth Davidson,
the new faces of Scottish Politics.

'I don't think I've ever really felt that being a woman in any way gets in the way.' – Theresa May

being feminine and needed to toughen up for the job. 'Tough? I chew tobacco for breakfast,' she replied.⁶

Her thick skin was to come in useful. In 1981 Boothroyd was elected to Labour's National Executive Committee, the party's governing body, at a time when a bitter rift had opened between the hard left and the party's more centrist MPs. Boothroyd was firmly in the latter camp. When she joined the inquiry into Trotskyist infiltration of the Liverpool party and council, she became a target for reselection. 'It was a very good excuse to get rid of me because I wasn't left wing enough or militant enough. I had the national problem and I also had the personal problem in my constituency.' It was a 'life-and-death struggle' for the party, Boothroyd believes. 'After it, the hard left was finished as a threat to our constitution.'⁷

At the time, however, 'It was hellish, it was absolutely horrendous.' She is concerned about the bitter splits under Jeremy Corbyn's leadership and, in particular, the role of Momentum – a political campaign group that supports Corbyn and has tens of thousands of members. 'We've had outside organisations before. I regard them as a party within a party and most destructive. I am concerned there may be moves to de-select some very good people.'

After the 1987 election, under Neil Kinnock's leadership, the wounded party began the slow healing process. Boothroyd decided to become one of three deputy speakers, shrugging off her party political work and putting on the mantle of impartiality. Not everyone was convinced she was up to the job. *Private Eye* said she had 'all the charm of carbon monoxide gas in an airtight room' and was as thick as 'two short planks'.⁸ She would prove them wrong.

When the female deputy speaker took the chair for the first time it sparked some confusion among MPs. Peter Pike, the Labour MP for Burnley, was reading from his notes before he looked up, unsure how to proceed. 'Oh, and what do we call you?' he asked.

Betty Boothroyd replied: 'Call me Madam.'

It was not the first time there had been a female deputy speaker. From 1970 to 1973 Betty Harvey Anderson had performed the role, referred to in Hansard as 'Mr Deputy Speaker'. No wonder Pike was uncertain how to refer to the new incumbent.

Boothroyd says Hansard was 'stuffy', adding incredulously: 'She allowed that to happen for so long. It wouldn't happen to me.'

The deputy speaker also had to make delicate decisions as to how she would dress: the traditional robes had been designed with men in mind. At the start of her third year as deputy speaker, Boothroyd commissioned the British designer Hardy Amies to create something distinctive for her to wear in the chair. From then on she wore a navy silk gown with Tudor roses embroidered on the sleeves and had half a dozen white collars, or weepers, made. She wore sparkling buckles on her shoes mainly for the benefit of the reporters gazing down from the press gallery. Boothroyd says she wanted to be formal in a feminine way. 'I always feel a sense of history. This is why I always dress correctly.'

The one thing Betty Boothroyd refused to wear, however, was the traditional speaker's wig. 'I said to the clerk, "I can't possibly wear the wig, because I find it too heavy and too imperious. I've got a sense of humour and I can't have a good laugh if I turn my face sideways."'

The clerk replied: 'Madam Speaker, you are the servant of this House and not its master and we must seek permission for you not to wear the wig.' When he wrote to the leader of the House and the shadow leader, they agreed to Boothroyd's request.

What does the most scrupulous of dressers make of what MPs wear today? 'I've no comment on that. I think you can imagine.'

Betty Boothroyd had not finished yet. Deputy speaker was merely a pit-stop on the way to her final destination. Lady Astor had been the first female MP to sit in the House of Commons; Margaret Bondfield had been the first female minister and

Margaret Thatcher the first female prime minister. There was one final glass ceiling to break through. When there was a vacancy for speaker of the House of Commons, Betty Boothroyd decided to apply.

She had sensibly sought cross-party nominations, with the Conservative MP John Biffen nominating her and her good friend the Labour MP Gwyneth Dunwoody seconding her. In her speech she begged MPs not to vote for her simply because of her sex: 'Elect me for what I am, not what I was born.'⁹

Boothroyd sat on the green benches to hear the results announced. She hadn't voted for herself and wasn't sure which way it would go. 'I didn't want to win by a handful, I wanted a majority – I needed the confidence of the House,' Boothroyd says. 'And I got it. Which was wonderful.'

Her achievement was remarkable not only because she was the first female speaker but because she won the election at a time when there was a Conservative majority in the House of Commons. More than seventy Tory MPs backed her, along with every minority party. Even the retired Sir Bernard Braine, a Conservative veteran of the old school, went around trying to persuade MPs from his own side to vote for Boothroyd. The new speaker was physically dragged to the chair, according to tradition – a reminder of the past dangers of the job, when falling foul of the sovereign meant execution. From that moment, Betty Boothroyd stifled her political allegiances to become the independent voice of Parliament. She sold her flat and moved into Speaker's House, nestled in Parliament, resplendent but lonely. Her new coat of arms was in the shape of a lozenge – the shields were reserved for men – and a forget-me-not bow indicated that she was single.

To Boothroyd, the speakership was the greatest honour. 'I love this Parliament. I am a great protector and I cherish what we've got and want to defend it. To me it's not a job, it's a calling.'

So seriously did she take the role that Boothroyd never had a day off when she was speaker. 'No matter how bad I felt, I just went through with it. If I had a big reception or a dinner party to give, I just put a bit more Polyfilla and a big smile on my face.'

The daily routine was exhausting. After finishing the morning business in the House at twelve thirty, she set aside half an hour to greet visiting dignitaries or ambassadors and serve them refreshments from a little drinks trolley in Speaker's House. At one o'clock she had lunch in ten or fifteen minutes, 'just a lettuce leaf and a tomato. I would never lunch with anybody apart from the governor of the Bank of England on Budget day.' Then, from twenty past one until ten past two, she would lie down – still wearing her full speaker's outfit – and try to get some sleep. Her secretary was instructed not to let anyone disturb her unless it was the clerk of the House or a minister.

Boothroyd would also try to snatch some time to herself in the mornings, when at 7.30 a.m. she would go for half an hour's solitary walk through St James's Park. It was the only time she could catch some fresh air and exercise. Many years later, after she had been elevated to the House of Lords, she greeted a policeman she recognised: 'Oh, hello! I've seen you in the Commons. Have you been transferred here?'

'Yes,' came the reply. 'I'm the one who used to ring up and say Madam Speaker is on walkabout again.'

'I thought I was on my own and nobody knew,' she said, 'but I was being watched.'

Betty Boothroyd is a legendary House of Commons character who smashed one of the final glass ceilings for women in Parliament. Objective, humorous and commanding, she became one of Parliament's most distinguished speakers. She has little tolerance for female MPs who complain of sexism. More than anything, Boothroyd sees herself as a defender of Parliament – even from attacks levied by her own sex. Asked whether female MPs get a tough time in the debating Chamber, she replied: 'No, they don't get abused and heckled. They've never been in life before, forget it, you won't find me going along with this. When I was in the chair, in the first few months I had a lot of points of order because they thought I'd roll over like a pussy cat. And I wouldn't. I'd give it back. That's what you have to do. In my experience there was no woman heckled. They never came to me to tell me about it if they were.'

Why, then, do some female MPs speak out about their bad experiences? 'Overly sensitive. Let's put it down to that,' she says. 'You might find somebody pulling a face at what you say. Well, that doesn't matter. Not everybody agrees with you, do they? I think one can be over-sensitive sometimes. If you're in politics it's a tough life and you've got to tough it out.'

In 1997, when Betty Boothroyd had been in the speaker's chair for five years, Parliament was transformed by the arrival of 101 female Labour MPs. Posing for a picture outside Parliament, the new intake was nicknamed 'Blair's Babes' in the press. Although she welcomed the increased number of women in the House, Boothroyd clashed with some individuals. 'I hated the title of "Blair Babes". I thought it was a disgrace,' she says. 'I don't want to have a dig but I thought it was undignified. I remember a photograph that was taken on the terrace. Rubbish.'

The introduction of all-women shortlists, when local constituency parties could only choose between a selection of female candidates, played a major role in enabling so many women to reach Westminster. For someone who had spent the best part of two decades trying to get elected, they were an aberration. 'I'm totally opposed to them, I don't believe in all-women shortlists,' Boothroyd says. 'If you can't compete with men, you regard yourself as a second-class citizen in my book. I wouldn't go to a selection meeting if it was a women-only shortlist. I deprecate what has happened to the Labour Party with them. I feel very strongly about it.'

Some backbenchers began to complain that Boothroyd was too tough with Labour's new women members. One cartoonist depicted the female speaker saying to a woman MP: 'If you can't stand the heat, get back to the kitchen.' Boothroyd found it so amusing that she hung it up in her home. The gap in attitudes between longer-standing MPs and the newcomers was tangible. Diane Abbott, the first black woman to be elected to Parliament in 1987, wrote to Boothroyd: 'As you know I am a diehard feminist. But I think it is an odd sort of feminism which involves women MPs attacking one of the most popular speakers that we have ever had – who also happens to be a woman!'[10]

In 2000 a group of female Labour MPs asked for a meeting with Boothroyd. 'For the first time that I can remember in history, the speaker received a deputation. You don't lean on speakers, speakers make the decisions, but anyway . . .' She agreed to meet with Julia Drown, MP for Swindon South, and Tessa Jowell, minister for education and employment, as well as others. The women MPs felt it was archaic that women were not allowed to breastfeed in the House of Commons Chamber and committee rooms and wanted the speaker to back their cause.

'Now, that was not on as far as I was concerned,' Boothroyd says. 'If their babies wanted breastfeeding they could either feed them in their own private office or they could take them to the Lady Members' Room. And I saw to it that in every room there was a changing table that you could pull out and a nursing chair.' She adds: 'They wanted to bring their babies in because it would be televised. I dislike using a Thatcher phrase, "the oxygen of publicity", but that's what it was.'

Julia Drown said she wanted to breastfeed in the committee room to make sure she didn't miss any important evidence. Boothroyd was unimpressed. 'I mean what a tale to tell me, I wasn't that naive.'

Tessa Jowell asked if Betty Boothroyd would reconsider the ban if the baby was really ill. 'If the baby was really ill I would expect the mother to be in hospital with it or to be at home with it,' she replied, adding: 'When they do it at Sainsbury's checkout, then I'll think about it.'

'That was facetious,' she admits, 'that was just my sense of humour, but I was being serious. They had all the facilities in the Lady Members' Rooms.'

Boothroyd was similarly unimpressed by the move to change Parliament's hours and stop MPs sitting late into the night. 'I think it's appalling,' she says. 'I don't know why they call them "family friendly hours" – how do people from West Bromwich get back to their families every evening? It's just London MPs. They're the only people who can do it.'

Baroness Boothroyd, who is still an active member of the House of Lords, believes that, as a result of the changes to the hours, MPs are failing to scrutinise legislation properly. Unlike in the House of Lords, where the government cannot limit the amount of time spent in a debate, 'programme motions' can now be used to set a strict timetable for how long MPs can spend on each stage of legislation. For Boothroyd, this is a major problem. 'I am appalled by the way it goes now,' she says. 'I do not think the scrutiny of the legislation is what it should be. They don't discuss all the amendments and clauses, they don't sit as they used to, they don't scrutinise the entire bill. They "programme" it. That's why we have all these amendments coming into the House of Lords, because they haven't looked at it, legislation is not thoroughly scrutinised.' She emphasises: 'Much of it has to do with the restricted hours.'

Boothroyd is not the only person to worry that the move to change Parliament's hours has curtailed its ability to scrutinise legislation properly. Cheryl Gillan, who was first elected in 1992, is the longest-serving female Conservative MP currently in Parliament. Asked her opinion on 'family friendly' hours, she replied: 'What family friendly hours? It's a myth! Most people have their families in another part of the country. It just means you've got more MPs down here kicking heels after seven o'clock.'

Does it also mean that the scrutiny of legislation is not as effective? 'Yes, that's exactly right. I find we don't scrutinise legislation in as much detail as we used to.'

The dissent is cross-party. Clare Short, a Labour MP from 1983 until 2010, says: 'The debating chamber has been diminished by the focus on short speeches with guillotines.'

Betty Boothroyd, like Margaret Thatcher, is not someone who readily identifies as a feminist.

'I'm not a bra-burning liberator,' she says. 'I'm not sure if I'm a feminist. I never know where I stand on it. I'm an egalitarian, I think if you want to make the grade you can make it. I never thought I'd be speaker – I left school at the age of sixteen. No excuses, just do the work.'

When I asked her why Labour has failed to elect a female leader, she replies, after a moment, 'I don't know.' Margaret Beckett, she says, 'really excelled herself' when she became acting leader after the sudden death of John Smith and 'rather deserved to have won' the subsequent leadership contest. She turns quickly to Clement Attlee, 'a great hero of mine', who was the Labour prime minister in 1945. According to her story, a junior minister went to see Attlee to complain that he hadn't been promoted. 'Attlee sat there, puffing his pipe, and he said, "Well, Bill, not up to it."' Concerned the parallel may be taken too far, she quickly adds: 'I don't mean there wasn't a woman who was up to it, but there were men who had other attributes.'

If Clement Attlee is her hero, Betty Boothroyd travels even further back in time to find her heroine. Queen Elizabeth I 'put up with those years as a young woman in the Tower', she says, 'pressured all the time to be married. There's a marvellous portrait of her – with this ring I wed the realm.' Like the Virgin Queen who inspires her, Boothroyd was to remain single – wedded to the Parliament she loves so ferociously. 'Politics and Parliament became the centre of my life in a way that I could not have managed as a wife and mother.'[11]

Now in her eighties, Boothroyd says: 'You make choices in life. It doesn't bother me at all. I travelled the world a lot and there is no young man going to wait at home until I come back from Hong Kong, or Ho Chi Minh City or Moscow – they'll probably find someone else. There's nobody going to take me on, because they'll only open the fridge door and the light will come on and there'll be nothing left in it.'

She adds: 'I had a very happy life and a very social life, I'm very fond of men and I had a lot of man friends and that was the end of it. Nobody wanted me and I didn't want them for keeps.'

When Betty Boothroyd decided to step down as speaker of the House of Commons in July 2000, she made the announcement exactly as tradition dictated. First to know was Margaret Beckett, who was then leader of the House, her eyes filling with tears at the unexpected news.

As she stepped up to address MPs, there was no advance warning, no briefing to the morning papers. Nobody saw her next sentence coming: 'I now wish to inform the House of my intention to relinquish the office of speaker immediately before the House returns from the summer recess.'

There was an audible gasp of disappointment, and someone let out an involuntary: 'Oh, no!'

'Be happy for me!' Boothroyd admonished them. Then the applause started. Clapping is not usually permitted in the Chamber but an unstoppable wave of MPs, front-bench politicians, civil servants and members of the public joined in almost instinctively. The noise continued for a full minute. Boothroyd blew a kiss to someone on the Labour benches, then dabbed beneath her eye.

'I felt really good. I thought to myself, How lovely,' Boothroyd says. 'I thought they'd say, we'd like to get rid of that fat old so-and-so. I thought they would listen in silence.' It is typical self-effacement from the woman who used to earn a few pennies scrubbing her neighbours' front doorsteps with a white pebble when she was a girl in Dewsbury.

Betty Boothroyd says the greatest moment of her life came when Nelson Mandela visited Parliament as the first president of free South Africa. Boothroyd and Mandela are both recipients of the Queen's Order of Merit – bestowed by the monarch, with only twenty-four members, it's known as the most exclusive club in the world. At a dinner at Buckingham Palace, one of the ushers asked if she would like to have a private word with the president. The next day he was due to give a speech in the creakily historic Westminster Hall, to which he would be accompanied by the speaker of the House of Commons. Boothroyd wanted to make sure he was prepared. 'When you get to Westminster Hall, pace yourself down those steps because they're a thousand years old,' she advised him. 'There will be thousands there to see you and millions on television, so you take your time and I'll follow you.' He thanked her.

The next morning, the crowds who gathered at Westminster felt the sun beating on their backs as trumpets sounded to greet the arrival of the president. Betty Boothroyd welcomed him at St Stephen's Entrance. 'You pace yourself and I'll follow you,' she reminded him.

'Don't worry, Madam Speaker,' he said. 'I came at six o'clock this morning to have a look myself.'

'What a man,' Boothroyd remembers. 'The trumpets sounded, he took my hand and we walked up the steps of St Stephen's and down into Westminster Hall. That was the proudest moment of my life. I have two or three pictures of us together holding hands on those steps. The speech he made afterwards was one of the best speeches I have ever heard, totally without bitterness.'

Boothroyd's own speech was also something to be proud of. She can still remember ending it with a flourish, and recites: 'As you cross Trafalgar Square to South Africa House tomorrow morning, it's a place that you were once vilified. Now you will enter as Head of State of a free South Africa.'

They are words that the first female speaker – once not permitted to enter the House of Commons – could have written about herself.

The Change-makers

'When I was first elected I was warned not to speak about women's concerns in case I might get pigeon-holed. But if there are so few women, those who are there have to speak up for women's concerns – who else will?'

– Harriet Harman

'Tony Blair, Ed Miliband, Gordon Brown – all of them had to be reminded to involve women.'

– Yvette Cooper

'The Labour Party is going backwards in terms of gender equality.'

– Jacqui Smith

In 1994, shortly after winning a by-election, the new Labour MP for Barking and Dagenham was having lunch with two journalists from the *Sunday Times*. As the cutlery clinked, she told the journalists that she thought it would be a very good idea if MPs could job-share. There were very few issues on which you voted against the party line, she explained, and the constituency case work could easily be divided.

Margaret Hodge was fifty; she might have been new to Parliament but she was experienced in the world of work. Her first job had been a well-paid graduate traineeship at Unilever. When she returned to work after her honeymoon, though, she had an experience that shocked her into a lifetime of feminism. 'I arrived back after getting married and found the girls had to do the research and the boys wrote the reports. It was extraordinary! I went to see HR to complain and they said to me, "If you want things to be different, you should just leave." So I left. My feminism was confirmed by my work experience at Unilever.' After that bruising experience she went to Islington Council and remoulded the working environment, setting up a crèche and scrapping the rule that you had to have worked at the council for two years before you were entitled to maternity leave. Hodge entered Westminster with that same eye on how she could effect change in working practice.

The following weekend, she picked up a copy of the *Sunday Times* and was surprised to see that her call for job-sharing had made the paper. She thought little more of it until, on Monday morning, she was called into the Whips' Office. As she entered the room, she saw a photograph of her face pinned to the wall and punctured with tiny holes. The Labour whips had been throwing darts at it. 'There are plenty of women who want your job, Margaret,' said a female whip, 'if you can't hack it.'

Margaret Hodge went on to a ministerial career before becoming chair of the Public Accounts Committee, where victims from top Google executives to HM Revenue and Customs officials were skewered by her questioning. But, more than twenty years later, it is the incident with the dartboard that she appears most affected by. 'I was really upset,' she says. 'I was a new MP and I was very nervous about being accepted.' Since then, however, her view that Parliament needs to change has only hardened: 'Westminster is such an anti-female place.'

In 1994, speaking out about 'women's issues', like job-shares, flexible working or childcare, exposed you to ridicule from male MPs and the tough female fighters whose political adolescence took place under Margaret Thatcher. At the time of Hodge's bruising encounter with the whips, women still made up less than one in ten MPs. Two years earlier, at the 1992 general election, just sixty women had been elected. They were expected to fit in, rather than question Westminster's structure and cultures. Not everyone obeyed.

Harriet Harman was first elected in 1982 to a House of Commons that was 97 per cent male: 'I was warned not to speak about women's concerns in case I might get "pigeon-holed". But if there are so few women, those who are there have to speak up for women's concerns – who else will?'[1]

While I was researching this book a clear divide emerged between the female MPs elected pre-1997, who believed that if women were tough enough they could make it, and those elected after 1997, who believed Westminster itself needed to change. The Labour MP for Peckham is an exception to that rule. Unlike many of her contemporaries in the 1980s, Harriet Harman is above all a change-maker, refusing to accept that women should knuckle down and quietly accept their lot. A committed feminist, who has always been prepared to do things that are unpopular, she would tell her staff: 'If you're not having a row about something then it's not working and you're not going far enough.'

Women in the Labour Party were about to have an almighty row that would transform Parliament and increase the number of female MPs on a scale that had never been seen before. Until that point, well-intentioned training programmes, mentoring and a policy to have a woman candidate on every shortlist had failed to increase the number of female MPs being selected and making it to Westminster. At the 1993 conference, members voted to exclude men from half of the shortlists in winnable constituencies.

As a result of all-women shortlists, the 1997 election – which Tony Blair won by a landslide – was a watershed in women's representation and changed the culture of Westminster. A total of 120 women were elected – 101 from the Labour Party. For most of the twentieth century women had made up less than 5 per cent of MPs. That number now jumped to 18 per cent. After 1997 women were no longer given their own separate area in the cloakroom because there were too many of them. More women's lavatories had to be installed. A hairdresser joined the barber. For change-makers like Harriet Harman and Margaret Hodge, the number of women elected in 1997 was a stunning victory.

In the hostile atmosphere of the Chamber, Conservative MPs would heckle Labour women they believed had been elected from an all-women shortlist. 'We could guess in the first few minutes,' says Ann Widdecombe. 'Then you could hear our benches yelling, "Positive discrimination!" We never got it wrong. If you come up through the proper selection process you are battle-hardened. But a lot of those women weren't used to it and found it all a bit of a shock.'

The post-1997 change-makers believed that institutional sexism in Parliament held women back. For the veterans, this was acting the victim. Widdecombe has little sympathy for women MPs getting special help. 'Six months after the Blair's Babes got elected – or the 101 Dalmatians as I used to call them – one of them came up to me in a corridor and said, "Isn't it horrible how the men are so rude to us?" And I replied, "Yes, and isn't it horrible how they are so rude to each other?"' That hadn't entered her head. She had just been roughed up in the Chamber and assumed it was because she was a woman. In fact, it was because she was a very, very poor performer.'

Edwina Currie, who lost her seat at the 1997 election, is similarly scathing: 'I'm totally against all-women shortlists because people who are discriminated against should not discriminate . . . If you bring people up through an easier route they are not hardened in battle and when they really get into battle, like in the House of Commons, they are bloody useless. That allowed them to be dubbed Blair's Babes. Pardon me.'

The cultural shift was almost immediate. One evening, when the Conservative MP Virginia Bottomley entered the House of Commons Chamber, a shout went up from the Labour benches: 'Who's looking after the children?' Margaret Beckett remembers two or three veteran Labour MPs turning around in alarm to reassure her that they weren't the culprit: 'It wasn't me! Don't blame me!' Beckett thought: Oh! Culture change . . .

'When so many women got elected in 1997 it felt amazing,' Beckett continues. 'It was appalling they called us Blair's Babes. But of course,' she can't resist adding, 'even so, not all of them stood again. In the end it wasn't for them.'

*   *   *

In the infamous 'Blair's Babes' photograph, ninety-six women cluster around the triumphant new prime minister, Tony Blair, on 8 May, just after the 1997 Labour landslide. Grinning at the camera, forming an adoring doughnut around their leader, the picture was ripe for parody. Clare Short, who had been instrumental in fighting for all-women shortlists, was one of only five Labour women MPs who didn't take part. 'I went along with everyone,' she says, 'And then I saw the mood of it, and how it was all these adoring women looking at Blair, so I slipped away.' Her absence was barely noticed at the time, but Short was not the only woman uncomfortable with being part of Tony Blair's adoring chorus. Harriet Harman, who had fought a lonely battle for women in Parliament for fifteen years, argued that Labour's 101 women MPs should be pictured without Tony Blair. Typically, however, she kept loyally quiet after being overruled.

Some future Labour stars stood outside Parliament on that May afternoon. New MPs like Caroline Flint, selected for the mining constituency of Don Valley, and Ruth Kelly, who would become the youngest ever female cabinet minister at thirty-six, were pictured alongside veteran survivors, like Margaret Beckett, at the front of the picture wearing shocking pink, and Diane Abbott. Abbott, who says 'Blair's Babes' is a 'horrible title', says: 'I was not a Blair babe, I joined in 1987, but I was glad that so many women came in at that time. It wasn't just an act of largesse from Tony Blair. Women on the left had campaigned for years to make it happen.' Jacqui Smith, who would become the first ever female home secretary, was elected from an all-women shortlist. 'In 1997 it felt like you were surrounded by a lot of other new women so there was a great sense of female camaraderie,' she remembers. 'Then, after you'd had a bit of time to look around the place, you thought, Oh, wow, blimey. It's fabulous that we're out on the steps having this photo taken, but wait a minute – they're calling us Blair's Babes, what the fuck's that about?'

Perched on the edge of the crowd was the new MP for Pontefract and Castleford. Just twenty-eight, Yvette Cooper was part of the new breed of female MPs determined to make change in Parliament. 'The Blair's Babes picture was such a headache,' she remembers. 'It ended up looking like a harem with a man in the middle. I remember being quite uncomfortable at the time.'

Cooper was born into a solid Labour family, the daughter of a trade unionist and the granddaughter of a miner. She was inspired to enter Parliament after being encouraged by other women, including Harriet Harman, for whom she worked when she was in her twenties. At the 1996 Labour Party conference she met female candidates who were preparing to fight the 1997 election, including Ruth Kelly and Lorna Fitzsimons, and decided to run herself.

The mining constituency of Pontefract and Castleford looked like a tough fight for a twenty-eight-year-old woman, particularly when the shortlist was revealed. The other candidates included the local council leader, a representative from the GMB union, an adviser to Tony Blair, and Hilary Benn, the son of Tony Benn; he would later become shadow foreign secretary. Even the most sceptical fighters of the eighties could not accuse Yvette Cooper of having had a leg up. Cooper, however, is a firm supporter of all-women shortlists: 'A lot of other women had been selected already so people's expectations of what a Labour candidate looked like had changed. If we hadn't had all-women shortlists, it would have been much, much harder for me to get selected.'

Her first hunch that she might be about to pull off an unexpected victory came when she was canvassing for support in Nottingley, and a former miner told her she could count on his vote: 'You know, I think it's time we had a woman around here.'

After winning the selection, Cooper was propelled to Westminster in the 1997 Labour landslide. As the number of women MPs rocketed overnight from sixty to 120, it took parliamentary staff a little while to get used to the new reality.

'I'm sorry, you're not allowed in there,' polite doorkeepers ushered Cooper away from areas restricted to MPs. 'Who do you work for, dear?' Cooper laughs about being mistaken for a secretary. 'It was a big change for them. I was quite young, as well.'

Tony Blair, the youngest prime minister since Lord Liverpool in 1812, quickly set about forming the first Labour government for eighteen years. Five women were appointed to cabinet positions: Margaret Beckett became trade and industry secretary, Clare Short international development secretary, Mo Mowlam Northern Ireland secretary, Ann Taylor leader of the House of Commons, while Harriet Harman became secretary of state for social security and the first ever minister for women.

For Harman, the triumph of women entering Parliament in 1997 wasn't just a step forward in female representation, it was a huge opportunity to make progress on the issues she had been championing for fifteen years – often in the face of mockery and criticism. She organised meetings between female MPs and journalists to try to make sure the new Labour women projected their political voices. 'It's not enough to just do good,' she told them, 'you have to tell people what you're doing and get the credit for it.'

One of Harriet's staff members was an ambitious young woman called Liz Kendall, who would later become an MP. 'Harriet has always known what she's in politics for,' she says. 'She brings issues to the table that would not have been there if it wasn't for her or women like her. She was laughed at. People thought she was difficult for what they saw as banging on about women's issues. But she did it because she had to and she made a difference.'

The wave of new women soon started to make a difference to government policy, with MPs including Harriet Harman, Patricia Hewitt, Margaret Hodge and Tessa Jowell pushing for new laws around childcare and equal rights for women in the workplace – issues that had until then been side-lined in Westminster. Nursery provision for three- and four-year-olds was rapidly expanded and Sure Start centres were set up to focus on childcare and early education. Paid maternity leave was extended from six months to nine months, and in 1998 Harriet Harman drew up the first ever national childcare strategy. 'In the early 1980s when I spoke in the House of Commons calling for more nurseries and after-school clubs, I was jeered – by my own side as well as the Tories,' Harman said in 2004. 'The overwhelmingly male Parliament just could not see the point of even discussing it. Now, we have a national child-care strategy to spread nurseries and a new children's minister to spearhead it. That would have been unthinkable in a House of Commons with only three per cent women.'[2]

When the Domestic Violence Bill was loudly backed by female MPs, Harriet Harman paid tribute to one of her fellow lonely female warriors when Parliament was a very different place. 'I remember only too well the response of the House to Jo Richardson's campaigns on domestic violence in the late 1970s and early 1980s. If you mentioned domestic violence once it could be ignored – mention it twice and you were regarded as obsessed.'[3]

One of the major political battles for the change-makers was over the right to request flexible working. Before 1997, when Harman had stood up in front of a sea of male MPs to make the case, she had been laughed at. Even her own side was hostile, with many Labour MPs visibly raising their eyebrows, arguing that the party was about full-time jobs, not part-time. Now a pincer move-ment of female ministers, with women working at Number 10, doggedly lobbied the prime minister and the chancellor, who were both initially hostile to the idea.

Margaret Hodge was one of the most vocal supporters. She says: 'It was our persistence and team work that forced Tony and Gordon – against their better judgement – to introduce the right to request flexible working, which was one of the most important reforms we introduced.'

The change-makers were also transforming culture in less noticeable ways. When Margaret Hodge was appointed culture minister in 2003, just 25 per cent of the appointments to cultural bodies, such as museums, were women. 'I thought, That's rubbish,' she says. 'So I made a list of capable women who could stand as trustees, and I got a hell of a lot of resistance from the officials.' Hodge let it be known that her expectation was that more women should be appointed and if they weren't she might turn down the recommendations. Within a year, 46 per cent of appointments were female. When she took a year off from ministerial duties to care for her ill husband, the number plummeted back to 26 per cent. 'You just can't let up,' she says.

Despite the achievements of women under the Tony Blair government, female MPs agree that they were unable to take their eye off the ball. When Yvette Cooper was a health minister, Labour were fighting the 2001 election. As the party became increasingly flustered about having too many all-male panels for debates, she found herself being increasingly called at the last minute by panicked press officers begging her to make late-notice appearances. This was even more of a hassle as she was pregnant at the time. 'It would drive me up the wall, actually,' Cooper says. '"If you want me that's brilliant, but why didn't you ask before?" Then you discover they've got nothing for you to say. I'm not just going to sit on this panel and allow the men to speak.'

Things came to a head when Cooper appeared at a health press conference alongside Tony Blair, Gordon Brown and the health secretary, Alan Milburn. Once again she hadn't been given any material to speak about, stoking concerns she was being used as a token woman. 'You've got to give me something to say,' Cooper demanded. 'You've got to let me speak because if I just sit there and am silent then it's worse than me not being there at all.'

Yvette Cooper won her battle to be given a topic to speak about and also butted in to answer a journalist's question. 'I just remember this moment of Tony turning around, like "Oh! Oh! Actually, that's quite a good answer!" And then, to be fair to him, he did laugh at himself for having done so. Tony Blair, Gordon Brown, Ed Miliband – all of them had to be reminded to involve women.

They would take it seriously but you always had to be reminding. You couldn't take your eye off the ball.'

At the end of a long week working in Westminster, Yvette Cooper was on the Friday-morning train back to her constituency with two children in tow. Juggling her work as a junior minister along with caring for her young family and continually hopping between Yorkshire and Westminster was exhausting. As the train waited to pull out of the London station, she could hear a convoy escorting the prime minister onto the train. Tony and Cherie Blair were coincidentally catching the same train up to Sedgefield, the constituency he represented. Cooper considered walking down the carriages to say hello to her boss, but decided against it. With two small children to look after, it was just too much hassle.

As the train swept north, Cooper needed to change her son's nappy. She didn't have much time before the train pulled into Doncaster, where she had to get off, so she dashed into the vestibule. Her little boy, however, had other ideas. Wriggling away from his mother, he started running down the carriage in the direction of the prime minister and his wife. 'Tony and Cherie were sitting on the train when suddenly a toddler runs by, with me running after him and I have to pick up this child!' Cooper remembers.

As more mothers were elected to Parliament they brought with them a very different set of experiences, juggling family responsibilities with their commitments in Westminster. More than ten years later, Cooper can laugh about the incident on the train. 'You only manage by being relaxed about chaos. Every weekend we would be back in the constituency, so the kids would come with us. We had potties on the train when we were potty training and they would go to part-time nursery in London and in Yorkshire.'

Cooper knew what she was in for after witnessing the fragile balancing act when she worked for Harriet Harman, who had a very young family at the time. 'She was continually juggling with the kids and was very matter of fact that, of course, they were the priority. If one of the kids was sick, well, she was just going to have to go and sort things out – no question. It wasn't a big deal. There were no contortions or great angst. That was just what you did.'

Harriet Harman has also spoken about the difficulties of being an MP and a mother. Her male colleagues advised her to hang out in the bar if she wanted to get on, to show she was 'clubbable'. 'I couldn't hang out drinking in the bar when I was feeling sick from pregnancy or rushing back home to put the babies to bed. Because I didn't conform, the punishment for being different was often nasty. When I came back after having my first baby I was reported to the serjeant-at-arms for breaking the rules by taking my baby through the division lobby under my jacket. Of course I'd done no such thing – I was still fat from being pregnant. What made it worse was that it was obviously my own side. I told the whips I'd have to miss a vote because I was ill – with mastitis. And they put it in the papers.'[4]

Less than two months after the 2001 election, Yvette Cooper became the first minister to take maternity leave. The Department of Health tried hard to make it a success, keeping her informed about any relevant decisions to help ease her return to work. Her responsibilities were carved up between other ministers, including the Redditch MP Jacqui Smith – who was less impressed with the department's efforts. 'Me and Hazel Blears were just expected to cover her work, which is typical – get the two women to pick up the slack!'

When Cooper took maternity leave for the second time in 2004, when she was a minister in the office of the deputy prime minister, she had a very different experience at the hands of the civil servants. 'Not only did they not try to make it possible for me to come back to work again, they were actively hostile to it. It was, like, stop her seeing any papers, actively exclude her from everything, give her no point of contact. Be gone and come back when you're not lactating. Really, really, bizarre.'

Cooper reveals that if she asked to see departmental business when she was on leave, the civil servants would refuse. 'The other ministers were really helpful but at official level there was no support. By the time I was preparing to come back they were trying to stop there being any job to come back to.' Panicked that she wouldn't be able to return, Cooper went to see Harriet Harman to ask her advice. The women's champion didn't need asking twice. Gus O'Donnell, then head of the civil service, helped shape a report looking at maternity-leave arrangements directly drawing on Cooper's experiences and requiring ministers to be kept up to date while away.

That would not be the last time Yvette Cooper battled with the civil service to reform working practices for ministers with families. Throughout her ministerial career, she refused to look at government papers in the evening. The 'red box' is the equivalent of a ministerial briefcase, containing documents prepared by the civil service. For any working mother, the convention that ministers would look at the red box overnight and make decisions by eight o'clock the following morning was simply impractical. Cooper's refusal was leaked to the papers, and the murmurings of disapproval grew louder.

'I got a bit of flak for not doing red boxes in the evening. Actually, making decisions when officials aren't around to answer questions is stupid anyway,' Cooper says. 'There was a bit of murmuring, from civil servants and other politicians – is she not taking the job seriously, not really on top of it, not working hard? If other ministers weren't on top of an issue nobody would have noticed, but if it was me, there was a sense of: "Ah, well, that's why . . ."'

Cooper was not the only woman of the 1997 intake who struggled with Parliament's dusty structures after having a child. Jacqui Smith had a four-year-old son when she became the MP for Redditch and a year later had another baby. When she went to tell Labour's chief whip Nick Brown that she would need time off work, he struggled to contain his shock. 'If I had unzipped my human body to reveal that I was an alien he wouldn't have looked more uncomfortable,' she says. 'He didn't say congratulations, he just hummed and hawed, "Er, right, oh, er, okay." I felt like saying, "Don't worry, I'm not about to give birth right now on the carpet."'

The speaker, Michael Martin, was equally concerned to see a heavily pregnant Jacqui bobbing up and down trying to get called in parliamentary debates. During a debate on the Education Bill in the spring of 1998, having watched her stand up and sit down for three hours, signalling that she wanted to speak, he could take it no longer and beckoned her to his chair. 'Don't worry, I've seen you,' he hissed. 'You don't have to keep standing up in your condition!'

'I think he was worried my waters were going to break on the leather seats!' Smith laughs. 'But he meant well, and I was relieved to be able to sit down.'

Just four months after giving birth, Jacqui Smith was back at work. She says: 'It is difficult to balance having a family and being an MP and I don't know what the answer to that is. If my husband hadn't been willing to give up his career and be the prime carer for our kids, I would have found it very difficult. The reality is, there are fewer men who are prepared to do that than women. When I look back, I'm not sure how four months after having my second child I was able to leave them for three days a week. I feel awful when I think about it. When my oldest son got his A levels my first reaction was "Oh, that's brilliant, love!" and then I said to my husband, "Thank fuck I didn't ruin his life!"'

If there had been few women MPs until then, there had been even fewer mothers. Jacqui Smith was not alone in struggling to balance family and career, and the new wave of change-makers joined to try to alter the hours to make them easier on parents. They were not all from the Labour Party.

Caroline Spelman was among the sparse band of thirteen female Tory MPs to be elected in 1997 and the only one with school-age children. The MP for Meriden was rejected by twenty-seven constituencies before winning her selection. 'It's not as bad as a former MP who applied for 50,' she adds. As a mother of three, she was asked 'regularly, all the time' how she would cope with the job while raising a family. 'Before we get too uptight about it, it's not a nine-to-five job and selectors are worried about whether the mother of children could handle what is essentially a vocation. It's not illegal for them to ask you and if you've got any sense you pre-empt it by explaining how you would learn to cope.'

The local association in Meriden made a further request of their candidate, asking that Spelman's children go to school in the constituency. 'That's asking a mother to be apart from her children, and that's tough. There are not many jobs where you're asked to do that.' Determined to make it work, Spelman agreed. She admits that being a mother as well as an MP has been harder than she imagined. 'If I'm really honest, I probably didn't realise how difficult it is with family life. I just thought, It's got to be possible!' As a result, Spelman is a firm believer in parliamentary reform and thinks the changes to the hours have not gone far enough. 'I don't think it needs to be as tough as it is on family life.'

She is full of shocking yet amusing stories of the juggling act. The time when she was sitting in a board meeting at the local hospital and the school decided to send all the children home because of an outbreak of nits. The occasion when she was sitting in a shadow cabinet meeting when a staff member of Michael Howard came rushing in to tell her that one of her children had fallen off a drainpipe at school. Her rather sanguine response impressed the men in the room: 'Which one?' On another occasion, Spelman was in the Chamber waiting to introduce a private member's bill when she was told her son had broken his wrist. When she asked for permission to go and look after him, she was told that she was not allowed to leave because her bill would be discussed shortly.

'The school always phones the mother, even if the mother is secretary of state – which has happened to me as well,' she explains. 'That is quite tough. Society hasn't changed that much.'

Coming from a career in agriculture, Spelman was used to working in a male-dominated environment but found the attitudes of some MPs puzzling. 'Compared to agriculture, I felt that some men could be more patronising. Farmers tend to be quite respectful of women because they run their business as a partnership with their wives. For a long time, I pondered why agriculture was so different from politics. Sometimes I found it a bit hard to take. Although it is the minority.'

Spelman believes the House of Commons is now a far more enlightened place than it was when she first entered in 1997. 'I think Parliament has moved on tremendously. I came in with dads of young children and we all struggled with missing our kids. We would sit around the table in the library, having a cup of tea, and they would find it just as hard as me: there goes the last train, I'm not going to get home tonight. I'll see them first thing tomorrow morning. That was quite heart-rending, really.'

She is not the only female MP who believes things have improved. Diane Abbott became the first black woman to be elected in 1987 and her son was born five years later. My son is now twenty-four and it is a little bit easier now that he can get his own dinner. There have been great advances since my son was a toddler. The best thing is that we now have a crèche and Speaker Bercow is to be thanked for that."

It's not the only change she's noticed. 'What I remember when I first entered Parliament is that security were always refusing to allow Bernie Grant and Paul Boateng in, because they couldn't believe that black men were Members of Parliament. They recognised me more quickly because my shoulder length braids made me stand out. The other bizarre thing was that security would always confuse Bernie Grant and Paul Boateng and you couldn't have two men that looked more different.'

In 1997, when many of the women MPs first entered Parliament, votes were still happening at two or three in the morning. Ed Balls, married to Yvette Cooper and working as an adviser to Gordon Brown, would sometimes wake up in the middle of the night to realise his wife wasn't at home. To put his mind at ease, he would telephone the House of Commons switchboard. 'Are they still voting?'

'Yes, they are still voting,' came the reply.

'Oh, that's all right then.'

Looking back, Cooper laughs. 'It was completely mad.'

As the long hours ticked slowly by, MPs turned to caffeine in the tea room or alcohol in the bars, while the solitary bed in the Lady Members' Room was frequently fought over. Meanwhile, two Labour MPs with offices next door to each other were going to extreme lengths to catch some sleep. When the Commons sat late, Caroline Flint had no chance of getting back to her Don Valley constituency, and Laura Moffatt would miss the last train to Crawley. The women pulled the cushions off an armchair and spread them out on the floor to create a makeshift bed. Two pillows donated by House of Commons staff finished the bedroom and a scribbled 'Do Not Disturb' sign was pinned to the door to warn the cleaners.

'We had sleeping bags in our office and an emergency kit of toiletries,' Flint remembers. 'Our biggest problem was that at six a.m. all the blinds in the room automatically came up, so we would be there in our pyjamas trying to pull them back down again! The hours were horrendous.'

The new generation of MPs fought to introduce a 10 p.m. cut-off time for debates and subsequently tried to change Parliament's finish on a Thursday from 10 p.m. to seven. There was initial resistance but for MPs like Caroline Flint, with constituencies a considerable distance from Westminster, it meant they could travel home on Thursday night to spend time with their families. 'Some of the men said Parliament would lose the clubby atmosphere,' Flint says. 'The whips believed you needed to have everyone here so they could know what the gossip is and influence what was going on. But I felt maybe the way we manage the parliamentary Labour Party is what has to change, rather than relying on little chats in corridors at one in the morning.'

Another victory for the change-makers came when a parliamentary crèche opened in 2010 in one of Westminster's former drinking dens, Bellamy's bar. Making the most popular bar into a crèche was a symbolic act, typical of a new breed of MP, who questioned tradition and was uncomfortable with the heavy-drinking masculine culture. Not everyone was happy. The Conservative MP Christopher Chope, for instance, reported the crèche to the National Audit Office for wasting money, describing it as 'gesture politics of the worst sort'.[5] But change was happening, slowly but inexorably.

In 2007, after ten years as prime minister, Tony Blair resigned. His chancellor, Gordon Brown, ran for the leadership unopposed and skipped unhindered from Number 11 to Number 10 Downing Street. Harriet Harman could not stomach an all-male shortlist for the deputy leadership of the party, so decided to launch her own campaign. 'We've got to reflect the fact that while the party used to be an exclusively men-only activity, that has changed,' she said in interviews. 'Women in the country regard themselves as equal and they expect to see a team of men and women making decisions.'[6] She added: 'My first instinct is that I object to the notion that when there's a difficult and important job to be done, you look around for the best man for the job.'[7]

With five MPs going for the deputy leadership it was a tough fight, particularly because, unlike some of her rivals, Harman had no trade-union support and had to take out a personal loan to fund her campaign. When the results were announced, she won by a whisker.

The new deputy leader expected to be appointed deputy prime minister as a result, like her predecessor John Prescott. However, when Gordon Brown formed his first cabinet he broke with tradition and failed to give Harman the job. 'Imagine my surprise when, having won a hard-fought election to succeed John Prescott as deputy leader of the Labour Party, I discovered that I was not to succeed him as deputy prime minister,' she later said. 'If one of the men had won the deputy leadership would that have happened? Would they have put up with that? I doubt it.'[8]

Harman's suspicion that she was being quietly side-lined grew when London hosted a G20 summit and she was relegated to looking after the leaders' wives at a Number 10 dinner – a role traditionally more suited to the prime minister's wife rather than his deputy leader. 'Imagine the consternation in my office when we discovered that!' she said. 'We must remember Caroline Flint's denunciation of women being used as window dressing.'[9]

Caroline Flint could not be further from the parliamentary gentleman with a red-carpet route to Westminster laid down by centuries of privileged ancestors. Wendy Beasley was just seventeen when she gave birth to Caroline in a home for unmarried mothers in 1961. Caroline's grandparents, who ran a pub in south-west London, played an increasingly important role in her life. 'My grandmother was always immaculately turned out and reminded me of Annie Walker in the Rovers Return – that was her stage,' Flint remembers. 'She was one of nine children and her family for generations had worked in the local paper mill. She wanted something more and with Grandad Frank became publicans managing pubs in the north before heading south to London.

'My grandparents were pretty amazing for their time as there was no question that my mum would have to give me up when she found herself pregnant at sixteen and all the family never made me feel any different. My maternal family was full of strong women rooted in an attitude of "Life may not be that great, but get on with it and do what you can."'

Flint never knew her biological father but when she was around thirteen years old her mother left Peter Flint, the only father she had known. In the following years, her mother became an alcoholic. She left home when she was seventeen, in the middle of her A levels, aware she wanted to make political change, and joined the Labour Party. 'I was angry about how little support my mum got, but at the same time I wanted to get away to university to have a different life from her too. I became more aware about inequality and how where you're born and who to affects your opportunities in life.'

When Flint was twenty-eight, her mother died from liver damage. Shortly afterwards her first marriage broke up, leaving her a single mother with two children. 'Honestly, the turning point came when my mother died,' she says. 'I had come out of a difficult marriage, got back on my feet and met Phil, who became my husband. I went about building my confidence with Phil's support, and got to a place where I felt in control of what I was doing. I've never been handed anything on a plate. I've had to work for everything I've achieved.'

As a result, Caroline Flint wasn't prepared to be silenced when she entered Parliament in 1997 as the Labour MP for Don Valley. After serving as a junior minister in Tony Blair's government, Gordon Brown promoted her to housing minister in 2008 and later minister for Europe, when she was told that she could attend cabinet meetings. In 2009, however, Flint sent shockwaves around Westminster when she resigned, claiming Gordon Brown was running a 'two-tier government' with few women allowed into his inner circle. Flint explains: 'When you sit around the cabinet table it is not a meeting of equals. There's a pecking order. As one of those "attending cabinet" it was obvious I was making up the numbers because I'm a woman. I was working my socks off and I didn't feel motivated to carry on.'

In her resignation letter, she said: 'Several of the women attending cabinet – myself included – have been treated by you as little more than female window dressing. I am not willing to attend Cabinet in a peripheral capacity any longer.'[10]

When the explosive letter was made public, Flint felt the full force of Brown's inner cabal moving against her with negative briefings appearing in the newspapers. 'If Tony was the great communicator, Gordon was the machine politician. MPs were constantly tested to prove which side you were on. You were either totally "for me" or "against me". It was destructive and didn't do

Gordon Brown any favours either. I believe this type of machine politics led to us losing in 2010, led to Ed Miliband, led to us losing the 2015 election and led to where we are now.'

One of the hardest things for Flint to stomach was the lack of support from other women MPs. 'There wasn't a huge amount of solidarity,' she says. 'Some women were actively sent to trash me.' Women close to Gordon Brown were quoted in newspapers at the time, claiming that Flint was more interested in her appearance than she was in the policies she presented.

Caroline Flint is not the only change-maker who was uncomfortable with the culture around Gordon Brown. Margaret Hodge describes him as 'just so paranoid', adding: 'There was a soft side to him but the team around him was very male and there was a culture of bullying. The way they used the press to punish people was disgusting.'

Even the most senior woman in Brown's cabinet agrees. Asked if there is some truth in Caroline Flint's statement that he used female cabinet ministers as window-dressing, Jacqui Smith replies: 'Yes. I will always be grateful to Gordon because he made me home secretary and treated me throughout – even when things got difficult – with the utmost respect and care for me and my family,' she says. 'But his inner team was almost completely male and had a male feel to it.'

Jacqui Smith became the first woman to serve as home secretary and only the third woman to hold one of the four great offices of state. She drove through significant changes including the first cross-government strategy on violence towards women and girls and began the change in prostitution legislation to focus on penalising the men who paid for sex rather than the women who sold it. 'I didn't spend all my time thinking that I was the first female home secretary,' she says, 'but you realise that other people think it's important so you have got to honour that. I thought that my time would have been wasted unless I did something on violence towards women and girls.'

Smith's first test came within twenty-four hours of her

appointment, when an attempted terror attack was carried out at Glasgow airport. She was inundated with politicians and members of the public telling her she had been calm and reassuring. 'A certain amount of people were thinking, She's the first female home secretary, the shit's hitting the fan, is she going to come running out of Downing Street shouting, "It's a nightmare"? And because I didn't, people thought, Blimey, you know what? A woman can do that job.'

When the 2010 election rolled around, Labour's problem with women became even more pervasive. After years of stubbornly pushing forward and demanding to be heard, women in the party felt they were going backwards. Even Yvette Cooper, who had loyally served Gordon Brown as chief secretary to the Treasury and secretary of state for work and pensions, says: 'The 2010 election was the one we were so angry about because we seemed to disappear altogether. We ended up having a series of panels without any women and there were a lot of men in senior positions in the campaign. There just were not enough women's voices, and given we had so many women ministers, given that we had so many women candidates, we had such a strong team of women, it was a massive missed opportunity for us. We had spent such a long time working really hard on changing the historic problem the Labour Party had with not winning support from women, so that by 1997 we were doing much better among women than men. And we saw that slipping back because we weren't raising the right issues and making it feel like politics was about everybody's life.'

After thirteen years in power, the Labour Party lost the general election and the Conservatives formed the Coalition government with the Liberal Democrats. David Cameron, the new prime minister, promised a different style of Conservatism: compassionate, liberal on issues like gay marriage, but with austerity running through the centre. Cuts to public spending soon followed. Harriet Harman, once again, found herself keeping the Labour leader's seat warm until a new man could be elected. When it seemed as though the leadership contest could be an all-male affair, Harman voted for Diane Abbott, despite their political differences, to help her receive enough nominations from MPs to make the ballot paper. When the results rolled in, Diane Abbott came in last place and Ed Miliband was duly elected leader of the Labour Party.

Abbott says: 'I did over fifty-two hustings with my four male rivals. There was a wonderful cartoon at the time of me as a Diana Ross figure and the other four as my backing group.' She adds: 'I think it's sad that Labour has never elected a female leader and I hope that I will see one in my lifetime.'

A record 143 new women were elected at the 2010 election, and the MPs grabbing a coffee in the airy Portcullis House or picking up an order paper from the Vote Office were a significantly more diverse intake even than the 1997 wave of change-makers.

Some of Westminster's veterans were playing catch-up. When Liz Kendall, freshly elected to represent Leicester West, got into a lift reserved for MPs, a Conservative colleague ordered her to get out. 'I'm an MP too!' she was forced to clarify.

She wasn't the only female MP struggling to make her way around the Hogwarts-style building of dusty book-lined corridors and stone staircases. Lisa Nandy, the new Labour MP for Wigan, tried to get into the House of Commons Chamber to hear a debate only to find her way blocked by a doorkeeper. After she had shown her pass, the official said bashfully: 'Oh, I am sorry, madam, please come in.' She had a similar experience when trying to access the terrace overlooking the river, reserved for MPs and their guests. 'None of it is dreadful,' she says, 'but when you put it all together you've got a battle to get around the building, let alone have your voice heard.'

Once, during a late vote, Nandy pushed through a door that said 'Members' Room' and entered a lavish bathroom, with towels and soaps set out neatly. A startled Conservative MP said: 'My God, what are you doing in here?' Nandy realised that she was in the men's bathroom and, when it came to Westminster, there were 'Members' and then there were 'Lady Members'.

'That's history. Traditionally you're a bolt-on,' she says. 'Thinking about women is not part of the DNA of the building and how it operates.'

Nandy emailed the parliamentary authorities to have the signs changed. It took ten months, but now they read 'Lady Members' and 'Gentleman Members'. 'These things aren't the most important things but I was determined not to let it go. It's a symbol of a bigger problem.'

The new Labour leader, Ed Miliband, included long-serving female MPs, such as Harriet Harman, Yvette Cooper and Caroline Flint in his shadow cabinet, alongside new faces such as those of Rachel Reeves, Liz Kendall and Lucy Powell. When Harriet Harman proposed that the substantial number of front-bench women should pose for a photograph at the Labour Party conference, her suggestion was hijacked by the leader's press team. They demanded Ed Miliband be pictured at the centre, just as Tony Blair had appeared in the infamous Blair's Babes shot. The inevitable 'Millie's Fillies' headlines soon followed.

Caroline Flint, who shadowed the communities and energy brief, said: 'Ed did improve things and had more women as shadow secretaries of state, but what we've seen with Gordon, Ed, Jeremy and David Cameron is making up new junior cabinet positions. That shouldn't be a shield for the fact you haven't got women in the top jobs.'

In 2011 Liz Kendall was appointed shadow minister for care and older people and invited to attend cabinet. For some, this may be seen as an example of how women were given subsidiary roles to make up the numbers. Kendall doesn't see it in that way. 'He was always interested in what I had to say,' she explains, a moment later adding: 'Although I do remember that many discussions on health and social care would be conducted by him, Ed Balls, Andy Burnham, all their team and I would be the only woman. I would think, Am I ever going to get to the point where I'm not the only woman in the room?'

While Ed Miliband's shadow cabinet was packed with women, his back-room team was almost exclusively male. The decision-making group around a leader is often more influential in policy terms than senior members of the cabinet or shadow cabinet. Margaret Hodge is blunt in her assessment of Ed Miliband's attitude to women in his shadow cabinet: 'They weren't there. He never talked to them. Did he ever talk to Harriet, his deputy leader? Probably never.'

As the 2015 election came into view, women began to worry that once again men would be at the centre of the Labour campaign. Ed Miliband was the leader, Ed Balls the shadow chancellor, and Douglas Alexander was the election co-ordinator. After feeling locked out of decision-making at the 2010 election and sensing the leader's office was planning to do the same in 2015, Labour's women decided to take matters into their own hands. Harriet Harman spearheaded the decision to create a women's campaign bus, coloured a much-mocked bright pink. Journalists criticised the shade as patronising, while members of Ed Miliband's press team were known to roll their eyes when it was mentioned. The Labour leader promised to spend a day campaigning on the bus – but failed to honour it.

For Caroline Flint, criticism of the bus is unfair: 'At least the pink bus got some attention and gave us a vehicle to do some independent campaigning as women, because the rest of it was very closed off. Our campaigning style was very old-fashioned with weekly themes that rarely cut through with strategy and appearances dominated by men jockeying for position.'

Yvette Cooper was a regular passenger on the pink bus. 'I suggested we should have the suffragette colours of green, white and purple but, to be fair to Harriet, she got far more attention doing something in wild, shocking pink and had far more impact as a result.'

Pink bus or not, the 2015 election ended in bitter disappointment for Labour. David Cameron won the majority his party craved. Ed Miliband resigned the next morning and Harriet

Harman found herself acting leader for the second time. The contest that engulfed the summer of 2015 would turn into one of the most astonishing and unexpected leadership battles. For once, there was no shortage of female candidates. First off the blocks was Liz Kendall, closely followed by Mary Creagh and Yvette Cooper. The front runner, however, was shadow health secretary Andy Burnham. Creagh failed to get enough nominations from her fellow MPs to make the ballot paper while Jeremy Corbyn – the left-wing outsider – scrambled over the line.

As 'Corbynmania' swept the Labour Party, hundreds of thousands of new members signed up to vote for the Islington North MP. Emotions flared while the tone of the debate sank as insults were traded on social media. Liz Kendall was brutally targeted after positioning herself as a centre-left candidate, who could attract Conservative voters. 'I was called a bitch, a whore, a "See You Next Tuesday" on Twitter,' she says. 'That's just a lot of sad, angry men on their keyboards. I have a pretty thick skin, and it never bothered me because I have a set of beliefs and a strong system of family and friends around me. But I thought, This is going to put young women off entering politics. I started to call it out on social media because nobody should have to deal with it and bullies have to be taken on.'

Far more affecting, she said, were comments and judgements made by journalists and some of her own colleagues. In an interview with the *Mail on Sunday*, the male political editor asked her how much she weighed. She responded: 'Fuck off.'

'I did think, dear God, we're in the twenty-first century!' she says. 'For me, what was unbelievable were the comments you got about your hair, your clothes, and your personal life. Not just from journalists but from your own colleagues. I had MPs tell me I should cut my hair, wear lower heels, wear trousers not skirts. That got my goat. Feminism tells us to value women for what they do and say, not for what they look like.'

Yvette Cooper entered the contest as one of the most experienced candidates, after serving in government jobs and regularly duelling as shadow home secretary with Theresa May. She was criticised for punching through only in the last couple of weeks of campaigning, and being risk-averse at the start. She admits: 'It was a slow start. Coming out of the general election, Ed [Balls] losing his seat, all of that was hard so it was difficult to keep going. It was also the process of pushing yourself forward as a candidate, and selling yourself. It's a hard one to adjust to. You have to shift into a different way of doing things and I didn't find that easy, is the truth.'

Was she affected by the abusive nature of the debate on social media? 'Liz faced more sexism than I did,' Cooper says. 'It was definitely apparent, you could see it happening.'

When the results came in, the Labour Party establishment was aghast. Jeremy Corbyn, the outsider, had won the contest with more votes than the other three candidates combined. Yvette Cooper was placed third after Andy Burnham, Liz Kendall was pushed into fourth. At the time of writing, no woman has ever been placed above a man in an election for the national leader of the Labour Party. Women have always come bottom.

The change-makers have done an extraordinary amount of heavy-lifting since 101 female MPs arrived in 1997, but for many, the work is gallingly incomplete. 'Because we are the party that's delivered a huge amount on equality for women we've got a blind spot,' Liz Kendall says. 'Today in the Labour Party we still have not voted a woman into the top job, which just isn't good enough. We need a long, hard look at ourselves as to why. You look at Diane Abbott, who had the same policy platform as Jeremy Corbyn and came nowhere near. We have a long and proud history of women who can't be controlled and know their own minds – Barbara Castle, Harriet Harman, Diane Abbott, myself, Angela Eagle. There's something in the culture of the party that finds it far more difficult to deal with than the Conservative Party.'

For Caroline Flint, first elected in 1997, the Conservatives are starting to catch up in terms of female representation. 'Our party operates in a way that acts against women because of the nature of our structure, with constituency parties, MPs, trade unions – there are so many groups you have to curry favour with to win approval. It can act as a brake on women because it's all about connections. We've had women leaders but it's always been by default. I think it has become more difficult for our party to be morally superior on equality, especially when you look at the benches opposite, which are completely different from their make up in 'ninety-seven. Today they do have more women, and they also have more Tory MPs who are black or Asian, working class or openly gay.'

When Jeremy Corbyn selected his first shadow cabinet, in 2015, for the first time more than half the positions were filled by women. He faced criticism, though, for appointing men to the three most prestigious roles: chancellor, foreign secretary and home secretary. At the time, the leader's office questioned whether the concept of 'top jobs' were out of date: 'The so-called "great offices of state" as defined in the nineteenth century reflect an era before women and workers even had the vote.'[11]

Asked whether Jeremy Corbyn is sexist, Margaret Hodge replies: 'I think it's never mattered to him. I don't think it's ever been high on his list of concerns. I've known Jeremy Corbyn for thirty-five years and I can't recall him ever talking about feminism. I don't think it's on his radar. He's got a totally macho team, it's all male. But it's not because he's sexist. He just doesn't think about it.'

Caroline Flint says several MPs came up to her after she made a contribution at a parliamentary Labour Party meeting to say that John McDonnell, the shadow chancellor and Corbyn's right-hand man, was making a hand gesture as she was speaking. 'He was making the yak-yak-yak gesture,' Flint says. 'I spoke to him about it afterwards. I said, "John, you know what that gesture means. That's what Jim Davidson and Bernard Manning used to do about the mother-in-law."'

Jacqui Smith, one of the success stories of all-women short-lists, stood down in 2010 after being engulfed by the expenses scandal. She believes the party is going backwards. 'We fought the 2010 general election with an almost wholly male front-facing set of people. It looked awful. We fought the 2015 general election with a largely male group of people and, guess what, people didn't like it. Jeremy Corbyn made appointments to his shadow cabinet, which meant he had no women in the top jobs, and, sorry, trying to claim that shadow home secretary isn't a top job – I mean, don't retro-fit your sexism. It isn't going to wash. There's a problem with the public face of the Labour Party and a problem with the key decision-making team. When you look at Jeremy's inner team, it's very male. The Labour Party is going backwards in terms of gender equality. The party thinks it's "job done", but it really isn't.'

After winning the 2016 leadership contest with an increased majority, Jeremy Corbyn added more women to his top team. Emily Thornberry was made the shadow foreign secretary, while Diane Abbott became shadow home secretary. The former director of Liberty, Shami Chakrabarti, was made shadow attorney general and Angela Rayner shadow education secretary. Jeremy Corbyn said at the time: 'For the first time, two of the three "great offices of state" are shadowed by women. Once again, the shadow cabinet has a majority of women, and has more black and minority appointees than any shadow cabinet or cabinet ever.'[12]

Diane Abbott adds: 'Jeremy Corbyn has had a bigger proportion of women in his cabinet than any of his predecessors. But there is always room for improvement.'

The New Rebels

'I feel very strongly we're potentially at a tipping point . . . but people like me have to keep pushing, it's not going to happen automatically.'

– Nicola Sturgeon

'I wasn't going to wear twin sets and pearls just to please them. They would be getting me unvarnished and whole or they would reject me. I've been in the closet, I'm not going back in for anybody.'

– Ruth Davidson

'There was a wonderful sense of standing on the shoulders of people who had gone before, who had put so much into making it happen.'

– Caroline Lucas

On 19 November 2014, members of the Scottish Parliament gathered to elect their first minister. The modern, airy room, built of oak, sycamore and glass, is a marked contrast to the crowded and adversarial lay-out of the House of Commons chamber. As the MSPs took their places in the semi-circle of desks, they prepared to prove that it was not only in its architecture that the Scottish Parliament was doing things very differently.

Only two candidates were running for the top job: Nicola Sturgeon of the Scottish National Party and Ruth Davidson of the Conservatives. Scotland was about to make history by electing the first woman as first minister. After the vote, it fell to the first female presiding officer, Tricia Marwick, to announce the result.

There was never any doubt of the winner. Ruth Davidson received fifteen votes from Conservative MSPs, while Nicola

Sturgeon picked up the sixty-six SNP votes. Labour abstained. As the applause filled the room, Sturgeon allowed herself a small, controlled smile before reaching out to hug her fellow MSP and friend Shona Robinson. She glanced over her shoulder to Alex Salmond, her mentor and former first minister, and gave him a wink.

Tricia Marwick stuck to the script, until the end. She took a breath. 'As the first woman presiding officer of the Scottish Parliament,' Marwick said, 'let me congratulate Nicola Sturgeon on being the first woman to be nominated to the position of first minister of Scotland.'

Now it was Sturgeon's moment. Addressing the 131 MSPs, she said what a proud moment it was for 'a working-class girl from Ayrshire'. Looking up at the public gallery, where her family were witnessing the historic election, she thanked her husband for his support. Then she directly addressed her eight-year-old niece, dressed in red just like her aunt, who had been enthusiastically clapping. Harriet, Sturgeon said, did not yet know about issues like the gender pay gap or the under-representation of women. 'My fervent hope is that she never will,' she continued, 'that by the time she is a young woman, she will have no need to know about any of these issues because they will have been consigned to history. If – during my tenure as first minister – I can play a part in making that so, for my niece and for every other little girl in this country, I can be very happy indeed.'

Nicola Sturgeon has been the most prominent politician in a new wave of women who are rebelling against the old, male-dominated structures in UK politics. In 2016, just seventeen years after the Scottish Parliament was first elected, the three largest parties all had female leaders: the SNP's Nicola Sturgeon, the Conservatives' Ruth Davidson and Labour's Kezia Dugdale. In 2012 Leanne Wood, socialist and proponent of Welsh independence, was elected as the first female leader of Plaid Cymru. Arlene Foster became the first female leader of the Democratic Unionist Party in December 2015 and the first female first minister of

Northern Ireland in 2016. The Green Party, Westminster's newest kid on the block, elected Caroline Lucas to be its leader in 2008 and she became its first MP in 2010.

After this dramatic breakthrough for women in politics, Nicola Sturgeon believes the UK is at a critical juncture. There is a chance, she says, that by the time her niece Harriet is a young woman some of the key feminist battles will have been won. 'Gender and equalities issues are very important to me and I feel very strongly we're potentially at a tipping point . . . but people like me have to keep pushing. It's not going to happen automatically. There's a lot to be proud about, but it's not enough just to have women leaders.'

Under Sturgeon's leadership, the SNP voted to introduce all-women shortlists for candidate selection. She has also campaigned for equal representation in boardrooms and worked with schools to try to encourage girls to take up subjects traditionally dominated by boys. 'Almost every day I come up against something,' Sturgeon says, citing a recent report on the gender pay gap. 'Lazy, stereotypical attitudes remind us we have a long way to go. Equal representation is still a long way off. I still hear attitudes being expressed about whether it's appropriate for women with children to be doing certain things. We've come a long way, but I still think we need to keep our shoulder to the wheel.'

One of Nicola Sturgeon's first actions as SNP leader and first minister was to announce a gender-balanced cabinet, with five men and five women. Her inbox was instantly flooded with reaction. Most of the messages were positive but some questioned whether the women were there on merit or solely because of their sex. 'Not a single person wrote asking if all the men were there on merit rather than to make up the numbers. That illustrates the way we've got to go.'

Nicola Sturgeon was born in 1970 in the north Ayrshire town of Irvine, growing up in a terraced council house that her parents later bought through Margaret Thatcher's Right to Buy scheme. Although her family benefited from one of Thatcher's policies, Thatcherism was to shape Sturgeon's politics for all the wrong reasons. As the miners went on strike and Ayrshire's coal industry declined, the forceful girl from Irvine sensed strongly that Scotland's future was being moulded by a prime minister the nation hadn't voted for. Nicola Sturgeon was just sixteen when she joined the SNP. 'I first got involved in politics when I was very young because I wanted to change the world, starting with the community I lived in,' she says. 'I grew up in a working-class community feeling the effects of the Thatcher government. That motivated me to get involved and make a difference.'

After studying law at Glasgow University, Sturgeon stood as the SNP candidate for Glasgow Shettleston in the 1992 Westminster elections. Aged just twenty-one, she was the youngest candidate in Scotland. During the fallow period of the early nineties, the future landslide victories of the SNP were unimaginable for even their most fervent supporters. Sturgeon was beaten by 15,000 votes. She didn't experience an election victory for another eight years, when she was elected as the MSP for the City of Glasgow, aged twenty-nine.

'When you're young and a woman in politics you really struggle to get taken seriously,' Sturgeon says. 'You're patronised because of your gender and you're patronised because of your age. That was a constant feature of my early days in politics. The positive effect it had on me was to make me more determined. One of the less positive effects is that – not consciously, but subconsciously – it encourages a very male pattern of behaviour. You emulate the men around you and become more aggressive and take yourself too seriously. That's one of the things I've learned as I've got older.'

Perhaps as a result, the MSP for the City of Glasgow quickly earned a reputation for being too cold and too serious. In 1999 the Labour MP Brian Wilson criticised her 'whingeing' and 'carping', saying, 'I've never heard that woman say a positive thing in her life.'[1] The Conservative MSP Brian Monteith agreed, saying in 2000: 'She really should learn to bite her tongue and smile more.'[2]

Sturgeon was nicknamed 'Nippy Sweetie' – Scottish slang, usually used by men, for a spiky and sharp-tongued woman. 'The person who mentioned it first meant it as a compliment! In Glasgow it means someone who fights your corner.' For Sturgeon, it's the perfect example of something intended as positive being 'twisted into something quite derogatory. Attributes that in a man are seen as real strengths – assertiveness, leadership – in a woman are seen as weaknesses.'

As the twenty-first century ticked on, the SNP was on a gilded path with its Nippy Sweetie propelled alongside. As Labour took its eye off the ball in Scotland, the Nationalist Party had a major electoral breakthrough in 2007 and formed a minority government. Alex Salmond was elected first minister, with Nicola Sturgeon serving as his deputy. She was also appointed health secretary: she handled an outbreak of swine flu in Scotland and steered through the scrapping of prescription charges. When it was announced that Scotland would have a referendum on independence from the United Kingdom, Sturgeon was given a key role in the Yes campaign, drafting the White Paper entitled 'Scotland's Future'. Sturgeon is a true believer: Scottish nationalism is the core force in her politics.

As a result, losing the referendum was a devastating blow for a woman who dreamed of an independent Scotland. Out of disappointment came opportunity. When Alex Salmond resigned as leader of the SNP, she dusted herself down. Sturgeon had been in government for seven years already so she knew the inevitable sacrifices of the party leader. Before deciding to run she spoke at length to Alex Salmond – who passionately encouraged her – but most crucially to her family. 'I thought long and hard about it,' Sturgeon says. 'The most important conversations are with the people closest to you – with my husband, my parents, my sister.

These are the people who have to live through it with you, and often the stresses and strains are felt more by the people around you than by yourself.'

On 24 September 2014, Nicola Sturgeon officially launched her campaign to be the next leader of the SNP. In a speech in Glasgow, she said she was putting herself forward to serve her country and because she believed she was the best person for the job. 'I also hope that my candidacy, should it succeed, will send a strong message to every girl and young woman in Scotland. No matter your background or what you want to achieve in life, in Scotland in 2014 there is no glass ceiling on ambition.'[3]

When the leadership nominations closed, Nicola Sturgeon was the only candidate. Her support was so overwhelming that nobody else had bothered to run. Formally instated as the first female leader of the SNP at the November conference, just days later Nicola Sturgeon was elected as first minister in the Scottish Parliament. One of her first actions after moving into Bute House, the official residence, was to hang more paintings of women. She also surprised the staff by asking where her husband, Peter Murrell, the SNP's Chief Executive, could find an iron and vacuum cleaner.[4]

Logging into her email, Nicola Sturgeon found it flooded with hundreds of messages. Little girls at primary school, teenagers studying for their exams and young women at university had felt compelled to write and express how inspired they were to see a female first minister. 'That was something that took me by surprise. It was hugely emotional,' she says. The messages are continuing even years into her tenure. 'A wee girl wrote who went to the same school as me, to say she now believes she could be first minister. That's so special.'

For Sturgeon, it was confirmation of the importance of female role models: 'You can't be what you can't see.' But she wasn't the only woman breaking perceptions of what a politician should be.

In 2011 another female politician in Scotland was feeling over-whelmed by the number of emotional emails she was receiving from young people. Ruth Davidson had just been elected leader of the Scottish Conservative and Unionist Party, at a time when the party was facing a crisis of stagnation and unpopularity. Many of the emails started, 'I'm not a Tory, but . . .'

Davidson's election as an openly gay woman had touched a nerve. Her correspondents wrote of how they hadn't told anybody about their sexuality, or said that their parents didn't know, or that they had always been interested in politics but until now hadn't thought it was for them. Like Sturgeon, Davidson was deeply moved. She sent an individual reply to every email. 'It was so touching,' she remembers. 'They were really raw, honest emails. From that point, even if it annoyed me, if I was ever asked in an interview about my sexuality I would never dismiss it. I would always discuss it and never push it to one side.' It was a turning point for a politician who had not wanted to be labelled by her sexuality.

Ruth Davidson was the first openly gay leader of a UK political party and in some ways an unlikely politician. The daughter of working-class Glaswegians, she was educated at a comprehensive school in Fife. 'We're not a political family,' she says. 'My family – unlike Ed Miliband's – didn't have Marxist philosophers around for the night. Our dinner conversations were about what had been on the telly.'

Before moving into politics Davidson worked as a journalist for ten years, presenting a current-affairs programme on Radio Scotland. 'It was a privilege,' she says, 'but I ended up getting frustrated because, as a journalist, you're not allowed to insert yourself into a story or be an agent of change. I thought, I've got no partner, no mortgage and no children. I either jump ship now or it's too late.'

At the time, the Conservatives were at risk of stumbling into insignificance in Scotland. The dizzying rise of the SNP and the visceral history of Labour pushed the Tories into a very distant third place, a mere pinprick on the political scene. 'The soggy left consensus, I thought, was damaging discourse in Scotland,'

Davidson says. 'I wanted to bring back proper debate – the white-hot crucible that forges policies – because you only know how firm your platform is when you have people attacking it from different positions.'

Davidson quit the BBC to join the Conservative Party and decided to throw her hat into the ring for the 2009 by-election in Glasgow North East. A year later she ran again for the same seat at the 2010 general election. She managed a respectable third with just over 5 per cent of the vote at a time when fighting elections for the Conservatives in Glasgow was about scrambling for swing rather than actually winning. Another lesson in failure came a year later, when she stood for the Scottish Parliament: 2011 was the Conservatives' worst ever performance in Scotland. Davidson managed to scramble into Parliament thanks to the regional list, only to see, on her first day in Holyrood, the leader of the Scottish Conservatives, Annabel Goldie, resign. The man who was the favourite to succeed her, Murdo Fraser, was so despondent after years of stagnation and decline that he wanted to separate the Scottish Conservatives from the national party and give it a completely new name and identity.

Ruth Davidson was aghast at the idea. Her decision to run for the leadership was the equivalent of the new kid at school deciding to be head girl, but her message, that the party could be proud of being Conservative, resonated.

The leadership campaign was tough for another, more personal, reason. The candidates she was running against were all referred to in the media by their occupation: Murdo Fraser was the deputy leader; Jackson Carlaw was the energy and transport spokesman; Margaret Mitchell was a committee chairwoman. The MSP for Glasgow, however, was invariably referred to as 'lesbian kickboxer Ruth Davidson'. For someone who had struggled with her sexuality in the past, Davidson admits finding this difficult. 'I was terrified when I first got elected,' she says, 'because I had come from nowhere, and no one really knew who I was. I was really worried I would be pigeonholed as the gay politician. Although I wanted to talk about lots of other things, I also wanted not to diminish that part of me, so I was quite conflicted. I didn't know how to get myself through it.'

The leadership contest was close, but in November it was announced that Ruth Davidson had beaten Murdo Fraser into second place. It was an astonishing victory for a woman who had only just entered the Scottish Parliament. 'I was the outsider. I was the black swan,' Davidson says. 'Some people didn't want someone telling them everything they'd done is wrong over the past twenty years – and I can completely see why, if it's the youngest and least experienced person suddenly deciding they can run the whole show. In many ways it was almost astonishing that someone who came from nowhere could win.'

Under Ruth Davidson's leadership, the Scottish Conservative Party has enjoyed success that seemed unimaginable in 2011. After the 2016 election they became the official opposition in the Scottish Parliament, with thirty-one seats compared to Labour's twenty-four. The personality cult around Davidson is part of the reason for that success. In 2016 her personal approval ratings surpassed even Nicola Sturgeon's. She is a politician who breaks all the rules, is partial to making *risqué* jokes and pulling faces in photographs. She has been pictured astride a tank, attempting to play the bagpipes, drinking pints (frequently) and riding a buffalo. Any initial concern about speaking of her sexuality appears to have dissipated. In 2015 Davidson appeared in a ground-breaking party election broadcast with her partner, Jennifer Wilson. A year later, in May 2016, she announced her engagement by posting a picture of the ring on Twitter. Asked whether she feels she is part of a new generation of politicians prepared to do things differently, Davidson says: 'It took me a long time to be comfortable in my own skin, possibly because I came out quite late. It's not been an unquestioning life, it's not a life unexamined. Having that level of acceptance gives you confidence to show more of yourself in public.

'When the leadership election was going on, I cut my hair really short – the shortest it's ever been – because I wanted people to know what they were getting. If I wasn't good enough, if they wanted someone other than me, with all my baggage, I didn't want it anyway. I wasn't going to wear twin sets and pearls just to please them. They would be getting me unvarnished and whole or they would reject me. I've been in the closet. I'm not going back in for anybody or for any job. Maybe that's part of being freer.'

With female leaders of the three biggest parties in Scotland, there are signs of a different type of politics emerging. Issues such as childcare and educational equality are given more prominence. Nicola Sturgeon, Ruth Davidson and Kezia Dugdale campaigned together during the EU referendum.

Sturgeon believes the tone of politics has also started to change. 'The three of us are kinder and nicer to each other. We're not bosom buddies, but we get on reasonably well and have a mutual respect.' She is careful, however, not to over-emphasise the difference it makes. 'Ruth, Kezia and I won't get all cuddly and collegiate. We'll tear strips off each other just as enthusiastically. Politics should be adversarial and challenging.'

Ruth Davidson agrees that there is mutual respect. 'It doesn't mean we're pals, we don't eat pizza together every night, but if there was an issue where I needed to have a quiet word with one of the others, I would.' She is less sure, however, that this is because of gender. 'The characters of the people is the biggest indicator as to how Parliament is conducted. There's a very big difference in the way Nicola Sturgeon goes about business and the way Alex Salmond goes about business. He's an incredibly Marmite politician, a complete bruiser. She's a bit more thoughtful, a bit less reckless. She's had to clean up after him for long enough so she understands the need.'

Ruth Davidson had experience of dealing with Alex Salmond when he was leader of the SNP. On a few occasions, all the party leaders met up to discuss issues such as managing the parliamentary estate or implementing the Leveson Inquiry into press regulation. As first minister, Alex Salmond would lead those discussions. Ruth Davidson believes he dealt differently with women and men. 'My impression was the way he treated [Labour Party leader] Johann Lamont and me was different from the way he treated the Greens' Patrick Harvie and the Lib Dems' Willie Rennie. He was a bit more disparaging towards Johann and me – dismissive is a better word. The only difference I could see was gender. Willie was on the same side of the argument as Johann and me. We were leading the second and third parties, while the two men were leading the fourth and fifth.'

The new generation of female politicians in Scotland shares cross-party concerns about the media portrayal of women. In Holyrood and Westminster, the political journalists who make up the 'lobby' are overwhelmingly male. For Ruth Davidson, that's part of the problem: 'We've not struggled to see women promoted in Scotland, but we are struggling to see women journalists. It's overwhelmingly male. When Wendy Alexander was the Labour Party leader there was a suggestion she was wearing low-cut tops that were too revealing. This was decided by the male journalists in the lobby. Parliament's cameras are mounted high in the ceiling, Wendy Alexander is five foot two, I'm five foot four, they're pointing down at you and you have to be pretty careful. You would never have had that about a man.'

Nicola Sturgeon is used to her appearance, hairstyles and fashion sense being meticulously unpicked in the press. Many column inches have been devoted to what the Scottish media have dubbed 'Project Nicola' – her transformation into an immaculately styled politician rarely seen without her trademark fitted dress and high heels. Her weight loss has been attributed to everything from Beyoncé's diet to Carole Vorderman's cookbook. She says she feels 'very conflicted' about how to handle the scrutiny. 'I get annoyed that for women there's a focus on what you wear or what your hair looks like. On the other hand, there's times you play on it as a way of engaging with people you might not otherwise. The only answer is to stop women being the exception in leadership positions.'

Sturgeon has spoken out strongly against the 'old-fashioned' media and the importance of 'challenging sexist portrayals of women'.[5] Being aware of the problem, however, does not mean she is immune from it. She wouldn't be human if she was unaffected, Sturgeon admits. 'I feel a constant pressure on how I look,' she says. 'It sometimes feels like every time I open the newspaper I feel a pressure because it's talking in some way about how I look. I've tried to resist that and not constantly change because of what they're writing. If I've changed anything about my own personal style it's more a feature of getting older. If you don't dye your hair it's grey. It's more about my own choices.'

She is most concerned about the impact negative media coverage has on her family. Her sister, in particular, finds it hard to read newspaper articles that she considers mean-spirited. 'Over the years I've developed a pretty thick skin. But there are moments when you're having a tough time and the media's being brutal, you just remember how difficult that is for your family. My sister in particular finds it really hard to read things about me that she thinks are unfair. There are occasions I've phoned up my sister and she's upset, and I've not even read the article.'

The fact that Sturgeon and her husband don't have children is also regularly brought up in the media. She points out that her predecessor, Alex Salmond, was not questioned in the same way about his family arrangements: 'While there's a variety of reasons why certain women don't have children, men don't get asked to justify that.' Some people assume that if a woman doesn't have children, she continues, 'you must have made a cold, heartless decision at some point to prioritise your career over children, and that's not usually how it works!' Even if it was, she adds, 'So what? Women are entitled to make a decision not to have children! You have judgements made about your personal choices in the way that men don't.'

The speculation over why Sturgeon does not have children,

which took on a dull persistence, led her to reveal that she had had a miscarriage. The SNP leader lost the baby when she was forty, shortly before the 2011 Scottish parliamentary election campaign period. Rather than grieve at home with her husband, Sturgeon decided to attend the fortieth anniversary commemoration of the Ibrox disaster, in which sixty-six Rangers football fans were crushed to death. She says she made the information public 'in the hope that it might challenge some of the assumptions and judgements that are still made about women – especially in politics – who don't have children. There are many reasons why women don't have children. Some of us simply don't want to, some of us worry about the impact on our career – and there is still so much to do, through better childcare, more progressive working practices and more enlightened attitudes, to make sure we don't feel we have to choose. And sometimes, for whatever reason, having a baby just doesn't happen – no matter how much we might want it to.'

Sturgeon adds: 'If the miscarriage hadn't happened, would I be sitting here as first minister right now? It's an unanswerable question. I just don't know. I've thought about it but I don't know the answer. I'd like to think yes, because I could have shown that having a child wasn't a barrier to all of this, but in truth I don't know.'[6]

In Westminster, too, a younger generation of female MPs is increasingly calling out what they consider to be sexism in the media. Shortly after being elected as the new MP for Wigan in 2010, Lisa Nandy was horrified to read an article claiming a top she had worn in the House of Commons was too low cut. The coverage was followed up by another newspaper running an online poll asking whether she was showing too much cleavage. 'Maybe I was a bit naïve, but I didn't expect to have to deal with that level of criticism,' she says. 'It felt particularly personal and difficult because the person who started it was a female journalist.'

It wasn't her only run-in with a hostile press. In 2013, when she was working as the shadow charities minister, Nandy became pregnant. One of the first calls she received was from a female journalist working for a trade magazine, who asked whether the fact she was having a baby and going on maternity leave signalled that Labour was no longer committed to the charity sector. 'The response from the public was much better. I was anxious about how my constituents would react, but people were amazing.'

There is also a cross-party camaraderie among female politicians who have shared similar experiences. The first person who came up to Nandy after the media focus on her cleavage was the Lib Dem MP Sarah Teather. 'Don't let the bastards get you down,' she said. Caroline Lucas, the Green MP for Brighton Pavilion, was another very supportive figure. Nandy believes women in a similar position should: 'Call it out, but don't let it distract you from getting on and doing your job.' While male politicians are asked their views on the economy, Nandy adds, female MPs are being asked what it's like being a woman in Parliament.

Caroline Lucas, leader of the Green Party between 2008 and 2012 and to date its only MP, has championed a very different kind of politics at Westminster – collaborative, less top down, and democratic in structure. It's the anti-establishment, feminist politics that she learned on anti-nuclear marches and at the peace camp on Greenham Common in the eighties. Beneath the shadow of the weapons base, women tied brightly coloured scarves to the fence surrounding it, scattered flowers and formed a rota of protesters chained to railings. They surrounded the nine miles of wire and pinned up teddy bears, baby clothes and photographs of their families.

'The degree of common connections you can make with people when you've got that sense of a common cause is something so fundamental,' Lucas says. 'There is something quite celebratory about forming quite strong friendships and in some sort of symbolic way, when you're putting the flowers on the fences, it really does emphasise that you're standing up for life versus the instruments of death. I know that sounds a cliché, but when you're outside some of those weapons places and you see how grey and lifeless they really are, there is something quite existential about it.'

Caroline Lucas has been a committed Green Party member since 1986. She was a member of Oxford Council and spent ten years in the European Parliament before winning Brighton Pavilion at the 2010 general election. It was a major breakthrough for a small party in the first-past-the-post system that is stacked against them. In 2015 Lucas was elated to win again in a tough-fought race against determined Labour opposition. 'The system is built to keep small parties out, so there was a wonderful sense of standing on the shoulders of people who had gone before who had put so much into making it happen. History is made – that was the front page of the local paper.'

Unusually, Lucas was fighting three female opponents to win Brighton Pavilion. Labour, the Conservatives, the Lib Dems and the Greens all fielded women. 'There were moments when you felt a degree of at least trying to do politics differently,' Lucas says. 'There was a sense that you could admit to being really nervous about a broadcast that you were about to do together, that you were all exhausted, and it wouldn't be used against you. Men very rarely, in my experience, say, "I'm really worried about *Question Time*." But you quite often bump into another woman on the programme who has gone to the loo just like you have because you're still feeling really nervous, and you're both saying, "God, it doesn't get any easier, does it?" "No, it's awful!"'

The Greenham Common culture of collaboration over common causes is part of the new politics that Lucas has tried to bring to Westminster. She has campaigned to make Parliament's hours more family friendly and has written a book spelling out the reforms she believes should happen. 'It's a bit like Hogwarts,' she says. 'It is so staggeringly inefficient.'

Filibustering and time-wasting is one of the milder forms of behaviour that Caroline has witnessed. Sitting in the Green Party office and talking about her experiences in the Chamber, Lucas says: 'I've come back here and cried a few times. I would never think of quitting. Sometimes it's more from anger and frustration. It just makes you feel angry that they get away with it.'

She gives two examples. In the autumn of 2012, Lucas secured an adjournment debate on market exposure to fossil fuels, like oil and gas. Adjournment debates can't change the law, but they can bring attention to an issue and force ministers to respond. The Conservative MP and energy minister John Hayes quickly made his position clear: 'The Honourable Lady made that case – I shall put it as generously as I can – with confidence,' he began, adding: 'I think that the Honourable Lady is not only outside the mainstream but, arguably, on the very fringe of the debate. I do not want that to be the case because, as I have said, I am generous and I am approaching the issue as paternally as I can. Dickens wrote about "a heart that never hardens, and a temper that never tires, and a touch that never hurts". I do not want to hurt the Honourable Lady.'

'The level of patronising arrogance coming from John Hayes!' she says. 'One of my greatest regrets is that I wish I had walked out. I just wish I had said, "This is out of order. I'm going to leave this Chamber until you treat someone with a bit more respect."'

Lucas also had a bruising experience when she argued against chancellor George Osborne's policy of austerity. 'He just deliberately tried to take me down, just to say, "What on earth can the Green Party possibly tell us?"' she remembers. 'It wasn't just him trying to make fun, but behind him all of the male Tories were yah-booing. When you're up there, it's really loud, you feel the whole thing is erupting around you to make you feel stupid and they would love it if you just crawled away. There are very few workplaces where that is the case. Even if you're in competition you're not actively willing the other side to dissolve.'

Despite the increasing number of women MPs, the behaviour in the Chamber is still raucous at best, sexist at worst. If a woman is seen to be wearing a low-cut top, some MPs will shout comments like 'Look at those!' or 'That doesn't leave much to the imagination, does it?'

'It's just horrible,' Lucas says. 'In any other workplace it would be grounds for very, very serious action, if not dismissal. It is intimidating. The architecture and the culture is based on confrontation.'

Examples of raucous behaviour are not hard to find. As there are significantly more MPs than seats in the House of Commons, members write their names on prayer cards and slot them into a space on the green benches to reserve a place. It's another parliamentary tradition that is foreign to new MPs, and Lisa Nandy realised she had left it too late to book a place to witness her first Budget. She had seen MPs sitting on the steps that form a gangway between the benches, so decided to take her place there.

Immediately, one of the nearby SNP MPs turned to her and said: 'You don't want to sit there. They'll shout, "Knickers," at you. Do you want my seat?'

Nandy was baffled – surely that couldn't be true? Besides, she was wearing a long skirt. It would be fine. She politely declined.

As the debate started, the noise began: Conservative MPs on the benches opposite were waving their white order papers and shouting, 'Knickers!'

'I was, like, what year is this?' Nandy says. 'I will always call it out when I hear it from our own side as well. The level of noise isn't the real problem, it's the abuse and some of it does get very personal. When you get intimidating behaviour it knocks you off your stride. People think it's having a laugh, all good sport, but you need extra reserves of resilience.'

Having a thick skin is now a prerequisite for a female MP. Social media has shaped and moulded the new generation of politicians perhaps more than any other recent development. At its best, it means a direct democracy where the public have access to their representatives and the power to hold them to account in a way that could not have been dreamed of in the days of Lady Astor.

'We are the social-media generation,' says Nicola Sturgeon. 'Perhaps it's to do with the fact we're a bit younger – Ruth and Kezia would probably jump in to say they're much younger than me, but I still think of myself as being quite young.'

In the far more informal setting of Twitter or Facebook, a very different sort of political conversation is allowed to develop. In January 2015, for instance, when Andy Murray was playing a tennis match that clashed with First Minister's Questions, Ruth Davidson tweeted: 'Hmm . . . FMQ prep vs tennis . . .'

A few moments later, Nicola Sturgeon responded: 'I'm sure we could come to some arrangement.'

Davidson replied: 'Okay, I'll bring the snacks – let's use your office. Kez, you in?'

The Labour leader tweeted: 'Yes, there in a minute, looking for the Pimm's.'

At its worst, social media has created a bullying and misogynistic atmosphere that can turn violent. When I ask Caroline Spelman whether she experienced any specific examples of sexism in Parliament, she bristles. What we should be talking about instead, she suggests, is the abuse women receive online. 'That's the serious version of "Oh, yes, I was so shocked that colleagues thought I was a secretary." I think we should move beyond that to the much more serious question of why we have this problem. We as a nation need to look into our hearts and minds – why do we think it's okay on social media to pursue female public figures in this hateful way? Particularly after the death of Jo Cox, which rocked me because she was a mum and her children were very little. Would I have gone into politics if I had known it could have put my children at risk of losing their mother? No way.

'The question back to society is, what's the matter with it?

What's the underlying problem? It's finding expression in a very uncivilised way with very tragic consequences.'

As emotions ran high during the Scottish referendum, an ugly level of abuse developed. The SNP stripped membership from one individual who aggressively abused Davidson over her sexuality, and Sturgeon intervened personally to condemn it. 'Action was taken,' Davidson acknowledges. 'We're quite robust in Scotland and we will weigh in for each other.'

While Davidson ignores the majority of aggressive comments on social media, she feels she has a duty to confront those who engage in homophobic abuse. She reveals that some people have told her she needs corrective rape to stop her being gay, while others have said she can't know what family is because she'll never have kids of her own and will have to use a turkey-baster. 'I get stuff about politics, party, my weight, my looks, something I've said, but I let all that pass me by,' she says. 'I do call out homophobic abuse, either by retweeting or answering back, just to lay down a marker. A lot of young gay people follow me and it's important that they see you just don't have to take that.'

Nicola Sturgeon says that if she went to look for it, the abuse she would find directed at her and her family 'would make your hair curl'. 'I make a conscious effort not to engage with it,' she says. 'If you get dragged into it you would get very affected by it. Some of it is vile and borders on criminal. But it's a mistake to forget that people who are abusive on social media are a tiny minority.'

If the 2014 Scottish referendum was a low point in social-media aggression towards women, another nadir was just around the corner.

In early 2016 Labour MPs who were exasperated with Jeremy Corbyn's leadership were casting around for a candidate who could challenge him. Angela Eagle, who had represented Wallasey since 1992, put her name forward with the required number of MPs backing her, prompting a leadership contest.

A campaign of aggressive abuse towards her followed. One man was arrested on suspicion of making death threats in emails and a brick was thrown through the window of her constituency office. She was forced to cancel surgeries with members of the public after receiving threats. Eagle, who was only the second openly lesbian MP to speak about her sexuality, also received aggressive homophobic abuse.

It isn't only Angela Eagle who has seen the ugly side of social media. Caroline Flint, who refused to serve in Jeremy Corbyn's shadow cabinet and backed Eagle's campaign, received abuse, including one tweet suggesting she should lie down on the road and let a car run over her. 'What I find distressing and upsetting is that I have spent thirty-seven years in the Labour Party as some-one who never thought they would be an MP. I still have to pinch myself,' she says. 'I spent years building up my confidence. One of the reasons I didn't want to be an MP or share more about my early life was that I was worried about people knowing my mum had me at seventeen, people knowing about the terrible marriage I had, people knowing about Mum's problems with drinking and being judged. It's taken me twenty years to be able to talk about these things. When I get stuff said about me on social media – that I'm a champagne socialist or Red Tory, I'm part of an elite – people are trying to say who I am when they don't know who I am. My mum was on and off benefits for years, we never owned a home. I spent time on my own with two kids on benefits. Reading these insults can be demoralising so I have got better at ignoring them.'

Flint adds: 'I don't think Jeremy Corbyn is directing this, but he's unleashed something. People are doing it in his name. That intolerance and ugliness, the harsh, intimidating language is violent. As a woman and as a feminist I find it unacceptable.'

In July 2016, forty-four female Labour MPs signed a letter call-ing on Jeremy Corbyn to try to stop the escalating abuse. The Labour leader has repeatedly said that he does not condone abusive behaviour and has demanded a 'kinder, gentler' politics, but some female Labour MPs feel he should do more. In 2016 Margaret Hodge authored a letter of no confidence in Jeremy Corbyn, which was backed by more than 80 per cent of Labour MPs. As a result, she was forced to refer some anti-Semitic emails she received to the police. 'Leadership is about the culture you permit and he's permitted that culture,' she says, before adding: 'It's one of the things that's stopped me thinking he's a decent man.'

On the morning of 18 July 2016, Labour MPs were deciding whether Angela Eagle or Owen Smith should be the unity candidate to challenge Jeremy Corbyn for the Labour leadership. Smith, the MP for Pontypridd since 2010, launched his own bid at late notice to the dismay of Eagle's cheerleaders, like Margaret Hodge. Later it was announced that Smith had received more support from Labour MPs than Angela Eagle. Despite doing the heavy lifting in mounting a challenge against Jeremy Corbyn, and receiving death threats as a result, Eagle announced she would step aside and throw her support behind his campaign.

When I ask Margaret Hodge whether the Labour Party has a problem with women, she replies simply: 'Yes,' then adds: 'We can't elect a fucking woman to lead the Labour Party. Look at Ed Miliband, who was absolutely surrounded by men. And so is Owen [Smith]. It's outrageous the stuff he's said about Leanne Wood.' She shows me a video that has emerged online showing Owen Smith telling Plaid Cymru leader Leanne Wood in 2015 that her 'gender helps' when it comes to being invited on *Question Time*.

'Will he put Angela in as chancellor, Owen, if he wins? I bet he bloody won't. It's really, really hard. It's depressing. Maybe it's because you've got me on the morning when Angela is about to go down. She had the guts.'

Prime Minister and Parliamentarian

'I don't think I've ever really felt that being a woman in any way gets in the way.'

– Theresa May

Theresa Brasier came home from school smarting. An air of excitement had whipped through the pupils when they learned the All Blacks – New Zealand's national rugby team – were due to play the Southern Counties in Oxford. A group of children from the Oxfordshire school would be able to go and watch the match, the head teacher revealed, while the rest would attend the carol concert as planned. As the daughter of the local vicar, Theresa Brasier held a deep affection and reverence for the Church that would last throughout her adult life. She was also a keen sports fan. There was no question in her mind as to what she wanted to do. 'I would like to go to the rugby,' she told the head teacher.

'No,' came the reply. 'That's for the boys.'

When Theresa returned home to the vicarage that evening, she told her father what had happened. The Reverend Hubert Brasier had encouraged her interest in sport and immediately took his daughter's side. 'My father wrote in,' Theresa May remembers, 'and he said that he thought I had been to a sufficient number of carol concerts and should be allowed to go to the rugby. The purport of this being, of course, that he was the local vicar!'

Ever conscientious, Hubert Brasier also made sure that his daughter would not feel self-conscious at being the only girl on the rugby trip. 'Fortunately he named in his letter two of my best friends who also liked rugby, so the three of us went to the rugby.'

As a child growing up in Oxfordshire in the 1960s and 1970s,

Theresa Brasier did not feel restrained by a gender strait-jacket. Barriers that limit other girls and women appear invisible to the UK's second female prime minister – either because she fails to see them or refuses to acknowledge they are there. The kernel of that mindset developed in childhood.

'I was an only child but I was very much brought up in the thinking that the important thing is to do the best you can in whatever you're doing and there was no suggestion that as a woman or a girl there were any boundaries to what I could do,' May says. The Oxfordshire vicarage was the Petri-dish for the prime minister's political philosophy: 'Where you go is up to you. It's about your talents and your willingness to put the hard work and effort in and do the best you can to be the best you can be.'

May is a female politician who defies categorisation. She differs from many of the fighters of the seventies and eighties because she identifies as a feminist and believes parliamentary reform must sometimes be viewed through a gender prism. As a result, she is in favour of changing Parliament's hours and reforming the selection process. However, her refusal to see boundaries puts her at odds with the many of the change-makers who entered Westminster, like her, at the 1997 election. Sometimes, May believes, women should just get on with the job. Her attitude is more comparable to that of female politicians like Betty Boothroyd or Angela Merkel. 'I don't think I've ever really felt that being a woman in any way gets in the way,' she tells me.

Theresa Brasier was born on 1 October 1956, in the lively seaside town of Eastbourne on the Sussex coast, popular with holiday-makers, who packed out its theatres, pier and bandstand. Amid the pleasure-making, Theresa grew up in a strongly Christian household where her father worked as a chaplain at All Saints Hospital. When Theresa was three the family moved to Church Enstone, a hamlet nestled in the picturesque Cotswolds, when her father became vicar at a local church. She attended Heythrop Primary School, one of only twenty-seven pupils, and later wrote: 'I remember arriving at school screaming my head off because I didn't want to leave my mother. So I had to be carried into the class in the arms of the headmistress, who announced to the rest of the class: "Look what a silly little girl we have got here."'[1]

Theresa Brasier's experience of the swinging sixties was very different from that of the generation tearing down boundaries in London. Hers was a rural, traditional existence. However, there were signs that the vicar's daughter was already gently pushing against gender stereotypes. Although she cooked and made scones with her mother, she also loved to listen to the cricket on the radio with her father. Her hero was a certain Yorkshire batsman. 'I've been a Geoff Boycott fan all my life. It was just that he kind of solidly got on with what he was doing.'[2] Immensely successful, Boycott was sometimes criticised for walking alone rather than rubbing shoulders with his team-mates. Theresa May, never one for Westminster's bars or Pall Mall's gentlemen's clubs, would also be an individual who got on with the job in front of her.

Political discussion around the dinner table was a key feature of her early life. She was a voracious reader and, as an only child, conversations with adults were the norm. Early debates with her father spawned her passion. 'Politics captured me,' May later said, adding: 'I wanted to make a difference. I wanted to be part of the debate.'[3]

When a twelve-year-old Theresa informed her parents that she wanted to be a politician, her father was supportive but firm. 'He was very clear, though, that as far as he was concerned he was the vicar for the whole parish so I shouldn't be out on the streets parading my politics. It was important to him that I could be involved but should do it in that behind-the-scenes sense.'[4] She got in touch with the local Conservative Association where she helped with unglamorous jobs, like stuffing envelopes, always carefully behind closed doors. Hubert Brasier's religious duties were felt by all the family. 'You don't think about it at the time,

but there are certain responsibilities that come with being the vicar's daughter . . . You're supposed to behave in a particular way.'[5]

Life in Church Enstone revolved around the church. In one firm memory of her childhood, Theresa was cooking in the kitchen with her mother when the idyll was abruptly disturbed by a group of people traipsing up the path to the back of the house. 'Just knock on the door, and that's it, they would expect to see the vicar. Some people would say that life as a vicar's daughter could have its ups and downs but I feel hugely privileged actually in the childhood that I had.'[6]

May is still a practising member of the Anglican Church and, with her husband, a regular church-goer. 'At no stage did I take issue with the Church,' she has said. 'I think that was partly because it was never really imposed on me by my parents.' Her religion inevitably shapes her politics. 'It is part of me, it is part of who I am, and therefore how I approach things.'[7]

Theresa Brasier attended the Holton Park Girls' Grammar School in nearby Wheatley, based in a historic manor house on a country estate. It was a highly successful school and many of the pupils went on to university. In 1971, when she was fifteen, the school was closed in the unpicking of the grammar system and became part of Wheatley Park Comprehensive School. One of May's most radical actions as prime minister has been to allow new grammar schools to open – a conviction that may have formed when she was a girl at Holton Park.

At school Theresa was a reserved, diligent student, who enjoyed reading and doing her homework. 'I shouldn't say it, but I probably was Goody Two Shoes.'[8] When the school ran a mock general election in 1974, she naturally stood as the Conservative Party candidate. Pitching to young people in the seventies was probably a lost cause from the start. 'In those days Liberal policies were much more appealing to a young audience than Conservative policies,' the winning candidate, Rosalind Hicks-Greene, told the *Daily Mail* in 2016. She remembers Theresa Brasier as being 'very serious and quite reserved' at school: 'I thought she would be a university lecturer or something.'[9]

In 1974 Theresa swapped the sleepy Cotswolds for Oxford University, the academic crucible that forges prime ministers. She studied geography at St Hugh's, at the time still a women's college, which boasted female alumni including Barbara Castle and Aung San Suu Kyi. In the early 1970s women made up just one in five undergraduates and around 43 per cent were from state schools.

May says she doesn't remember feeling surrounded by public-school boys, once again (perhaps wilfully) blind to gender boundaries. 'The only thing that did strike me was . . . I remember thinking that those girls who had been to boarding school had had an experience of living away from home that I hadn't had. So it was quite different.' The grammar-school girl had had other advantages. 'I actually went to my local university, because I was brought up in Oxfordshire and went to Oxford, so if I had forgotten anything at the beginning of term I could ring my mother and say, "Please could you bring . . ."'

Warring with words against other political hopefuls at the Oxford Union debating society, Theresa Brasier honed the skills she would later deploy in the House of Commons. The second female prime minister is, above all, a parliamentarian with an intense respect for the debating Chamber. 'If you have the opportunity to debate prior to coming into Parliament that's very helpful, because obviously part of it is about being able to enter into the discussions, challenge other people and so forth.'

It was during her time at Oxford that Margaret Thatcher was elected leader of the Conservative Party. Pat Frankland, a university friend of Theresa Brasier, said in 2011: 'I cannot remember a time when she did not have political ambitions. I well remember, at the time, that she did want to become the first woman prime minister and she was quite irritated when Margaret Thatcher got there first.'[10]

It's a moment the prime minister cannot remember. 'I knew I wanted to try and become a Member of Parliament, because that had been part of my thinking from quite an early age. I don't recall ever telling anybody I wanted to be PM but I certainly would say, and people would know, that I was interested in coming to Westminster.'

That ambition was given perhaps its greatest leg-up when, at Oxford, Theresa Brasier made one of the most important decisions of her political life, a choice that made her dream of being prime minister possible. At a Conservative Association disco she was sitting talking to Benazir Bhutto, who would go on to be the first female prime minister of Pakistan. As a young man approached, Benazir turned to her and said: 'Oh, do you know Philip May?'

'And the rest is history, as they say,' Theresa May would later say.[11] The couple, who danced together that night, would become one of Westminster's most steadfast couples. 'He was good-looking and there was an immediate attraction.'[12] Philip May even persuaded his girlfriend to return to Oxford after she had graduated to speak at debates he organised, most famously opposing the motion in June 1978: 'That sex is good . . . but success is better.'[13]

In 1980 the couple married. Philip's importance in Theresa's life would soon be brought into sharp and painful relief. In 1981 the Reverend Hubert Brasier set off to conduct a Sunday evening service at the local church, driving his Morris Marina. As he edged forward from a central reservation, he was hit by a Range Rover. Aged sixty-four, he died from head and spine injuries. 'I got a phone call saying he was in intensive care. I saw him before he died but he wasn't able to speak,' she later said.[14]

Zaidee Brasier, Hubert's wife, was a wheelchair-user, suffering from multiple sclerosis. A few months after her beloved husband was killed, she also died. Their daughter was twenty-five and an orphan. 'I had huge support in my husband and that was very important for me,' May said. 'He was a real rock for me. He has been all the time we've been married but particularly after the loss of both parents within a very short space of time.'[15]

A supportive husband links some of the most successful women in politics. Philip's quiet dedication to his wife's career has not gone unnoticed in Westminster. Caroline Spelman, a Conservative MP and former cabinet minister, says May has a 'very supportive' husband. 'I think a man could get away with doing politics if their wife wasn't that interested in it, but I think it is very, very hard for a woman to do politics if her husband is not interested or support-ive. I know that sounds a rather old-fashioned reflection on the genders but I think without that it would be extremely difficult, especially at times of crisis.'

Theresa May's path to Westminster was not fast-tracked through the slipstream of being a special adviser or getting onto an all-women shortlist. Her first job after university was at the Bank of England, where she was seconded to the Treasury to work on a committee to review the functioning of financial insti-tutions. Later she went to Interbank Research Organisation, which then became part of the Association of Payment Clearances. If the financial world seems a traditionally male career path, May did not find it so. The head of her unit was a woman: 'For me, there seemed to be quite a lot of women around.'

Throughout her time at the Bank of England, her political ambition continued to burn. 'I always took the view, though, that you should try and do something else first and not just come into politics because that gives you a different experience that you can then bring into the political world.'

When the opportunity came to serve as a Conservative coun-cillor in Merton, south London, in 1986, she seized it. 'I'm not somebody who has set out on the back of an envelope a career path, I'm going to do this and so forth. So what happened was, I was interested in getting into politics, my husband and I were involved in the local Conservative Association, and then a vacancy came up, as it happened, in the ward that we lived in for somebody to stand as a councillor and I thought I would do it.'

She took the decision, she says, partly because she thought it would be good practice before running for election as an MP and partly to try to help the local area. 'For me, being in politics is about making a difference, it's about trying to improve people's lives, and you can do that at a local level as a councillor and you can do it as a Member of Parliament and you can do it as somebody in government.'

Philip May had been heavily involved in politics at Oxford University and was at the time active in the local Conservative Association with his wife. Did the couple ever have a conversation to say Theresa would go for the councillor's job while Philip would play a more supportive role?

'It was never that sort of arrangement. I mean, the opportunity came up. At the time, I guess, it was slightly easier for me work-wise to stand so I decided to go for it.' In retrospect, the seemingly innocuous decision to run as a councillor was a turning point not only in the direction of May's career but in the future of the country. She had caught the political bug, and fighting for a constituency was the inevitable next step.

In 1992 Theresa May fought hopelessly in North West Durham, a safe Labour seat, and in 1994 she lost to Labour's Margaret Hodge in the Barking by-election. In her typical manner, she does not believe this was because of her sex. 'I don't remember any questions that were specifically related to being a woman as I went through the selection process,' she says. 'I took the approach that I should never think – because I wasn't selected for a number of seats – I should never think I wasn't selected because I was a woman. I should always analyse the interviews I had done, the questions I had answered. Were there particular subjects I needed to mug up on a bit more? Were there things I'd done well and not so well? I should go through it in a rigorous way, rather than thinking, "Oh, they obviously didn't want me because I'm a woman."

'It's back to what I was saying about my parents and my father,' she explains. 'Do the best that you can and always try to say, How can I ensure I'm giving of my talents and my hard work in whatever I'm doing, and not see it as something that's about being male or female?'

Eventually the hard work paid off. Theresa May caused an upset when she won the selection for the safe Conservative seat of Maidenhead, beating off more established competition in the form of Sir George Young and Eric Forth. After a tough selection for a Tory stronghold, winning the 1997 election was the easy bit. Around her, however, Conservative MPs were falling under Labour's landslide victory. 'In a sense it was a party almost in mourning for a lot of people who had lost out because of the political tide turning against the party.' As usual, May focused on the job at hand. 'Of course, there weren't many women on the Conservative benches – one or two characters like Teresa Gorman who was still in when I came in – but I just approached it in the same way as I did everything else.'

A record number of women entered Parliament in 1997 but May was one of only five new Conservative women to win seats. Despite the small numbers, she joked in her maiden speech that she should wear a name badge to avoid being confused with the fellow Conservative MP Teresa Gorman. 'People used to sometimes get us mixed up,' she says. 'They used to think I was the MP for Billericay and it was sort of, oh, no, that's the other Teresa!' The confusion is harder to understand when you consider that at the time there were only thirteen female Conservative MPs.

The new MP for Maidenhead also found herself muddled with Ann Widdecombe, the MP for Maidstone. 'A lot of people would say, "Who are you the MP for?"

'"Maidenhead."

'"Oh, that's in Kent, isn't it?"

'"No, that's Ann Widdecombe!"'

May was also, bizarrely, muddled with another Teresa. The

new MP for Maidenhead had a namesake in the porn industry and would receive rather peculiar calls to her office asking for an altogether different woman. 'We do get telephone calls from time to time from people who want to book me to do programmes which are perhaps not about politics,' she said at the time.[16]

Unlike many of the 101 Labour MPs who entered Parliament at the same time, Theresa May doesn't remember any incidents of overt sexism: she wasn't mistaken for a secretary or patronised by MPs. 'I genuinely don't think I had any experience like that,' she says, adding: 'But then, I've always taken an approach – and I think this is important in business and in politics, indeed in anything that women are doing – to just get on with the job in the way you want to do it. I think sometimes people come into politics – less so now, but sometimes people have come into politics or will do this in business as well, and it probably happens in the media – thinking they've got to do the job in the way that the men do it, and actually you don't. You must be your own person and do it in your own way. It's one of the things I say to business groups: don't feel that you've got to be that stereotype of the way a man does a job. Women may do the job in a different way, but it's an equally valid way, an equally good way and gets the results. It's just different.'

Theresa May's way of doing the job was almost immediately successful and the MP for Maidenhead was quickly pinned as one to watch. Caroline Spelman remembers: 'She's a good friend and she stood out very early on. I noticed that the people who had been in local government had an advantage because they already had some practice in speaking in a chamber with the dynamics of government and opposition. That was very new to me as a business person, and probably cost me a year of coming up to speed, whereas Theresa had been at Merton Council. She hit the ground running and was promoted very quickly.'

May agrees that mastering the Chamber was vital – and believes it offers some particular challenges for female MPs. 'As a Member of Parliament that is such an important place because that's where you put across your views. That's where you can make a difference in terms of legislation. So what happens in the Chamber is hugely important and it can be a robust and boisterous place on occasions,' May says. 'I think there's a challenge for women which is simply a physical thing, that when it's very noisy and you're trying to make your voice heard, often the natural thing for a woman is for your voice to go up and then, of course, people assume it's a shrill note that's being sounded, but actually it's just something that happens. So you have to consciously think about how you are putting the message across.'

More widely, however, May does not accept that women get a harder time in the House of Commons Chamber than men. 'You hear people tell stories about things but I'm not sure I've ever seen or witnessed anything myself. There's banter across the Chamber, male or female – it's not necessarily a gender thing at all. Sometimes we women can give as good as we get.'

With a career spanning two decades, May does acknowledge some fraught and difficult moments in the House. 'I always say with the House of Commons Chamber that you never know when you walk into it what the atmosphere is going to be.' As an example, she talks about a moment when Jack Straw, as leader of the House, was giving the government's response after London had won its bid to host the 2012 Olympic Games. As his shadow, May stood up to speak for the Conservatives. 'I gave what I thought was a perfectly positive response, it's great that we've got the Olympics and so forth, and I put in a phrase that was something like, "Of course it's going to be a big budget and we'll have to make sure it's spent properly, but that is not for tonight. Tonight is for the celebration of getting it."

'Suddenly, just like that, the atmosphere in the Chamber turned as being much more negative towards me. And it was just – you know – I thought it was a perfectly reasonable thing to say. It wasn't about being a woman, it was just about the whole atmosphere of the Chamber at the time.'

As the noise levels increased, May found herself in an

unexpectedly hostile environment. Even for an experienced politician, standing at the despatch box surrounded by a sea of scepticism can be lonely and intimidating. 'There was just this grumbling, that I had made the slightest suggestion . . .' Was the noise also coming from Conservative MPs? 'I think it probably was, on a sort of a general . . .'

Despite May's acute reverence for the Chamber, she has clearly had difficult moments. Another came when MPs were denied an expected vote on the European arrest warrant. Eurosceptic MPs were incandescent and it was feared that May, then home secretary, could lose the vote on EU law. Amid rowdy and sometimes farcical late-night scenes, the prime minister David Cameron dashed back into the Chamber wearing white tie after a dinner function because the vote was so tight. 'On the European arrest warrant I had to be prepared to speak on a motion I hadn't expected, that we hadn't known was coming, and keep the debate going. It was a high tense moment. Were we going to get the vote through? I always said we would, and we did. But you have to be prepared to deal with the situation as it comes.'

Female MPs, she believes, have to accept the gladiatorial nature of Westminster. 'In politics you have to be prepared for the cut and thrust. There's a lot of serious debate and a lot of serious discussion, but there's a lot of banter and a lot of cut and thrust as well, and you have to be prepared to deal with the situation that comes to you.'

Theresa May was the first of the 1997 intake to be promoted to the shadow cabinet when, in 1999, she was appointed shadow education and employment secretary. In July 2002 she became the first woman appointed as chairman of the Conservative Party. Her speech to the Bournemouth party conference was her bravest and most distinctive political action yet. In front of an elderly, right-wing audience she urged Conservatives to face the fact that they were seen as 'the nasty party'. The Conservatives needed to reflect twenty-first-century Britain, she argued, instead of hankering after 'some mythical place called Middle England' and descending into 'Punch and Judy politics', 'glib moralising' and 'hypocritical finger-wagging'.

As the audience listened in shock, she said: 'Twice we went to the country unchanged, unrepentant, just plain unattractive. And twice we got slaughtered. Soldiering on to the next election without radical, fundamental change is simply not an option.'[17]

The speech caused resentment and anger that proved sticky to shake. Party members and MPs felt she had publicly decried the Conservative brand. In reality, her speech set the template for future attempts to detoxify the party's reputation. Electoral success would remain elusive until that happened.

Less noticed under the clouds of controversy surrounding the 'nasty party' allegation was her passionate call for more female candidates. 'How can we truly claim to be the party of Britain when we don't truly represent Britain in our party?' she asked the sceptical audience in front of her. 'As a Tory woman I'm instinctively suspicious of positive discrimination. I'm a passionate believer in meritocracy. But are we in the Conservative Party really choosing our candidates on merit? Isn't it time we were more open-minded about what makes the best candidate?'

The independence of local Conservative Associations is something to cherish, she continued, 'but with independence comes responsibility. When selecting a candidate you aren't simply choosing someone to represent your association or your area. Your candidate becomes the face of the Conservative Party.'

In a direct plea to audience members who would select the MPs of the future, the unabashed chairman continued: 'So don't ask yourself whether you would be happy to have a drink with this person on a Sunday morning, ask instead what this person says about us.'[18]

In 2001, a year before May's explosive conference speech as chairman, the number of Conservative women had ticked up by one to fourteen. May is not a demonstrative politician who reveals her soul in interviews, but in her speech to the party conference, you could hear the emotion. 'At the last general election thirty-eight new Tory MPs were elected. Of that total only one was a woman and none was from an ethnic minority. Is that fair? Is one half of the population entitled to only one place out of thirty-eight? That's not meritocracy – that's a travesty and it will never be allowed to happen again.'

The speech was one of the most passionate in a career not known for emotion and opens a window into May's priorities for making change. A couple of years later, in 2006, she was involved in a drive to increase the number of Conservative women in Parliament. Dispirited after the 2005 election, at which just seventeen Tory women won seats, it was decided that affirmative action had to be taken. Along with Baroness Jenkin, she co-founded the organisation Women2Win, providing advice and mentoring for women interested in becoming candidates for the party. Anne Jenkin had stood unsuccessfully as a Conservative Party candidate in 1987 and was the granddaughter of Joan Davidson, the only woman to win a seat for the party at the 1945 general election. In Jenkin's view, not enough had changed since then. The two women called a meeting and invited Eleanor Laing MP, Laura Sandys, who would win a seat at the next general election, Shireen Ritchie, the chair of Kensington and Chelsea Conservative Association, and Anne's husband, Bernard Jenkin MP. With no budget or structure, Women2Win was launched on 23 November at Millbank Tower. More than two hundred women attended, including MPs like Maria Miller and Caroline Spelman, alongside a scattering of supportive men. Academics, journalists and Sandra Howard, wife of party leader Michael Howard, were also there.

May explains the motivation: 'It was out of the concern obviously for the small number of women that we'd had on the Conservative benches in the House of Commons and it was around the time of the 2005 leadership election. A number of us thought, Actually there's an opportunity here to raise this as an issue for the two leadership candidates. So we got together and co-founded Women2Win.'

The launch was deliberately timed to coincide with the leadership election between David Cameron and David Davis. May and Jenkin hoped that by highlighting the lack of female Conservative MPs, the two candidates would be forced to prioritise it. Shortly afterwards David Cameron – who went on to win the contest – made a speech on gender representation and launched an A-list that helped push female candidates forward.

After receiving the support of the party leaders, Women2Win morphed into a mentoring scheme: 'Then we were able to take it on to become an organisation that was providing practical support for women, not just women who wanted to be parliamentary candidates but running sessions for women who were interested in politics to show them the different ways they could be involved – as councillors, as MPs, on the voluntary side of the party – opening people's eyes to the opportunities.'

In the 2010 general election, the number of Conservative women MPs swelled to forty-nine (although still limping behind Labour's eighty-one). After the 2015 vote, there were sixty-eight. For the prime minister, numbers matter. 'If you don't have women in politics you're losing out on talent,' May says forcefully. 'Women also bring a different approach, a different experience into politics, and I think that, generally speaking, you get better decisions if you've got a diverse group of people. I've also said, in politics I think it's important to have people from different backgrounds, different experiences, coming into politics as Members of Parliament.' May has never directly criticised what some see as her predecessor David Cameron's 'chumocracy' or 'Notting Hill set', but she adds: 'If sitting around a table you have that diverse group, I think you end up with a better result just from that process of discussion and consideration.'

Do any specific examples illustrate the need for better representation? 'Often women will listen in a different way from men and I think be willing sometimes to try and be more creative in terms of solutions to things.'

The shockwaves created by Theresa May's speech to the Conservative Party conference as chairman temporarily shook her from her perch. In 2003 Michael Howard demoted her and sent her to Transport and the Environment. Then, in 2004, she was shunted sideways to shadow secretary of state for culture, media and sport. It wasn't until David Cameron unexpectedly won the Conservative Party leadership election that she recovered from her brutally honest spell as chairman, and her star was on the ascendant again. The rise started slowly, with the post of shadow leader of the House of Commons in 2005, but in 2009 she was promoted to shadow work and pensions secretary.

A year later Gordon Brown called a general election. It was a tough and hard-fought battle in the shadow of the financial crash. David Cameron's new brand of compassionate Conservatism limped over the line but stopped short of an overall majority. Teaming up with the Liberal Democrats to form a coalition meant MPs from both parties were scrapping over the same number of ministerial jobs. The Liberal Democrats failed to nominate a single woman for a cabinet position. Female MPs were given relatively junior positions slanted towards 'women's issues', with Sarah Teather becoming minister for children and families and Lynne Featherstone parliamentary under-secretary for equalities. Nick Clegg frequently moaned that his party was too 'male and pale' but chose a cabinet team that was exactly that.

Shirley Williams is scathing about the Lib Dems record on women, describing it as 'not good' and saying she is 'cross with them'. 'They are good in theory, and they support all the right things, like parental leave, maternity benefit. All of that is very liberal. But because what we have is a very localised system of choosing MPs . . . very often it means the local hero will be selected for the candidate and the local hero is more often likely to be male than female. We had piles of local government people, councillors, mayors, but because of this localised thing it was much more difficult to get some tremendously able young women.'

Does she think the lack of women has held the Lib Dems back? 'Oh, yes, it held the Lib Dems back. I was the one that fought it.' Like Theresa May, Williams believes the key lies in candidate selections. In the 1980s she pushed for a system in which women would have to be selected in one out of four constituencies. A counter movement was organised with young women wearing T-shirts saying, 'I'm not a token woman.'

'None of them had a clue about how hard it was going to be. They all thought, I'm jolly good, so I'll be swept in. All of them were not yet married and had no children, so they had no idea what they were going to run into. All these luscious young girls who were very pretty took to the platform wearing lovely T-shirts saying: "I'm not a token woman." Mrs Williams may be a token woman but I'm not. And so I lost the vote. I had to put up with it, but I knew it wasn't going to work. I knew with my deepest knowledge and experience of being an MP. They rushed around the place chirping and being bought drinks by nice young men who would become an MP rather than them. Now a lot of them say to me, "You were right."'

David Cameron's highest-profile female appointment was Theresa May. When the new home secretary was unveiled, many surprised journalists and politicians underestimated her. She had been nicknamed 'Theresa May . . . then again she may not' by Tory backbenchers – a fundamental misreading of her character – and some Conservatives dismissed her promotion as a politically correct appointment that would soon come unstuck. David Laws, then a Lib Dem cabinet minister, first met her in 2010 shortly after the election. 'I was sitting in my Treasury office, overlooking St James's Park, me in one armchair and the home secretary in the other, with no officials present. She looked nervous. I felt she was surprised to find herself as home secretary. Frankly, I didn't expect her to last more than a couple of years.'[19] In fact, it would be David Laws who would make history as the shortest serving cabinet minister in modern history when he resigned over expense claims after just seventeen days. Theresa May, in contrast, was to be the longest-serving home secretary since Henry Matthews in 1892.

Around the cabinet table the new home secretary gained a reputation as a quiet but forceful woman who held her ground. She frequently clashed with the education secretary, Michael Gove, and was also prepared to take on the chancellor, George Osborne. As she grew into the role, she became too powerful for David Cameron to either move or demote. He knew she was the biggest challenge to his chosen successor, George Osborne, and Number 10 often eyed the very independent home secretary with suspicion. Unsurprisingly when William Hague resigned as foreign secretary, a role often viewed as a springboard to prime minister, the job went to the less threatening Philip Hammond.

Meanwhile, like her hero Geoffrey Boycott, Theresa May was getting on with the job in front of her. On immigration, the thorniest of political issues, she failed to reduce net migration to the tens of thousands as the prime minister had promised but positioned herself as tough and uncompromising. She also bulldozed through controversial changes to policing. In 2014 she addressed the Police Federation, who had loudly resisted the reforms, and tore into police corruption, racism and 'contempt for the public'. They listened in stunned silence as May delivered the second speech in her career that left her audience aghast.

At the Home Office she became known as a hard-working minister who would often stay up until 1 a.m. working on her red box before getting up at six. The diligent schoolgirl had become a fastidious adult. Nick Herbert, who worked with her as a Home Office minister, said in 2014: 'I've seen people wither under a very steely glare in meetings. You know, she has the ability to command a meeting by sheer force of personality and not to let an issue go. People can't bluff their way through because she'll be on top of the detail.

'Theresa is a fierce manager of her team,' he continued. 'She's more of a micro-manager. It's not always easy for the people working with her.'

Herbert compares Theresa May to Margaret Thatcher, saying that both women 'reached the summit by virtue of tremendous hard work, or being on top of the detail'.[20]

He is not the only Conservative MP to draw parallels between the first and second female prime ministers. In early 2016, when Theresa May was a candidate in the leadership election, the former Conservative chancellor Kenneth Clarke was caught on camera by Sky News making some rather unguarded remarks to Sir Malcolm Rifkind. 'Theresa is a bloody difficult woman, but you and I worked with Margaret Thatcher,' he said, then added: 'I get on all right with her . . . and she is good.'[21]

The two women, however, are as different as they are similar and Theresa May is wary of overstating the parallels. 'I've never compared myself to Margaret Thatcher,' she has said firmly. 'I think there can only ever be one Margaret Thatcher.'[22] While Thatcher famously claimed to owe nothing to women's lib, May has been happily pictured wearing a T-shirt made by the left-leaning Fawcett Society with the slogan: 'This is what a feminist looks like.' As home secretary she rarely lunched or gossiped with journalists but took the time to hold a drinks reception exclusively for female lobby hacks in the Press Gallery bar, jokingly wagging her finger at male reporters who tried to enter.

Theresa May has also prioritised issues that disproportionately relate to women. As home secretary she set up a unit to focus on female genital mutilation and created the first law to tackle modern slavery. In 2007, as shadow minister for women and equality, she launched a report on gender inequality called *Women in the World Today*. It focused on fairness in the workplace – 'one of my passions' – and the gender pay gap. In an interview at the time, she said: 'We tend to take equality between men and women for granted as if it is a box that was ticked years ago. This is not the case. While it is true that we have come a long way with the equality agenda we still have further to go.'[23]

Legislation, for this very Conservative feminist, is not always the answer, which has put her at odds with some women's-rights campaigners. As the shadow minister for women and equalities from 2010 to 2012, one of May's first acts was to scrap 'Harman's Law' – named after her predecessor Harriet Harman – which would have made it a legal requirement for public bodies to help reduce inequality. For Theresa May, stubborn problems like the gender pay gap exist 'because its causes are deep and complex, and yet the tools we have to fight it are blunt and inadequate'.[24] Tackling cultural issues, rather than imposing new laws on businesses, is the answer. She is in favour, therefore, of 'soft' action, such as encouraging girls to make more ambitious career choices at school. Under May's brand of feminism, the law can help women by encouraging flexible working and shared parental leave. Women of child-bearing age will only stop facing discrimination in the workplace after a cultural shift has taken place in which more men take time off work to raise children.

Although she is not a regular face in Westminster's tea rooms and drinking dens, May has quietly nurtured relationships with other female MPs. When Karen Bradley was a Home Office minister May mentored her and, as prime minister, appointed her to her first cabinet. When David Cameron sacked Caroline Spelman and Cheryl Gillan from his cabinet in 2012, Theresa May reached out a hand. Gillan says: 'She's very collected and reserved, I would have almost said she was shy. She's not showy. I sat in cabinet with her and have a great deal of respect for her. When Caroline Spelman and I left cabinet she was the only one that came and had dinner with us. That was nice.'

Cheryl Gillan was only the fifth woman ever to be appointed as a Conservative cabinet secretary when she took the Wales brief in 2010. David Cameron's first cabinet also included Baroness Warsi as Conservative Party chairman and Caroline Spelman as secretary of state for environment, food and rural affairs.

In September 2012 when both Gillan and Spelman were sacked, according to reports David Cameron mentioned Caroline Spelman's age when he dismissed her – she was then fifty-four. This was strongly denied by Number 10 and Spelman has refused to comment. Other articles claimed that three ministers had cried after being dismissed from cabinet. It was widely assumed that the women, Gillan and Spelman, were two of the three.

'I don't cry. It certainly wasn't me. Rubbish,' responds Cheryl Gillan. 'I was really cross with the media because I just thought it was another way of having a go at women. Particularly as I happened to see one of the men who cried!'

Cheryl Gillan refuses to speculate on the reasons for her dismissal. Asked about David Cameron's record with women, she replies: 'I think if you start making an issue it becomes an issue. I'm slightly old-fashioned. I think it's not a question of how many women you've got in the cabinet, it's how competent are the people you've got in the jobs. And I think Theresa will be like that as well.'

The first tremor came shortly after midnight on 24 June 2016: people in Sunderland had resoundingly voted to leave the European Union. As the night rolled into the early hours of the morning, it became clear that the complacent political establishment had made a major miscalculation. Many of Westminster's politicos had gone to sleep already, dreaming merrily of a vote to remain. For those who stayed up to watch the results come in, each announcement pierced the comfort of the status quo until it became clear that the UK had voted to leave the EU.

The next morning things moved at a breathtakingly rapid pace. Journalists scrambled to Downing Street where the prime minister, David Cameron, was due to make a statement. As soon as the door of Number 10 opened and Samantha Cameron walked out to accompany her husband, it was clear that he was to step down. Calling for 'fresh leadership', Cameron continued: 'I will do everything I can as prime minister to steady the ship over the coming weeks and months but I do not think it would be right for me to try and be the captain that steers our country to its next destination.'

The process of choosing a new leader was expected to take three months. In the new post-referendum reality, it would be fewer than three weeks.

The two clear front runners in the race to succeed David Cameron were Theresa May, who had kept a low profile during the referendum campaign, and Boris Johnson, face of the Leave campaign. Just three hours before nominations closed on 29 June, a bombshell hit. The Brexit-supporting justice secretary Michael Gove withdrew his backing for Boris Johnson and announced he was running himself. It was an audacious act from a man who had stood shoulder to shoulder with the former London mayor during the referendum campaign. As the tornado continued, Boris Johnson made a speech in front of a room packed with journalists and MPs who were expecting him to announce his candidacy. 'My friends, you have waited for the punchline of this speech,' he said, then told a shocked audience that he was to withdraw from the race.

Five contenders were left: Theresa May, Michael Gove, work and pensions secretary Stephen Crabb, Leave campaigner and energy minister Andrea Leadsom and former defence secretary Liam Fox.

On 30 June, wearing a tartan suit and standing at a lectern in the library of the Royal United Services Institute, Theresa May attempted to portray a vision of stability and calm in the midst of head-spinning events. 'My pitch is very simple: I'm Theresa May and I'm the best person to be prime minister.' She continued: 'I know I'm not a showy politician. I don't tour the television studios. I don't gossip about people over lunch. I don't go drinking in Parliament's bars. I don't often wear my heart on my sleeve. I just get on with the job in front of me.'

The home secretary easily won the first ballot with 165 votes from MPs, half of the parliamentary party. Michael Gove came a disappointing third and became known as the 'suicide-bomber candidate' – in killing off Boris Johnson's chances, he also blew himself up. As the other candidates were gradually eliminated and their votes redistributed, only Theresa May and Andrea Leadsom were left standing.

Whatever happened in the expected ballot of Conservative members, the party was about to elect its second female prime minister. To date, a woman has never placed below a man in any modern election to the national leadership of the Conservative Party. The opposite is true of Labour. At the time Theresa May said: 'I think it's a very good thing that the Conservative Party has come up with an all-women shortlist for prime minister without being told to.'[25]

Asked why the Conservative Party, not Labour, has sent two women to Number 10, Theresa May replies: 'I'm not sure I can put my finger on it, actually. Maybe the Conservative Party has just had much more of a view that they want the right person for the job regardless of gender. I think it's a question for the Labour Party, actually, rather than for me. Why are the Labour Party so bad at this? Both Margaret Beckett and Harriet Harman have been interim leaders, just standing in as caretakers, but the party has never been prepared to actually elect a woman for the permanent job.'

There was another twist still to come in an extraordinary race. Energy minister Andrea Leadsom had impressed during the referendum campaign and was pitching strongly for the support of Conservatives who had voted to leave the EU. One hideously misplaced step was to destroy her bid for the leadership. In an interview with *The Times*, Leadsom implied that she was better suited than Theresa May to the role of prime minister because she was a mother. Below the headline 'Being a Mother Gives Me Edge on May – Leadsom', she was quoted as saying that Theresa May 'possibly has nieces, nephews, lots of people. But I have children who are going to have children, who will directly be part of what happens next.' An outburst of disgust quickly followed. Leadsom initially denied the quotes, until *The Times* produced a recording of the interview.

Andrea Leadsom's comments were particularly painful because Theresa May had spoken before about her sadness that she and Philip had never been able to have children.

'It just didn't happen,' she told the *Daily Telegraph*. 'This isn't something I generally go into, but things just turned out as they did.' With a rare glimpse of emotion, she added: 'You look at families all the time and see there is something there that you don't have.'[26]

After Leadsom's explosive comments, it was as if the leadership race had hit the fast-forward button. Just days later, Leadsom announced she was withdrawing her candidacy and would support Theresa May as prime minister. She would later be rewarded for clearing the path to power with a job in May's first cabinet.

Theresa May acknowledges the highly emotionally charged campaign. 'This was a contest to elect the leader of the Conservative Party and the person who was going to be prime minister, so there were strong feelings on all sides and people passionate about what they were doing. I think had the campaign gone the length it was originally intended to be, you would have seen more speeches about policy development and things like that coming through, so there was a very intense period at the beginning of the contest. But then, I think that's what you expect from something that's so important.'

Speaking about infertility is painful and private, but Theresa May knows she is public property. 'I like to keep my personal life personal. We couldn't have children, we dealt with it and moved on. I hope nobody would think that mattered. I can still empathise, understand people and care about fairness and opportunity.'[27]

The couple sought medical help to try to conceive, but have since accepted their position. 'Of course, we were both affected by it. You see friends who now have grown-up children, but you accept the hand that life deals you. Sometimes things you wish had happened don't or there are things you wish you'd been able to do, but can't. There are other couples in a similar position.' She added: 'I'm a great believer that you just get on with things. There are lots of problems people have. We are all different, we all have different circumstances, and you have to cope with whatever it is, try not to dwell on things.'[28]

Does she think that she would still have become prime minister if she had had children?

'Well, Margaret Thatcher did,' comes the reply.

When Andrea Leadsom withdrew from the race it was only a matter of time before Theresa May became prime minister. Bruised after the bitter referendum campaign, the Conservatives were in no mood to reopen the leadership contest. In the wake of the vote, Westminster was craving stability.

The day before she became prime minister, David Cameron showed Theresa May around Number 10. Ruth Davidson happened to be in Downing Street when Cameron was giving the incoming premier a tour of her new flat. 'It felt quite historic. One of the interesting things was, knowing Theresa relatively well, I had expected that the weight of the office would make her quite tense about what was coming, as it would for any human being. But, actually, that was almost the most relaxed I've seen her. There was a sense of serenity and calm about her, the idea that she knew exactly what she was going to do.'[29]

The next day, standing outside the door of Number 10, Theresa May delivered her first speech as prime minister, promising to 'make Britain a country that works not for a privileged few, but for every one of us'. 'That means fighting against the burning injustice that if you're born poor you will die on average nine years earlier than others. If you're black, you're treated more harshly by the criminal justice system than if you're white. If you're a white working-class boy, you're less likely than anybody else in Britain to go to university. If you're at a state school, you're less likely to reach the top professions than if you're educated privately. If you're a woman, you will earn less than a man.'

The public pronouncements over, the rehearsed and polished speech finished, what went through the new prime minister's mind as she shut the black door, with the lion knocker, behind her, leaving the cameras flashing on the street outside?

'Well, I was partly thinking about the job that had to be done: this is all very well, thank you for the applause, it's all very nice, but there is a job. And pretty soon I came in and started doing it, in terms of getting the cabinet together.'

Did she feel a moment of history, becoming the second female prime minister? 'It comes back to the way I've always approached things through my life, which is not so much to think, Gosh, here I am, I'm a woman, but to think, Here I am, I've got a job to do, let's do it. I step back and think, What a huge honour and privilege it is to be in this position, and second, We've got a lot of work to do. There are some challenges ahead. It's a huge responsibility to get this right for the UK. I don't think, Gosh, I'm a woman doing this job. I just think, There's a job to do.'

Does that go back to her father, who taught his daughter not to feel limited by her sex? 'I think that's right. It's about not seeing barriers and just saying, "Okay, how can I put my best efforts in?"'

The prime minister acknowledges that perceptive boundaries may exist. 'One person said to me that their daughter, I think she was six or seven, had said to her: "I didn't know a girl could become Prime Minister." I hope that helps to remove any potential perceptive boundaries that there are and actually says to girls, "You can do this."'

Unprompted, Theresa May adds: 'But what I think is nice is, I've had quite a lot of letters from people who have known me over the years, and knew my family, who had said how proud my parents would have been. They never saw me even become a Member of Parliament. They died when I was quite young so it's really nice to think . . .' She pauses for a moment, then adds, with a slight smile, 'You know, I think they would have been proud.'

Theresa May's first cabinet did not achieve the gender balance that some had predicted. Men filled the clear majority of posts, including those of chancellor and foreign secretary. Amber Rudd was appointed home secretary, Liz Truss justice secretary and Karen Bradley went to the Department for Culture. However, noticeably, Theresa May has surrounded herself with women behind the scenes. Along with Nick Timothy, Fiona Hill is her closest adviser and joint chief of staff – a tribal political street-fighter who gets involved in the fray her boss appears to rise above. Three women – Katie Perrior, Lizzie Loudon and Liz Sanderson – make up the political press team, with Helen Bower the prime minister's spokeswoman on the civil service side.

The new prime minister is a private person who has refused to use the emotive parts of her back story for political gain. 'Today, there's an expectation that you get to know public people,' she says. 'In the past, it was much more what you did and how you presented yourself.'[30]

She has been forced to accept life as a public figure, and admits she has 'perhaps less chance' of doing the normal things that she is used to. 'Let's say there are more people surrounding me when I do the normal things. The protection team get to know what Philip's getting for his birthday before he does because they see me buying it.'

At home, traditional roles are roughly maintained. 'I do the cooking, because I enjoy cooking, and Philip puts the bins out.' If the prime minister is away with work, however, 'He's got one or two recipes that he can rustle up for himself. Life as a political husband does mean that you've got to learn to do a bit of cooking for yourself.'

Having a supportive partner, May says, is crucial, and Philip's political influence should not be underestimated. 'He's been a huge support to me. Of course, because he's been involved in the party, he understands politics. He's in a different world career-wise but he understands politics, which I think is very, very helpful. I think it must be very difficult if you have a partner who perhaps doesn't understand what politics is about because there are pressures. There are the dinners that he comes to, the events that he comes to with me. I do think it's very helpful.'

We know a little about the very private prime minister. She loves cooking, owns more than a hundred recipe books, and prefers Jamie Oliver's chuck-it-all-in approach to the precision of Delia Smith. She can seem stand-offish but her quietness is an excellent negotiating tactic, while others babble on to fill the silence. Queen Elizabeth I is the historical figure she most admires, 'a woman who knew her own mind and achieved in a male environment'. She has said she dislikes her nose and was most happy in church on her wedding day.[31] She has type one diabetes, and must inject herself with insulin twice a day for the rest of her life. She went public about her condition after increasing gossip in Westminster about her weight loss – which some put down to getting herself in shape to mount a leadership challenge against David Cameron – and has been known surreptitiously to break the House of Commons rule about not eating in the Chamber to keep her energy level topped up with nuts. Her response is 'to just get on and deal with it . . . you just have to get into a routine'.[32]

Rather than lazy comparisons to Margaret Thatcher, Angela Merkel is a more similar political sister. Both women love holidays hiking in the Alps and are the daughters of Protestant clergymen. Both are said to be non-ideological but a steady pair of hands. Of the German chancellor before she became prime minister, May said: 'There are still people who don't rate her, are a bit dismissive, perhaps because of the way she looks and dresses. And she goes walking in the Tyrol and all that sort of stuff. What matters is, what has she actually done? And when you look at her abilities in terms of negotiation, and steering Germany through a difficult time, then hats off to her.'[33] They are words Theresa May might like to be spoken of herself. The prime minister may have understandable empathy with someone dismissed over the way they dress.

The laser focus on Theresa May's clothes, hair and – above all – shoes began when she gave the infamous 'nasty party' speech. 'Suddenly I was the first woman chair of the Conservative Party, so the press were presented with a different image of somebody there,' she rationalises.

'After that speech I was walking down the corridor and somebody was rushing after me with a media pass on – dare I say it, from *The Times*. They said, "Help! We've got one question!"

'I thought, Oh, right, they're going to ask about elements of the speech.'

She assumed wrong. The journalist cried: 'There's only one question we need the answer to. Where did you get the shoes from?' As she tells the story, there is a subtle undercurrent of frustration that her message was drowned by the packaging.

The next day's press coverage was dominated by her £120 pair of Russell & Bromley leopard print heels. The *Daily Telegraph*'s front page, for instance, carried a picture of the shoes with the headline: 'A Stiletto in the Tories' Heart'. When she was out canvassing ahead of the 2005 election, according to her campaign manager she would wear comfortable shoes in the car, changing into a pair of heels before she got out. 'If she turned up at a meeting and she wasn't wearing them, the first thing people would say is, "Where are the shoes, Theresa?"' Sam Olsen revealed in a *Guardian* interview, adding: 'The shoes are a leopard-print curse because she's now expected to wear them all the time.'[34]

May believes women should not attempt to ape their male colleagues, but be themselves. Women can be serious politicians while wearing leopard-print kitten heels. I suspect she is more relaxed about the attention her shoes receive than many realise. Sometimes she may even enjoy it. 'It has, I think, a different aspect to it that many people who comment on it don't kind of appreciate. First of all, it can be quite an ice breaker for people who aren't sure about meeting a politician. A few years ago I was in a lift in the House of Commons and there was a young woman in the lift and obviously from her pass she was working in the House. I think she was a researcher for somebody. I happened to look down and said, "Oh, nice pair of shoes." She said, "I like yours as well." And she looked at me and said, "Your shoes got me interested in politics." And here she was working in the House of Commons. So it's not a bad thing.'

Her cleavage has also been a regular item for discussion. When she was the shadow leader of the House in 2006, Simon Hoggart wrote of her in the *Guardian*: 'She was dressed entirely in black but, far from covering up her body, her clothing revealed a great deal more of it – more, to be frank, than I can recall any woman MP showing before . . . a quantity of cleavage that would not have disgraced a page-three stunner opening a nightclub.'[35] In 2016 the media judged Theresa May's cleavage to have stolen the show from George Osborne's Budget as she sat alongside the chancellor in the House of Commons. 'I had no idea the photographs would come out like that,' she said in an interview. 'It was a female photographer – I could see her moving around and I thought, Surely she must have enough shots of George Osborne already. Why is she taking more?'[36]

If she is irritated by the focus on her appearance, publicly Theresa May stifles her feelings. Besides, this is a woman who is genuinely interested in fashion and says she would take a subscription to *Vogue* as her luxury item on a desert island. 'I always tell women, "You have to be yourself, don't assume you have to fit into a stereotype," and if your personality is shown through your clothes or shoes, so be it.'[37]

Since May became prime minister, the attention has only intensified with a series of newspaper articles on the 'power bob' – or 'pob'. Apparently the short haircut signals 'dependable, no nonsense, tough on immigration'.[38] Nicola Sturgeon admits being flabbergasted to see herself featured in an article alongside fellow 'power bobbers' Theresa May, Hillary Clinton and Angela Merkel. 'You look at the pictures and think, These are four completely different hairstyles! Most people looking at them would probably have the same reaction as me.'

Theresa May is far more sanguine about the focus on her appearance. 'I think people should be true to themselves and what they are. I enjoy clothes, I enjoy fashion, and I've had various descriptions of what I wear over the years, some positive, some not. You get more used to it and take it in your stride a bit more easily but of course it's frustrating.'

Journalists criticising her favourite clothes are irritating. 'If you feel you've bought a really nice outfit and you look great in it and somebody makes some disparaging comment about it, you do feel a bit, well, hang on a minute . . . That's just natural.'[39]

Theresa May entered Parliament in 1997 but she shares some qualities with the earlier generation of female fighters, who refused to accept they were victims. She wrote in 2009: 'I have worked in two traditionally male-dominated careers, firstly in banking before moving into politics. In both professions I have never allowed being a woman to be an excuse or an obstacle. When I was working in the City I tried to see myself as a person, achieving what I did on my own merit not because of or in spite of my sex. And it has been the same in politics.' She added: 'We tend to focus on the lack of women in business or politics or how tough it can be to balance work and family life when really we should be celebrating the great things being done by the women who are there.'[40]

The prime minister is a feminist, who believes it is a travesty that women are so poorly represented in Parliament and has prioritised legislation on issues that disproportionately affect women. 'You do have to be tenacious,' she once said, 'Things don't move quickly and there's an inbuilt inertia in the system. If you take your foot off the pedal, it will move back to where it was. You just have to keep going, not give up basically, until you achieve the ultimate goal.'[41]

Theresa May backs recent changes to Parliament including reforming the hours that MPs sit. 'There have been some changes to the times of Parliament sitting since I came in, which I think personally is important. I think each generation changes Parliament slightly. What I would say is, there is less sitting around in smoke-filled bars – partly because people aren't able to smoke in most of the rooms. Lots of people think the hours are about women but actually it's about the men, these days, who very often have young families that they would want to get to see. Each generation brings a slightly different approach to it.'

Reforming the selection process has been another personal crusade. 'I think it's been important to ensure that the selection process values the different skills that women and men have, and recognise the variety of skills that are needed for a Member of Parliament. There are many fine examples of female MPs being out there doing fantastic jobs in the constituency, and that hopefully gets the message across that this is a job that's not about gender, it's about the merits of the individual.'

May's approach to female-focused political reform is complex. She chose not to appoint a gender-balanced cabinet, scrapped some equality legislation and rejects the idea of all-women short-lists. 'Being a woman is not a barrier to anything,' she once said. Not all women would agree with her particular brand of feminism.

To understand Theresa May's philosophy, it can be helpful to return to the Geoffrey Boycott mantra that sometimes you should stop complaining and just get on with the job. 'My whole philosophy is about doing, not talking,' she says.[42] 'I think the aim must be – and this is partly what my aim was in terms of selections in the Conservative Party – the point at which nobody looks at gender, they just look at the merits of the individual. I think that's the important thing.'

The implication is that there can be too much focus on gender. If true equality is gender-blind, sometimes women should simply knuckle down, stop talking and start doing, or, to use a Theresa May mantra, 'just get on with the job'. That is all very well, as long as it is possible for them to reach the job to get on with it. That Theresa Brasier, the rugby-mad vicar's daughter from Oxfordshire, could achieve the greatest position in the United Kingdom is because she is standing on the shoulders of the queens, the writers, the campaigners, the suffragists, the militants, the pioneers, the class warriors, the ceiling smashers, the fighters, the change-makers and the rebels who have gone before her.

Notes

The Queens

1 http://www.parliament.uk/about/living-heritage/evolutionofparliament/parliamentwork/offices-and-ceremonies/overview/the-speaker/
2 Agnes Strickland, *Lives of the Queens of England: from the Norman Conquest*, vol. X (Lea and Blanchard, 1847), p. 189.
3 Quoted in ibid., vol. XI, p. 117.
4 Quoted in John Van der Kiste, *William and Mary* (History Press, 2003), p. 113.
5 Ibid., p. 114.
6 Ibid., p. 115.
7 Quoted in Chris Bryant, *Parliament: the Biography, Volume One: Ancestral Voices* (Random House, 2015), p. 350.
8 Quoted in Joyce Marlow, *Votes for Women: The Virago Book of Suffragettes* (Virago, 2001), p. 17.
9 Disraeli, Hansard, House of Commons, 20 June 1848, vol. 99, col. 950.

The Writers

1 http://spartacus-educational.com/STUlevellers.htm
2 Paula McDowell, (ed.), *The Early Modern Englishwoman: Essential Works: Elinor James* (Ashgate, 2005), p. 130.
3 Ibid., p. 223.
4 John Dunton, *The Life and Errors of John Dunton, Citizen of London*, vol. 1 (London, 1705; reprinted New York: Burt Frankling, 1996) pp. 252–3.

5 Mary Beth Norton, *Separated by their Sex: Women in Public and Private in the Colonial Atlantic World* (Cornell University Press, 2011), p. 74.

6 Quoted in Catherine Mason Sutherland, *The Eloquence of Lady Astell* (University of Calgary Press, 2005), p. xiii.

7 George Ballard, *Memoirs of several ladies of Great Britain, who have been celebrated for their writings of skill in the learned languages, arts, and sciences* (Oxford, 1752), p. 387.

8 Mary Astell, *A Serious Proposal to the Ladies Part I and II*, ed. Patricia Springborg (Broadview Literary Texts, 2002), p. 51.

9 Ibid., p. 54.

10 Florence M. Smith, *Mary Astell* (Columbia University Press, 1916), p. 34.

11 Mary Wollstonecraft, *Thoughts on the Education of Daughters* (J. Johnson, 1787), p. 94.

12 Barbara Taylor, *Mary Wollstonecraft and the Feminist Imagination* (Cambridge University Press, 2003), pp. 26–7.

13 Ibid.

14 Mary Wollstonecraft, *A Vindication of the Rights of Women* (London, 1792), p. ix.

15 Ibid., p. 329.

16 Mary Wollstonecraft, *Letters Written In Sweden, Norway and Denmark.* (Oxford University Press, 2009), ed. Tone Brekke and Jon Mee, p. xxii.

17 Virginia Woolf, *Mary Wollstonecraft, The Common Reader*, https://ebooks.adelaide.edu.au/w/woolf/virginia/w91c2/chapter13.html#section17

The Campaigners

1 Quoted in Augustus Hare (ed.), *Life and Letters of Maria Edgeworth*, vol. 2 (Arnold, 1894), pp. 66–7.

2 Christopher Silvester, *The Literary Companion to Parliament* (Sinclair-Stevenson, 1996), pp. 587–8.

3 Millicent Garrett Fawcett, *Some Eminent Women of Our Time:*

Short Biographical Sketches (Macmillan, 1889), p. 9.

4 Mary Carpenter, *Reformatory Schools: For the Children of the Perishing and Dangerous Classes, and for Juvenile Offenders* (Cambridge University Press, 2013), p. vi.

5 *Morning Chronicle*, 23 June 1836.

6 Diane Atkinson, *The Criminal Conversation of Mrs Norton* (Arrow, 2013), pp. 9–10.

7 K. Chase and M. Levenson, *The Spectacle of Intimacy: a Public Life for the Victorian Family* (Princeton University Press, 2008), p. 38.

8 Mary Lyndon Shanley, *Feminism, Marriage and the Law in Victorian England* (Princeton University Press, 1993), p. 23.

9 Quoted in ibid., p. 26.

10 Quoted in Elizabeth K. Helsinger, *The Woman Question* (Manchester University Press, 1983), p. 15.

11 Shanley, *Feminism, Marriage*, p. 22.

12 Quoted in Kristine Wardle Frederickson, *Josephine E. Butler and Christianity in the British Victorian Feminist Movement* (ProQuest, 2008), p. 38.

13 Ibid.

14 Jane Jordan and Ingrid Sharp, *Josephine Butler and the Prostitution Campaigns* (Taylor & Francis, 2003), p. 4.

15 Ibid.

16 Dale Spender, *Josephine Butler: Sexual Economics* (Routledge and Kegan Paul, 1982), p. 340.

17 Jordan and Sharp, *Josephine Butler*, p. 6.

18 Margaret Forster, *Significant Sisters: The Grassroots of Active Feminism 1839–1939* (Vintage, 2004), p. 192.

19 Robert Lacey, *Great Tales from English History* (Little, Brown, 2006), p. 179.

20 'White Slavery in London', *The Link*, no. 21 (Saturday, 23 June 1888).

21 Lacey, *Great Tales*, p. 181.

22 Quoted in Elizabeth Longford, *Eminent Victorian Women* (Weidenfeld & Nicolson, 1981), p. 146.

23 Sheila Rowbotham, *Hidden from History: 300 Years of Women's Oppression and the Fight Against It* (Pluto Press, 1977), p. 74.

24 Roger Manvell, *The Trial of Annie Besant and Charles Bradlaugh* (Pemberton, 1976), p. 91.

The Suffragists

1 Quoted in Henry Hunt, *To the radical reformers, male and female, of England, Ireland and Scotland* (Oxford, 1820), p. 38.

2 Hansard, House of Commons, 3 August 1832, vol. 14, col. 1086.

3 *Morning Post*, 8 August 1832.

4 *Bell's Life*, August 1832.

5 *The Times*, 11 August 1832, p. 13.

6 Quoted in Sheila Rowbotham, *Hidden from History: 300 Years of Women's Oppression and the Fight Against It* (Pluto Press, 1977), p. 35.

7 John Stuart Mill, Hansard, House of Commons, 20 May 1867, vol. 187, col. 820.

8 Quoted in Sandra Holton and Dr June Purvis (eds), *Votes for Women* (Taylor & Francis, 2002), p. 72.

9 *The Englishwoman's Review*, January 1868.

10 Quoted in Holton and Purvis, *Votes for Women*, p. 67.

11 Quoted in Joyce Marlow (ed.), *Votes for Women! The Virago Book of Suffragettes* (Virago, 2001,) p. 14.

12 Ibid., p. 8.

13 Peter Catterall, Wolfram Kaiser, Ulrike Walton-Jordan, *Reforming the Constitution: Debates in Twentieth-century Britain* (Routledge, 2014), p. 161.

14 Quoted in Cheryl R. Jorgensen-Earp, *Speeches and Trials of the Militant Suffragettes: The Women's Social and Political Union, 1903–1918* (Fairleigh Dickinson University Press, 1999), p. 281.

15 Hansard, House of Lords, 12 June 1907, vol. 175, col. 1355.

16 www2.warwick.ac.uk/fac/arts/.../women_and_politics_ after_1850.pptx

17 Quoted in Ruth Adam, *A Woman's Place: 1910–1975* (Chatto & Windus, 1975), p. 29.

18 Quoted in Andrew Rosen, *Rise Up Women! The Militant Campaign of the Women's Social and Political Union* (Routledge, 2013), p. 157.

19 Millicent Garrett Fawcett, *The Women's Victory – and After: Personal Reminiscences, 1911–1918* (Cambridge University Press, 2011), p. 22.

20 Ibid., p. 8.

21 Millicent Garrett Fawcett, *Common Cause*, 14 August 1914, p. 384

22 Fawcett, Garrett *The Women's Victory*, p. 115.

23 Quoted in Gerry Holloway, *Women and Work in Britain Since 1840* (Routledge, 2005), p. 127.

24 Millicent Garrett Fawcett, *What I Remember* (T. Fisher Unwin, 1924), p. 247.

The Militants

1 Quoted in Joyce Marlow (ed.), *Votes for Women! The Virago Book of Suffragettes* (Virago, 2001), p. 35.

2 *Manchester Guardian*, 16 October 1905.

3 Karen Lynnea Piper, *Cartographic Fictions: Maps, Race, and Identity* (Rutgers University Press, 2002), p. 21.

4 *Guardian*, 16 October 1905, https://www.theguardian.com/ century/1899-1909/Story/0,,126368,00.html

5 E. Sylvia Pankhurst, *The Suffragette Movement* (London, 1931), pp. 52–3.

6 Hannah Mitchell, *From The Hard Way Up* (Faber & Faber, 1968), quoted in Marlow, *Votes for Women!*, p. 36.

7 Ibid., p. 37.

8 Christabel Pankhurst, *The Policy of the WSPU, The Suffragette*, 18 October 1912, p. 6.

9 Quoted in Marlow, *Votes for Women!*, p. 267.

10 Lady Constance Lytton, *Prisons and Prisoners: Some Personal Experiences* (William Heinemann, 1914), p. 39.

11 Ibid., pp. 239–41.

12 Quoted in Cheryl R. Jorgensen-Earp, *Speeches and Trials of the Militant Suffragettes* (Fairleigh Dickinson Press, 1999), p. 107.

13 Lytton, *Prisons and Prisoners*, p. 269.

14 Lyndsey Jenkins, *Lady Constance Lytton: Aristocrat, Suffragette, Martyr* (Biteback Publishing, 2015), p. 170.

15 Christabel Pankhurst to Ada Flatman, 19 January 1910, in Ada Flatman Papers, Suffragette Fellowship Collection, Museum of London.

16 Emmeline Pankhurst, *The Times*, 28 January 1913.

17 Quoted in Marlow, *Votes for Women!*, p. 151.

18 *Daily Herald*, 4 July 1912.

19 Quoted in Marlow, *Votes for Women!*, p. 195.

20 Robert Lacey, *Great Tales from English History* (Little, Brown, 2006), p. 206.

21 Ibid., p. 208.

22 Ibid., p. 208.

23 Jill Liddington, *Rebel Girls: How Votes for Women Changed Edwardian Lives* (Virago, 2006), p. 212.

24 Stephen Wade, *Foul Deeds and Suspicious Deaths around Doncaster* (Wharncliffe Local History, Pen and Swords Books, 2010), p. 96.

25 Liddington, *Rebel Girls*, p. 216.

26 Cheryl R. Jorgensen-Earp, *The Transfiguring Sword: The Just War of the Women's Social and Political Union* (University of Alabama Press, 2015), p. 1.

27 Ibid., p. 1.

28 Ibid., p. 2.

29 *The Times*, 4 November 1972.

30 E. Sylvia Pankhurst, *The Suffragette Movement - An Intimate Account of Persons and Ideals* (Read Books, 2013), p. 455.

31 Elizabeth Crawford, *The Women's Suffrage Movement: A Reference Guide 1866–1928* (Routledge, 2001), p. 342.

The Pioneers

1 *Journal*, 28 July 2012, http://www.thejournal.ie/my-favourite-speech-mary-lou-mcdonald-532830-Jul2012
2 'St Patrick's Day Manoeuvres of the ICA', *Workers Republic*, 1 April 1916.
3 Ann Matthews, *Renegades: Irish Republican Women 1900–1922* (Mercier Press, 2010), p. 129.
4 Gina Sigillito, *The Daughters of Maeve: 50 Irish Women Who Changed the World* (Kensington Publishing, 2007), p. 89.
5 Karen Margaret Steele, *Women, Press and Politics During the Irish Revival* (Syracuse University Press, 2007), p. 123.
6 Quoted in Susan Ratcliffe, *The Concise Oxford Dictionary of Quotations* (Oxford University Press, 2011), p. 18.
7 Lady Astor, *My Two Countries* (Doubleday, Page, 1923), p. 4.
8 Quoted in Adrian Fort, *Nancy: The Story of Lady Astor* (Random House, 2012), p. 161.
9 Ruth Adam, *A Woman's Place, 1910–1975* (Persephone Books, 2000), p. 91.
10 Fort, *Nancy*, p. 169.
11 Hansard, House of Commons, 24 February 1920, vol. 125, col. 1621.
12 Ibid., col. 1624.
13 Astor, *My Two Countries*, p. 5.
14 http://www.independent.co.uk/news/uk/home-news/my-dear-you-are-ugly-but-tomorrow-i-shall-be-sober-and-you-will-still-be-ugly-winston-churchill-tops-8878622.html
15 http://www.plymouth.gov.uk/20_winston_churchill_biog_final.pdf
16 *The Times*, 29 November 1919.
17 Fort, *Nancy*, p. 170.
18 Shirley Williams, *Climbing the Bookshelves* (Virago, 2009), p. 147.
19 Astor, *My Two Countries*, p. 52.
20 Ibid., p. 57.

21 Hansard, House of Commons, 9 November 1921, vol. 148, cc. 467–8.
22 J. P. Wearing (ed.), *Bernard Shaw and Nancy Astor* (University of Toronto Press, 2005), p. 14.

The Class Warriors

1 Margaret Bondfield, Hansard, House of Commons, 29 March 1928, vol. 215, cc. 1416–17.
2 Matt Perry, *'Red Ellen' Wilkinson: Her Ideas, Movements and World* (Manchester University Press, 2014), p. 209.
3 *Guardian*, 4 January 1998.
4 Quoted in Lise Sanders, *Consuming Fantasies: Labor, Leisure and the London Shopgirl, 1880–1920* (Ohio State University Press, 2006), p. 46.
5 http://www.bbc.co.uk/news/magazine-28104806
6 Matt Perry, *Red Ellen Wilkinson: Her Ideas, Movement and World* (Manchester University Press, 2014), p. 209.
7 Quoted in Peter Hennessy, *Never Again: Britain 1945–51* (Penguin Books, 1992), p. 159.
8 Ibid., p. 162.
9 Quoted in Susan Penderson, *Eleanor Rathbone and the Politics of Conscience* (Yale University Press, 2004), p. 2.
10 Quoted in David Marquand, *Britain since 1918 – The Strange Career of British Democracy* (Weidenfeld & Nicolson, 2008), p. 138.
11 Quoted in Lynda McDougall, *Westminster Women* (Vintage, 1998), p. 191.
12 Barbara Castle, *Fighting All the Way* (Macmillan, 1993), p. 364.
13 Quoted in Sheila Rowbotham, *A Century of Women* (Viking, 1999), p. 53.
14 BBC interview, 1 October 1967. https://www.ft.com/content/470a8d67-8f94-3361-a223-30c3bfa37e65
15 Castle, *Fighting All the Way*, p. 339.
16 Ibid., p. 417.

17 *Guardian*, 4 May 2002. https://www.theguardian.com/news/2002/may/04/guardianobituaries.obituaries

18 Quoted in Andrew Marr, *A History of Modern Britain* (Pan Macmillan, 2009), p. 321.

19 Kevin Jefferys, *Labour Forces: from Ernie Bevin to Gordon Brown* (I. B. Tauris, 2002), p. 178.

20 Bernard Donoughue, *Downing Street Diary* (Pimlico 2009), p. 34.

21 Ibid., p. 362.

22 Quoted in Sheila Rowbotham, *A Century of Women* (Viking, 1999), p. 47.

23 Ibid., p. 51.

24 Lisa Martineau, *Politics and Power: Barbara Castle* (Andre Deutsch, 2000), p. 17.

25 Castle, *Fighting All the Way*, p. 489.

The Ceiling Smashers Part 1

1 John Campbell, *Margaret Thatcher: The Iron Lady*, vol. 2 (Vintage, 2008), p. 473.

2 http://www.telegraph.co.uk/finance/comment/alistair-osborne/9980292/Margaret-Thatcher-one-policy-that-led-to-more-than-50-companies-being-sold-or-privatised.html

3 Campbell, *Thatcher*, p. 114.

4 Jonathan Aitken, *Margaret Thatcher: Power and Personality* (A. & C. Black, 2013), p. 73.

5 John Blundell, *Margaret Thatcher: A Portrait of the Iron Lady* (Algora, 2008), p. 38.

6 Aitken, *Thatcher*, p. 78.

7 Margaret Thatcher, *The Path to Power* (HarperCollins, 1995), p. 94.

8 Aitken, *Thatcher*, p. 79.

9 Ibid., p. 81.

10 Ibid., p. 98.

11 Tony Benn, *The Benn Diaries* (Arrow, 1996), pp. 363–4.

12 Campbell, *Thatcher*, p. 44.

13 Thatcher, *Path to Power*, p. 144.

14 *Guardian*, 8 April 2013.

15 Earl A. Reitan, *The Thatcher Revolution* (Rowman & Littlefield, 2003), p. 16.

16 Hansard, House of Lords, 10 April 2013, vol. 560, col. 1169.

17 *Guardian*, 8 April 2013.

18 Thatcher, *The Path to Power*, p. 277.

19 Hansard, House of Lords, 10 April 2013, vol. 560, col. 1186.

20 Bernard Donoughue, *Downing Street Diary* (Pimlico, 2009), p. 310.

21 Hansard, House of Lords, 10 April 2013, vol. 560, col. 1163.

22 Campbell, *Thatcher*, vol. 2 (Vintage, 2008), p. 473.

23 Hansard, House of Lords, 10 April 2013, vol. 560, col. 1160.

24 Hugo Young, *One of Us* (Macmillan, 1989), p. 245.

25 Hansard, House of Lords, 10 April 2013, vol. 560, col. 1128.

26 Quoted in Campbell, *Thatcher*, vol. 2, p. 474.

27 Ibid., p. 477.

28 Quoted in Brian Walden, 'Why I Can Never, Never Let Up', *Sunday Times*, 8 May 1988.

29 Barbara Castle, *Fighting All The Way* (Macmillan, 1994), p. 458.

30 Campbell, *Thatcher*, vol. 2, p. 474.

31 Hansard, House of Lords, 10 April 2013, vol. 560, col. 1635.

32 Ibid., col. 1136.

33 Ibid., 10 April 2013, col. 1137.

34 Campbell, *Thatcher*, vol.2, p. 124.

35 Aitken, *Thatcher*, p. 562.

36 Ibid., p. 129.

37 Quoted in Sheila Rowbotham, *A Century of Women* (Viking, 1999), p. 294.

38 *Guardian*, 8 April 2013.

39 Aitken, *Thatcher*, p. 86.

40 Margaret Thatcher, *The Downing Street Years* (HarperCollins, 1995), p. 855.

41 Walden, *Sunday Times*, 8 May 1988.

42 Campbell, *Thatcher*, vol. 2, p. 472.

The Fighters

1 Shirley Williams, *Climbing the Bookshelves* (Virago, 2010), p. 119.
2 Ibid., p. 235.
3 Ibid., p. 300.
4 Ibid., p. 116.
5 Ibid., p. 394.
6 Alan Clark, *Diaries in Power* (Phoenix, 1994), p. 29.

The Ceiling Smashers Part 2

1 Betty Boothroyd, *Betty Boothroyd: The Autobiography* (Arrow, 2002), p. 38.
2 Ibid., p. 50.
3 Ibid., p. 56.
4 Ibid., p. 61.
5 Ibid., p. 140.
6 Ibid., p. 149.
7 Ibid., p. 159.
8 Ibid., p. 184.
9 Ibid., p. 229.
10 Ibid., p. 404.
11 Ibid., p. 62.

The Change-makers

1 Sarah Childs, *New Labour's Women MPs: Women Representing Women* (Routledge, 2004), p. viii.
2 Ibid., p. vii.
3 Ibid., p. vii.
4 http://www.theguardian.com/politics/2014/jul/08/harriet-harman-gordon-brown-inequality-labour-sexism
5 *Daily Mail*, 8 February 2012.
6 *PM*, BBC Radio 4, 15 September 2006.
7 BBC Radio Northampton, 15 September 2006.

8 http://www.theguardian.com/politics/2014/jul/08/harriet-harman-gordon-brown-inequality-labour-sexism

9 Ibid.

10 http://www.scotsman.com/news/just-female-window-dressing-full-text-of-caroline-flint-s-resignation-letter-1-469301

11 http://www.huffingtonpost.co.uk/2015/09/14/jeremy-corbyn-defends-failure-to-appoint-women-to-top-shadow-cabinet-jobs_n_8133064.html

12 https://www.google.co.uk/amp/www.independent.co.uk/news/uk/politics/jeremy-corbyn-labour-reshuffle-shadow-cabinet-reelection-purge-mps-a7351196.html

The New Rebels

1 David Torrance, *Nicola Sturgeon: A Political Life* (Birlinn, 2015), p. 97.

2 Ibid., p. 97.

3 http://www.telegraph.co.uk/news/politics/SNP/11117913/Nicola-Sturgeon-predicts-independence-one-day-as-she-launches-bid-to-replace-Alex-Salmond.html

4 https://www.holyrood.com/articles/inside-politics/full-interview-nicola-sturgeon

5 Nicola Sturgeon, Alternative MacTaggart Lecture, Edinburgh International Television Festival, 2015.

6 http://www.bbc.co.uk/news/uk-scotland-scotland-politics-37270135

Prime Minister and Parliamentarian

1 http://news.bbc.co.uk/1/hi/in_depth/education/2000/first_day1741078.stm

2 http://www.telegraph.co.uk/news/politics/9762170/Theresa-May-interview-I-probably-was-Goody-Two-Shoes-at-school.html

3 Theresa May, *Desert Island Discs*, BBC Radio 4, 2014.

4 Ibid.

5 http://www.telegraph.co.uk/news/politics/9762170/Theresa-May-interview-I-probably-was-Goody-Two-Shoes-at-school.html

6 May, *Desert Island Discs*, 2014.

7 Ibid.

8 http://www.telegraph.co.uk/news/politics/9762170/Theresa-May-interview-I-probably-was-Goody-Two-Shoes-at-school.html

9 Quoted in Virginia Blackburn, *Theresa May: The Downing Street Revolution* (John Blake, 2016), p. 52.

10 http://www.bbc.co.uk/news/uk-politics-36660372

11 May, *Desert Island Discs*, 2014.

12 http://www.dailymail.co.uk/news/article-3671725/We-affected-not-having-children-coped-Exclusive-interview-Theresa-reveals-softer-steely-favourite-PM-says-EU-chiefs-talk-UK-Brexit.html

13 http://www.theguardian.com/politics/2014/jul/27/theresa-may-profile-beyond-the-public-image

14 http://www.dailymail.co.uk/news/article-3671725/We-affected-not-having-children-coped-Exclusive-interview-Theresa-reveals-softer-steely-favourite-PM-says-EU-chiefs-talk-UK-Brexit.html

15 May, *Desert Island Discs*, 2014.

16 http://news.bbc.co.uk/news/vote2001/hi/english/key_people/newsid_1179000/1179350.stm

17 http://www.theguardian.com/politics/2002/oct/07/conservatives2002.conservatives1

18 Ibid.

19 http://www.bbc.co.uk/news/uk-politics-36660372

20 https://nickherbert.net/2014/07/11/my-interview-about-theresa-may/

21 http://news.sky.com/story/watch-ken-clarke-ridicules-tory-candidates-10423744

22 http://www.standard.co.uk/lifestyle/london-life/theresa-may-on-the-conservative-leadership-election-and-being-the-next-uk-prime-minister-a3288226.html

23 http://news.bbc.co.uk/1/hi/business/8033607.stm

24 Ibid.

25 http://www.telegraph.co.uk/women/politics/theresa-may-interview-red-boxes-are-very-much-banned-from-the-be/

26 http://www.telegraph.co.uk/news/politics/9762170/Theresa-May-interview-I-probably-was-Goody-Two-Shoes-at-school.html

27 http://www.telegraph.co.uk/women/politics/theresa-may-interview-red-boxes-are-very-much-banned-from-the-be/

28 http://www.dailymail.co.uk/news/article-3671725/We-affected-not-having-children-coped-Exclusive-interview-Theresa-reveals-softer-steely-favourite-PM-says-EU-chiefs-talk-UK-Brexit.html

29 http://www.theguardian.com/politics/2016/aug/21/ruth-davidson-never-been-caught-out-tells-you-something-interview-leader-scottish-conservatives

30 http://www.telegraph.co.uk/news/politics/9762170/Theresa-May-interview-I-probably-was-Goody-Two-Shoes-at-school.html

31 http://www.essentialsurrey.co.uk/culture/interview-theresa-may-prime-minister/

32 May, *Desert Island Discs*, 2014.

33 http://www.telegraph.co.uk/news/politics/9762170/Theresa-May-interview-I-probably-was-Goody-Two-Shoes-at-school.html

34 http://www.theguardian.com/politics/2014/jul/27/theresa-may-profile-beyond-the-public-image

35 http://www.theguardian.com/politics/2006/oct/13/immigration-policy.houseofcommons

36 http://www.telegraph.co.uk/women/politics/theresa-may-interview-red-boxes-are-very-much-banned-from-the-be/

37 Ibid.

38 https://www.theguardian.com/fashion/2016/jul/26/pob-power-haircut-women-theresa-may-political-bob

39 http://www.dailymail.co.uk/news/article-2380142/My-shocking-illness-Home-Secretary-Theresa-May-reveals-Type-1-diabetes-needs-daily-injections--vows-continue-political-career.html

40 http://news.bbc.co.uk/1/hi/business/8033607.stm
41 http://www.dailymail.co.uk/news/article-2380142/My-shocking-illness-Home-Secretary-Theresa-May-reveals-Type-1-diabetes-needs-daily-injections--vows-continue-political-career.html
42 http://www.telegraph.co.uk/women/politics/theresa-may-interview-red-boxes-are-very-much-banned-from-the-be/

Acknowledgements

Writing this book has been a joy and a privilege but writing the acknowledgements is an exercise destined to fail. It is impossible to thank everyone who has helped to shape the story of women in politics. Every day I am inspired by the remarkable and diverse bunch of female MPs in Westminster – many of whom have made significant personal sacrifices in order to represent their constituents and causes – and the many journalists and campaigners who influence politics in the UK. Delving into the histories of the remarkable women who have gone before us has been a humbling experience. We are all standing on their shoulders, and owe them more than we can know.

I would first like to offer my most sincere thanks to the women who have agreed to be interviewed as part of this book. I was amazed to find so many towering female politicians accept my request to speak to them.

Theresa May, Britain's second female Prime Minister, kindly hosted me in Downing Street at a time when she would have been forgiven for having more pressing engagements in her diary. Some of the other women politicians who generously gave their time include Diane Abbott, Dame Margaret Beckett, Baroness Betty Boothroyd, Baroness Lynda Chalker, Yvette Cooper, Mary Creagh, Edwina Currie, Ruth Davidson, Caroline Flint, Cheryl Gillan, Patricia Hewitt, Dame Margaret Hodge, Liz Kendall, Caroline Lucas, Lisa Nandy, Clare Short, Jacqui Smith, Dame Caroline Spelman, Nicola Sturgeon, Ann Widdecombe and Baroness Shirley Williams. During my time as a lobby correspondent I have had countless conversations with other female politicians who have also helped to shape my understanding of what it means to be a woman in Westminster.

This book would not have been written without the help of James Saville, my agent and friend, who told me it was about time that someone wrote a book telling the story of women in politics and that I should step up and do it. He put me in touch with the crack team at Hodder: the brilliant Fiona Rose, Hazel Orme and Rebecca Mundy. I would also like to thank my friend Faye Jones for reading my drafts and making sure I didn't miss every deadline.

Sky News have – as always – been tremendously supportive throughout. Particular thanks go to John Ryley, Esme Wren, Lucy Aitkens and Lucy Ellison.

My biggest thanks are saved for the people who always deserve my biggest thanks. To the rock of my family: my mum, dad and brother. And to Ben, as ever, I couldn't have done any of this without you.

The mistakes and unforgiveable omissions – and there will be many – are mine alone.

Index

198–200, 203, 204, 206–7, 228

Flint, Peter 198

Flynn, Pul 161

Foot, Michael 111

force-feeding 2, 72, 73–4, 80–81, 90

Ford 116–17

Forsyth, Michael, Baron 127

Forth, Eric 238

fossil fuels adjournment debate 224

Foster, Arlene 210–11

Fox, Liam 251

franchise *see* suffrage

Frankland, Pat 234

Fraser, Murdo 216, 217

French Revolution 23, 25

Gandhi, Indira 122

Gang of Four 145

Garrett, Agnes 59

Garrett, Elizabeth 57

Garrett, Millicent *see* Fawcett, Millicent, née Garrett

gay sex 143, 155

  see also homophobia; homosexuality

gender pay gap 210, 211, 248–9

George V 77, 104–5

Gilbert, John, Baron 128

Gillan, Cheryl 131–2, 158–9, 177, 249–50

Girton College, Cambridge 57

Gladstone, Herbert 75

Gladstone, William 58

Glasgow 212–13, 214, 216

Glorious Revolution 8, 10–11, 17

Godwin, William 28

Goff, Sir Park 97

Goldie, Annabel 216

Goodman, Elinor 3–4

Goodman, Len 161

Gorbachev, Mikhail 121

Gore-Booth, Sir Henry 86

Gorman, Teresa 156, 238

Gove, Michael 247, 251, 252

Gow, Ian 133

Grant, Bernie 195

Great Depression 105

Great Reform Act (1832) 51

Green Party 211, 222–4

Greenham Common 222, 223

Grey, Sir Edward 67

Guardian 258–9

Gunter, Ray 144

Hague, William 247

Halsbury, Hardinge Giffard, 1st Earl of 60

Hamilton, Neil 156

Hammond, Philip 247

Hardie, Keir 81

Hare, John 122–3

Harman, Harriet 2, 182–3, 185, 186, 187, 188, 190–91, 192, 201–2, 203, 204–5, 206, 252

  and Cooper 190–91, 192

  as deputy leader 197–8

Manchester Society for
  Women's Suffrage 54, 61
NUWSS 61, 64
and the Reform Acts *see*
  Reform Acts
suffragettes 2, 4–5, 59, 61,
  62–3, 67–83, 85, 90, 92, 103
suffragists 47–65
universal 47, 48, 56, 58, 63
and the voting system 48
Women's Suffrage Bills *see*
  Women's Suffrage Bills
and the working class 14,
  48–9, 53, 59, 83, 103
and the WSPU 61, 63, 66–7,
  70, 75–6, 78, 79, 80
Summerskill, Edith 109
Sun 126
Sunday Graphic 122
Sunday Times 181, 182
Sure Start 187–8

Talfourd, Thomas 36–7
Taverne, Dick 147
Taylor, Ann 148, 187
Teather, Sarah 222, 245
Tebbit, Margaret 133
Tebbit, Norman 127, 132–3
Thatcher, Carol 137–8
Thatcher, Denis 123, 124, 137,
  138
Thatcher, Margaret 1, 114, 115,
  119–29, 130–39, 145, 150,
  151, 152, 154, 166, 167, 173,
  212, 234, 248, 254

autobiography 124, 129
statue 4
The Times 52, 74, 75, 78, 92,
  252–3, 258
Thornberry, Emily 208
Tiller Girls 167
Timothy, Nick 256
trade unions 48, 86, 102, 114,
  143–4, 197, 207
Trench, Sir Francis 52
Troup, Sir Edward 74
Trumpington, Jean Barker,
  Baroness 131
Truss, Liz 256

unemployment 103, 105, 106
benefit 105
Insurance Fund 105
Union, Act of 12–14

Victoria, Queen 14–15
Villiers, Elizabeth 9
Votes for Women 78–9

W. Hetherington's 100–101
Walden, George 136–7
Walpole, Horace 25
Walpole, Robert 167
Walton Prison, Liverpool 72–3
Warnock, Mary, Baroness 134
Warsi, Sayeeda Hussain,
  Baroness 250
Webb, Beatrice 108
Wells, John 124
West, Rebecca 70

Do you wish this wasn't the end?

Join us at www.hodder.co.uk, or follow us on
Twitter @hodderbooks to be a part of our community
of people who love the very best in books and reading.

Whether you want to discover more about a book
or an author, watch trailers and interviews, have the
chance to win early limited editions, or simply browse
our expert readers' selection of the very best books,
we think you'll find what you're looking for.

And if you don't,
that's the place to tell us what's missing.

We love what we do, and we'd love you to be part of it.

www.hodder.co.uk

 @hodderbooks

 HodderBooks

 HodderBooks

Photographic Acknowledgements

The author and publisher would like to thank the following for permission to reproduce photographs:

©NILS JORGENSEN/REX/Shutterstock, Pictorial Press Ltd / Alamy Stock Photo, ©History collection 2016 / Alamy Stock Photo, ©JUSTIN TALLIS/AFP/Getty Images, ©Jeff J Mitchell/Getty Images, ©Universal History Archive/UIG via Getty Images, ©Jeff Overs/BBC News & Current Affairs via Getty Images, ©Ann Ronan Pictures/Print Collector/Getty Images, ©Rolls Press/ Popperfoto/Getty Images, © SZ Photo / Scherl / Bridgeman Images, ©Manchester Art Gallery, UK / Bridgeman Images, ©Private Collection / Bridgeman Images, © Devonshire Collection, Chatsworth / Reproduced by permission of Chatsworth Settlement Trustees / Bridgeman Images, © Mirrorpix / Bridgeman Images, ©Franz Xavier Winterhalter/Getty Images, ©Topical Press Agency / Getty Images, © Eve Arnold/Magnum Photos, ©Ben Birchall PA Archive/PA Images, ©PA Archive/PA Images, ©Private Collection / Bridgeman Images, ©Estate of Rosalind Thornycroft/Image courtesy of The Stapleton Collection/Bridgeman Images, ©ART Collection / Alamy Stock Photo, National Portrait Gallery, London